CITIZEN

By
JOHN WOOD

Copyright © 2012 John Wood
All rights reserved.

ISBN-10: 1878964097
EAN-13: 9781878964090

This novel is dedicated to Walt and Milly Woodward, who lived this story and wrote these editorials. I did not know the Woodwards or any of the Japanese American families, so the personal lives and relationships depicted here are purely fiction.

Issei – the immigrant generation from Japan or "first" generation
Nisei – children of the Issei, or "second generation"
Nikkei – the entire ethnic group in America
Kibei – Japanese who have returned to Japan for education in the language and culture

"Racism is man's gravest threat to man – the maximum of hatred for a minimum of reason."

ABRAHAM JOSHUA HESCHEL
Jewish theologian, American rabbi

CHAPTER ONE

Will pulled his old terrycloth robe around his lean body and walked slowly out of the bedroom and into the living room. He could feel the grains in the aged wooden floor on his bare feet as he made his way to the front door. He looked through the small window to the outside with a mix of anticipation and reluctance. He knew the early December air was going to be cold and he saw the bright sunlight streaming down on the front porch, promising some warmth. He could almost feel the sting of the air flowing through his nostrils before he opened the door. He turned the worn brass knob and stepped outside. The sun hit his face and he squinted, and then closed his eyes, and in a moment he felt the sun on his forehead, cheeks and neck. The air nipped at the top of his ears.

He was not what most people would call a big man, lacking the weight and musculature that would warrant that description, but he was tall and his long limbs, black hair and the intense look in his dark eyes gave him a presence that caught the attention of most women, and men, in a room of strangers.

Sunday morning. Close to eight o'clock. He and Molly had just had Sunday morning sex and she was still wrapped up in the big down comforter, in the steel frame bed, enjoying what she called "dessert sleep." He pulled the powder blue robe tighter around his torso and closed his eyes. A light breeze tickled the needles of the large Douglas fir trees across the dirt road that ran by the front of the house. He opened his eyes and looked at the light slicing down through the trees. The sun was low in the eastern sky, having just cleared the Cascade Mountains and the shafts of light seemed to be like searchlights scanning the forest floor for someone missing. Who could they be looking for this morning, in this forest, in the quiet, in the peace, he thought.

Will enjoyed these quiet moments in the morning. He liked the mix of the chill of the winter air and the warmth of the direct sun, smelling the evergreen needles and the rotting forest floor, listening to the small red squirrels chatter and the blue jays greet the day. He took a deep breath and exhaled slowly. There was no evidence of other human beings save the twin tire tracks left by himself and his neighbors to the north.

From the trees across the road he heard the *dee-dee-dah-dah* of a towhee, telling the rest of the world where it was. A quail called from the woods off to his right. And, as nearly always, an ink-black crow squawked at him from the dead limb of a fir tree in front of the house.

He turned, and flexed his toes, up and down and looked down at his feet on the old porch. How white they were, what funny appendages, those toes, lumpy and crowded together by too many years in shoes too narrow, he thought. The doorknob was cold. He opened the door and slid quickly back through the narrow opening into the house and headed for the bedroom. Molly, her auburn hair standing out like rust on the white pillow case did not move and spoke in a soft voice, muffled through the comforter that was pulled up to her nose:

"Get back in here you." Her voice was raspy and low and sweet. It touched something deep inside him, just the tone and her intent.

Will dropped his robe on the wooden chair beside the bed and crawled under the covers beside his wife. He pulled the old, white comforter up high and skidded his body across the sheets, pushing the bedsprings down in a creaky chorus. He inched his loins up behind her soft twin buns, spooning her lithe body into his and cupping her left breast in his right hand. He kissed the nape of her neck, tickling his nose with the soft hair there. A deep breath. Molly sighed. They both sunk into a comfortable, drowsy reverie, apart from the rest of the world, alone inside these wooden walls, holding out the chill of early December.

Will and Molly Whitman owned and published The Bainbridge Review, a weekly newspaper. They had purchased the paper in the fall of 1939, moving over from Seattle where Will was a sports and city desk reporter for The Seattle Times. Their house, originally an island summer home for Molly's family, had for years been lived in and treasured by her grandmother. But that ended nearly ten years ago with her nana's death and the board-and-batten house in the woods was in need of tender loving care. Molly inherited the house and, after two years of marriage, she and Will had made the leap to this island in Puget Sound, eight miles west of Seattle.

The cottage was a project. Soundly built but neglected, it needed leaks plugged, windows caulked, doors sealed, walls painted and a new furnace. For Will and Molly, when they had the time, it was a labor of love. The newspaper was a project too. They counted almost 1,000 people on the island as subscribers, out of nearly 7,000 men, women and children who lived there. Subscriptions and local advertising didn't make a lot of money, but the island was growing and so were advertisers, as islanders gradually moved from agriculture and shipbuilding to running small groceries, nurseries, barbershops and hardware stores. Summer homes were turning into more permanent residences and the island, overwhelming rural and undeveloped, was beginning to get the feel of a real community.

Will and Molly were reporters, editors, copy editors, typesetters, printers, distributors, advertising sales reps, accountants, bill collectors and publishers. The paper was—in the words that Will chose to run beneath the nameplate -- "The Only Newspaper That Cares About Bainbridge Island," a claim no one disputed.

Will had been an English major and was a graduate of the University of Washington. Tall and athletic looking, he had a hunk of straight black hair on his head that he didn't bother to control most of the time. It hung loosely around his ears and forehead and he was continually brushing it back with both hands, a habit Molly had quickly gotten used to and watched with some affection. Molly was two years behind him as a history major. They met when Will was covering a high school basketball tournament in Bellingham, about two hours north of Seattle. Molly had volunteered to chaperone some of the students and stationed herself low in the wooden bleachers, just behind the team.

Will, seated behind her and to her left side, had a hard time taking notes on the game and he kept looking over at Molly, lingering on her wavy auburn hair and her body as it pushed against her cotton flowered dress. He saw the blush in her cheek and the soft fine hair at the base of her neck. She caught him looking at her more than once and smiled. After the game, fumbling with his notepad, Will walked over to her, sure that his face was pink, feeling his cheeks getting warmer.

"Hi, I'm Will."

"Hello," she said, extending her hand.

"May I know your name?"

"Molly."

"Molly, I realize we don't have a lot of time right now. Can I see you again, back on Bainbridge?"

Will watched a small smile form on her face as she looked down at her feet.

"Well, I think that would be fine. But I must tell you, I'm not looking for a man just now." She raised her eyes to meet his.

"OK." He paused. "Neither am I," Will said and smiled broadly, proud of his own little joke.

She let out a burst of air through her nose and shook her head. "I guess we'll have to find some other interests then."

Will laughed out loud, then wrote down her phone number in his notebook.

Driving home he thought he just might marry her. He did not believe in love at first sight, but he didn't completely dismiss the idea either. Eight months later he did marry her, after one request, made as they walked along the beach at Crystal Springs. And it was just the kind of relationship he had imagined it would be, the kind he wanted, the kind his parents had had. He felt in Molly his equal, equal in intelligence and equal in a desire for living life to its fullest, not holding back, not withholding from the other. He loved her mind and he loved her sense of humor. Molly was equal, he knew, but different, different in her way as a woman. She had a way of embracing the world, seeing everyone and everything as somehow acceptable, taking others in, almost taking them into her own being. He could not do that. He discriminated too much, he saw the differences between himself and others and all to often allowed those differences to keep him apart, from another man or a woman. He used his judgment to separate himself from another, when he wanted to and needed to. Perhaps this was the function of a man's judgment, he thought, to create a distance between himself and another man, so as not to join with him. But with Molly there was no distance. He had the feeling from the beginning, and it remained true over these many months, that he needed no distance from her. He could let himself go, let himself merge with her and he would be safe. His mind, his spirit, his body could move into hers and he could withdraw when he wanted to. This was freedom, he thought to himself, the willingness and the ability to let one's self go into another, without fear and emerge again from that other when one chose. In this way, surrender, in love, was a part of freedom because one has the freedom to choose. And so he chose, as Molly did, to give himself – all he had and all he was, and he still felt free.

In their first year on the island, the couple wanted to make it clear to long-time residents that this newspaper business wasn't going to be just a hobby. They wanted it known that the Whitmans were here to stay, were part of the community and not just interlopers from the big city eight miles and a ferry ride to the east. In his first editorial Will wrote with obvious emotion:

> We're together now in this business of publishing The Review. We've taken a deep breath, drawn up our own Declaration of Independence, cut all business connections we had with Seattle and thrown our permanent lot with Bainbridge Island. Our pledge to you is this: A Review which will be crammed to the column rules with news, while it is still news; a Review which will be bright, sparkling and thought provoking in its features, photographs and columns; lastly—and perhaps most important—a Review which will always strive to speak the truth, unafraid, whether it be on a national issue or something purely local. We seek the Island's friendship and support, for we intend to make The Review our life's work.

Bainbridge Island, twelve miles long and four miles wide, rose up out of the deep water west of Seattle and nestled up against a broad arrowhead of land called the Kitsap Peninsula. It was populated by a surprisingly diverse collection of men and women from all over the world, drawn by the work of building the large wooden sailing ships that criss-crossed the Atlantic and Pacific oceans. The island, it seemed, was the perfect location for gathering the huge fir and cedar logs that were harvested from all over the Pacific Northwest, shipped into the island's bays and fashioned into two and three-masted ships. A hundred years before Will and Molly moved there, the island was home to the world's largest shipyard. Poles, Germans, Italians, Chinese, Scandinavians, Japanese and Filipinos made the island home, along with landowners from Seattle who kept summer houses there. The winters were relatively mild and the air was almost always damp.

Later that same December Sunday morning, Will and Molly were in the kitchen. Molly had climbed out of bed and into her robe, relishing each moment of a rare day off. They had just finished a breakfast of eggs -- from neighbors Frank and Colleen's hens – with sausage, rye toast and black coffee. Molly was at the sink, cleaning the dishes with a worn pink dishrag and Will was at the big window on the west side of the cottage, applying caulking to an old glass pane.

The kitchen was warm. The small wood stove in the corner heated up quickly and kept at least the kitchen toasty most of the day. The small brown radio on the round table was on, playing Harry James' "You Made Me Love You." Molly had a pleasant buzz in her chest as she contemplated a day off with Will, something that didn't come along that often since they had jumped into the weekly newspaper business. She hummed along with the tune.

The music stopped abruptly. A man's voice, tense and hurried, filled the little room. Will and Molly stopped and looked at the radio.

"We interrupt our regular programming to bring you this bulletin. Japanese airplanes have attacked American forces on the Hawaiian island of Oahu. Japanese dive-bombers, torpedo planes and fighters have bombed US naval ships at Pearl Harbor and other facilities at Hickham Airfield. Hundreds of Americans are believed dead. The attack, apparently launched from Japanese aircraft carriers in the Pacific, was unprovoked and took the island by surprise. First reports indicate the bombing went on for two hours. More details when they are available."

The music resumed, as if nothing had been said, giving the listeners the feeling that they were in another distinct reality. Was this real? Was Harry James' trumpet real or was the brutal attack on American territory real? The whole world had changed.

Will immediately stepped quickly across the kitchen floor to Molly. He set the caulking gun down on the old wooden floor and came up behind her. Molly's hands were motionless, hanging in the soapy water. She stared out the window at the bare limbs of the apple trees, the sun playing off of the moist branches. Will stepped up to her back, nestled his face down to her neck and shoulder and put his arms around her.

"Oh Will."

Tears welled up in her blue eyes and dropped one by one down into the dishwater. He held her.

"The Japanese," she said. "Why?"

He held her and slowly nodded, not knowing what to say, not knowing what to think.

"What will we do?" She whispered. He slowly shook his head from side to side and breathed in the smell of her body. He drew her closer to him.

Hideki Tojo, who had risen steadily through the Japanese army, was appointed Army Minister in the summer of 1940 and named Japanese prime minister in October of 1941. He was a resolute supporter of the alliance between his country, Germany and Italy. He stepped into his power quickly, continuing to expand Japan's war in China. For six months he had been building support and plans for taking on the American naval fleet in the Pacific, which he saw as a hindrance to Japan having its way with the weaker nations around it. Tojo's plan for dominance in the Pacific went on while the United States and Japan were in continuing diplomatic negotiations, revolving around Japan's aggression in China and the presence of Japanese troops in French Indochina. As the mood around the diplomatic table darkened, the US decided to impose a total embargo on oil and gas exports to Japan. During the fall of 1941, unknown to the western world, the Japanese Navy stepped up practice landings on aircraft carriers and bomb runs over water, gearing up to cripple the US Navy as it sat idly in the waters of Pearl Harbor.

Americans, still reeling from a nation-wide depression and trying to regain their national confidence, watched while Germany and Italy gobbled up countries in Europe, shocked as Poland, Holland, Greece and Belgium fell and England was attacked. They watched as Germany invaded Russia. Still, the American President and Congress maintained an official policy of non-involvement, unwilling to be drawn into a war that would drain their resources and further test their national will. On two sides of the world, military dictators imposed their power on nations and indeed continents while Americans looked on, most believing they were protected by two vast oceans.

Despite the wars raging in Europe and Asia, despite the language floating in the air of international discourse, and despite a warning from the US ambassador to Japan in November of "a sudden and unexpected attack," Americans were shocked at the audacity and bare aggression shown by the Japanese. The attack itself was brazen and without warning. American forces on Oahu were taken by complete surprise, even on that early morning of Dec. 7, as incoming planes were spotted on radar and assumed to be US planes returning from reconnaissance flights. American innocence and the policy of non-involvement were quickly and rudely shattered.

The attacking planes came in two waves, launched from Japanese aircraft carriers 270 miles north of Hawaii. The first wave, coming directly over the island and watched by Hawaiians on the ground, hit at 7:50 a.m. The second wave, coming an hour later and circling the island to the east, flew directly into the mouth of Pearl Harbor.

On the ground, all ammunition was under lock and key. Anti-aircraft guns were unmanned and American fighter planes were silent and still, parked wing-to-wing to prevent sabotage. Rifles and handguns were not widely distributed around the base, in order to avoid upsetting local landowners. Submarine nets were not in place in the erroneous belief that the harbor's shallow waters were a natural defense.

Japanese bombers and fighters destroyed two hundred American planes, the vast majority on the ground. Eight US battleships, including the USS Arizona with 1,400 men on board, were sunk or badly damaged, lying in the harbor or on the bottom of the Pacific.

By ten that morning the Japanese had killed 2,403 Americans.

By one that afternoon the Japanese carriers, with their attack planes back on board, were on their way back to Tokyo. America had taken a gut shot and was badly bleeding.

CHAPTER TWO

That same afternoon Japanese planes attacked American facilities in the Philippines and, farther west, struck Hong Kong, Thailand and Malaysia, attempting, in one day, to stun the world and disable any America ability to stand in Japan's way. Two days later the British battleships, H.M.S. Wales and H.M.S. Repulse, were sunk off the Malay Peninsula. Japan's successes continued without interruption. On the 13th of December, Guam was captured and on successive days, December 24th and 25th, the Japanese captured Wake Island and occupied Hong Kong.

The hostility between the United States and Japan had not begun with the attack on Pearl Harbor in December of 1941. Although America resisted entering the war in Europe for a long time, it had its irons in the fire for some months, even years, before that "day of infamy." The US had supplied the Chinese with goods and material since the Japanese invaded China in 1937. The American political structure had looked with a scornful eye at Japanese expansion in Asia and, by the summer of 1941, the relationship between the two nations was so strained that President Roosevelt clamped an oil embargo on Japan and closed US ports to Japanese ships. Talks at the highest levels of both governments continued until November, then deteriorated rapidly, leaving some of those around Roosevelt warning of some kind of attack. No one thought an attack would be so aggressive, so sudden and so complete.

Will and Molly walked the 100 yards to Frank and Colleen's house in the December sunlight, past the bare apple trees, past the clucking hens in the chicken coop and up the stone walk. Frank Viola was Italian and his father had settled on Bainbridge Island at the turn of the century to help haul the large Douglas firs to Port Blakely to be cut into beams and planks that would become the hulls and masts of American merchant ships.

The two couples had already had spirited discussions over dinner about Mussolini, Hitler and the Italian-German axis that was gobbling up Europe. Frank was angry and embarrassed about the course of events in his home country.

"Hey, have you heard?" Will said as Colleen opened the door.

"Yes, my god. We had the radio on. This is horrible," Colleen moaned as she waved them into the house. Colleen was a bright, attractive blonde who was a match for her husband's passion and enthusiasm for life. Frank walked in quickly from the kitchen.

"Holy shit Will, the whole world is going to be at war. We're going to have to get into this. We're gonna be at war with the Japs, the Germans and – God forbid—the Italians, all of them. This is crazy. This is really crazy. What are we going to do?"

"I'm not sure Frank, but we can't just take this sitting down."

Frank seemed dissatisfied with Will's response. He looked down at the floor and stuck his hands in his pants pockets. He was shorter than Will, close to 5'8", just about the same as Colleen. He was muscular and carried himself with an air of confidence, although he deferred to what he believed was Will's higher intelligence and easy way with the English language.

"Well," he said, looking Will in the eye, "I'm not in much of a position to do anything—if you know something please tell me – but you, you've got the paper, you and Molly."

"Yeah, we've got a small weekly newspaper Frank, but we're nothing compared to the Times and the Chronicle and the LA Times." Will seemed a little perturbed. "We reach a thousand people."

"That's a thousand more than I reach," Frank fired back. Colleen edged up next to her husband and put her arm in his. She could smell him perspiring and she saw the stubble of a beard on his cheek. She spoke softly into his ear:

"Frankie, Will's going to do something, I'm sure of it. We don't have to push him at all. Let's calm down." Frank glanced at his wife, who met his eyes, and then looked back at Will. He was quiet for a moment and it came to him that he was feeling guilty and, if he admitted it, afraid. He had watched, over the last months, as his countrymen teamed up with the Nazis and marched over the smaller countries in Europe. He felt deep in his gut a shame for his country and, perhaps more than that, a fear that now the entire world was going to be sucked into a terrible war. And he felt unable to do anything about it.

"You're right sweetie." Frank took a deep breath and blew it out between pursed lips. "I gotta admit, I feel a little helpless. Hell, I feel a lot helpless." He took Will by the arm and Molly stepped closer to them both, joining in the palpable emotion that was in the room. "You know what's going to happen don't you? We're going to be in a very big war and the Japs are coming for the West Coast."

That afternoon Will sat at his kitchen table, drumming his fingers on the worn wood. He got up and went out in the yard. He circled the space that would be this year's vegetable garden. He looked at the apple trees, gray, wet and bare. He came back into the house, smiled weakly at Molly and walked slowly into the living room. He paced. He contemplated the bookcase. He pondered. He thought about Frank. He thought about his small newspaper. And, again and again, his thoughts circled back to the Japanese population on their little island.

Surely Roosevelt will ask congress to declare war tomorrow, he thought. The whole nation knows about the attack by now. There won't be any hesitation, any turning back. Everyone will have the radio on all day. The big city newspapers are already all over this. What can I say? What can a small weekly newspaper hidden away in the Puget Sound say about a world war?

"Molly," he called into the kitchen, unaware that she was leaning up against the doorframe watching him.

"Yes, Will?" Their eyes met and both smiled. Molly's eyes were wet.

"How many Japanese are on the island?"

"Oh, I'd say two hundred. Maybe more. Maybe even three hundred."

"That's a big chunk of the population."

"You bet."

"People are going to be all over them."

"I think you're right. And not just here," Molly said, "but all up and down the West Coast."

They both moved back to the kitchen and took their regular chairs at the kitchen table. It was early afternoon. Sunshine filtered in through the window over the sink. Will's large hands rested on the table. Soon he was drumming the tabletop with both hands.

"I think we have to stay local," Will said. "Everyone is going to have the big picture covered. We've got to stick to Bainbridge."

"OK, what's your headline?"

"Let me think a little more. Whatever it is, I think we need a special edition. Tomorrow."

Molly and Will worked all that December afternoon and into the night. The cold, wet air coming off the water surrounded their little office near Rich Passage, on the south end of the island. The 100-foot fir trees dwarfed the small wooden building and swayed easily in the wind. Will, in khakis and a blue corduroy shirt with his sleeves rolled up and Molly in her signature flowered dress with a white sweater on, bounced around the small offices, setting type, laying out the front page and writing. Molly took a break to go back to the house and make a couple of tuna sandwiches. Somewhere around nine, Will sat down at his friendly old Royal typewriter and grew quiet. He stared up, at the line where the wall met the ceiling. He typed slowly at first, carefully considering his words. As he wrote, he picked up speed, gathering momentum, nodding his head. In half an hour he was finished and said simply: "Yeah."

He rolled the last page out of his typewriter, pulled the carbon paper from between two sheets, and handed the pages to Molly.

"Read it out loud sweetie," he said to his wife.

"If ever there was a community which faced a local emergency growing out of something over which it had no control, it is Bainbridge Island this Monday morning in December, 1941.

This is no time to mince words.

There are on this island some 300 members of 50 families whose blood ties lie with a nation that, yesterday, committed an atrocity against all that is decent.

The great American democracy is a slow-moving creature, at best. We Americans dilly-dally around, talk a lot, fool with labor strikes and in many other ways give apparent evidence that we are not as efficient as a smooth running machine.

But you don't treat Americans the way Japan treated America without swift, sudden and sure action.

And in such a recoil of sentiment, there is danger of a blind, wild hysterical hatred of all persons who can trace ancestry to Japan. That some of those persons happen to be American citizens, happen to be loyal to this country and happen to have no longer a binding tie with the fatherland are factors which easily could be swept aside by mob hysteria.

So, The Review points out to Island Japanese that they cannot change their names, as did Germans in the last war. They must stand on the facts as they are. They are Japanese Americans and America is at war with Japan.

Island Japanese, as never before, must prove their mettle as loyal Americans. They must realize they will be the objects of intense scrutiny. They must not resent this. They must welcome it. They must do everything in their power to ferret out those among their number - if any there be -who do not have an abiding love and loyalty for this America of ours.

To other Islanders, The Review says this: These Japanese Americans of ours haven't bombed anybody. In the past, they have given every indication of loyalty to this nation. They have sent, along with our boys, their own sons - six of them - into the United States Army. They, in this edition, are quoted as pledging anew their loyalty.

So, of all Islanders - Japanese and otherwise - The Review would seek as calm an approach to this emergency as possible. Let us live so in this trying time that when it is all over loyal Americans can look other loyal Americans in the eye with the knowledge that, together, they kept the Stars and Stripes flying high over the land of the brave and the home of the free."

"Whew," Molly said. "You certainly *didn't* mince words, as you said."
"No time for that."
"One thing; isn't it the land of the free and the home of the brave?"
"Huh, maybe. How can we find out?"
"I'm not sure. Maybe it doesn't make too much difference."
"Well," Molly said, "I'll look that up. Also, I'm a little uncomfortable with 'blind, wild hysterical hatred.' Don't you think that's a little inflammatory?"
Will paused and thought. "Maybe. Maybe not. I think by saying something that strong we do a little more to head off the possibility. I just know there's going to be people crying for their heads."
"OK. And you say something about 'in this edition they are quoted as pledging their loyalty.' What's that?"
"Oh, I guess I didn't show you. Sorry. I've got statements from two of the Kouras and a Nakata —pretty strong statements—talking about their personal feelings and the loyalty of the other families on the island."
"Good, I'd like to see those. And, Will."
"Yeah?"
"Great job, honey. I'm with you all the way."
He grabbed Molly around the waist and pulled her to him, pulled her to his chair and buried his face under her breasts.
The next morning, barely 24 hours after the attack, The Bainbridge Review rolled out its first special edition. "Island Defenses Set" spanned the top of the front page, in fact the only page. "Leaders Prepare for Blackout...Japanese Leaders Here Pledge Loyalty to America...Church Bells Hushed." What made that December 8 edition special was not the news regarding the defense of the island and neighboring Bremerton Naval Base, but the editorial. Will Whitman had set a tone and articulated principles that he -- but very few others in the Fourth Estate -- would follow throughout the war. Little did the Whitmans know how they would be tested.

CHAPTER THREE

On that same cold December night, Bert Kobiyashi and his wife Linda sat at the kitchen table talking. They leaned forward over the old wooden table that had held so many of their meals and they warmed their hands around cups of hot tea. The wind nipped at the edges of the small wooden house that sat on the front border of five acres of strawberry fields. Bert and Linda talked in soft voices.

"They <u>will</u> come after us," Bert said. "I don't have a question about that. It's just when and how."

"How are you so sure? This is America in the 20th century." Linda brushed back her long blonde hair and took a sip of tea.

"Look at my face Linda," Bert said and pointed to his eyes. "This is now the face of the enemy. Trust me, this is the face people will hate. I know. I walk around with it every day. It's hard to hide."

Bert, his face the color of copper pipes, burnished rosy by his outdoor life, seemed in pain as he said it. Inside he was seething, angry at the nation of Japan and angry about the situation he now found himself in. His black eyes were fixed on the wooden table.

"But sweetie, we know a lot of people on this island. They don't hate us. I don't know a single soul who believes you would do something against our country."

"I don't think you know what I know," Bert said, and raised his head to look his wife in the eyes. "You don't hear the whispers, the names—'slant eyes, moon face, yellow eyes, Jap.' You're not there on the street when men do this." He raised his hands to his face, put his thumbs on his chin and his middle fingers on the outside corners of his eyes and pushed back. "They don't have to say anything." He shook his head and his eyes welled with tears.

"Oh, Bert that's awful. I'm sorry honey." She paused and looked intently into her husband's eyes. She saw the pain and the anger and opened her heart to him. "Maybe you're being pessimistic. Maybe this will work out, especially here. I mean, we're not the big city you know."

Bert was one of several Japanese American men on Bainbridge Island that had married a Caucasian woman. He and Linda were high school sweethearts, Bainbridge High School, class of 1934, holding hands in the hallways, going to basketball games, and taking long walks in the woods that were so much a part of their island home. They married two years after graduation. He loved her open heart, generous nature and ability to talk about what she thought and felt. She loved his quiet sweetness, his inner strength and solid integrity. He had been a wrestler in high school and Linda, in her senior year, had gone to every match, home and away, and rooted him on.

"Sweetie?" She looked at his face as she asked, to see if he was ready to talk. Watching him, her body ached and her mind reeled with what he was saying. "Who do you think, as you put it, would come after you?"

He looked hard in her eyes. "The police, the FBI, the army. Maybe just ordinary people. It really doesn't matter what organization it is. They will be white and they will have the power of the US government behind them. And they will come. That much I know."

The Whitman cottage smelled of old wood, musty and a little damp; a smell Will and Molly had become very familiar with, so familiar that they rarely noticed it. They were aware of the smell when they returned home after some time away, not a usual occasion, as trips off the island put too much pressure on them to get the paper out on time. The weekly deadline, the newspaper itself, had become both a jail cell and an open door. It held them to the island, to their house and the small offices, pulling them like an old mule pulls a plow to phone calls, meetings, feuds between neighbors, weddings, deaths and accidents. It also freed their voices, their opinions and values, and gave the couple a way to speak that their neighbors did not have. They could take a photograph of anything they pleased and print it. They could write headlines and stories with only their integrity guiding them and give their words to a thousand neighbors. Will sometimes thought of himself as a tethered mule, tied loosely to a stake and braying at passersby on a regular basis. But, all in all, he loved the freedom, the power, the responsibility and the connection to the community. This was why they had bought the paper in the first place.

Will rolled both shoulders forward and buttoned his old tweed sport coat. Then he pulled on his black knee length raincoat and yelled to Molly in the bedroom. "You ready babe?"

"One minute." Her sweet voice drifted through the cool air in the cottage and he smiled at the sound of it.

They were headed for the small offices at the south end of the island. A Wednesday edition had to be to put out and neither Molly or Will had had much sleep.

"Did you see what Odo wrote?"

"Not yet," she said.

"Something like: 'My only purpose in life is to raise my six children to be good members of American society.' and he added 'I am positive that every Japanese family on the island has an intense loyalty for America and stands ready to defend it. My American citizenship is what means the most to me.' Will leaned through the doorway to see if Molly was coming. "We need more statements like that," he said. "Come on babe."

"Well, we've got at least one," Molly said, striding toward the front door and pulling on her large tweed sweater. Look what I pulled out of the Seattle Courier this morning." She handed a copy of a Japanese community newspaper to Will.

We Cannot Fail America

"No matter what develops involving the United States in the present tragic world situation, we Americans of Japanese ancestry must be prepared and remember that there are certain fundamental truths from which we cannot depart. One of them is that we were born in these United States as

American citizens. Now that we have become involved in the Far Eastern conflict that is going to test our worth and mettle as citizens, and we cannot fail America.

"There is a remote possibility of our becoming the victim of public passion and hysteria. If this should occur, we will stand firm in our resolution that even if America may 'disown' us – we will never 'disown' America.

"One inspiring example of the contribution of Americans of Japanese ancestry to the national defense effort is that more than 3,000 American soldiers of Japanese ancestry are now serving in the military training camps The percentage in proportion to population is greater than any other racial group, such as Italian Americans, German Americans and French Americans.

"It is easy for us at this time to shout our patriotism and declare our loyalty. But we must do much more than mere lip service. Our biggest job, and the hardest, will be to go ahead doing our work as diligently and as efficiently as we can, to contribute to America's defense. This is a time for calm thinking and quick action, in behalf of America."

"Wow. Perfect," Will said. "Let's try and find a spot for that." Will was touched by the patriotism in the editorial and it fed his hope for a growing unity in the Japanese community.

"Let's get cracking."

Will pulled their 1939 Pontiac two-door into the dirt driveway of their offices near Rich Passage. Waiting for them on the steps and in the yard were half a dozen young Japanese American men -- Nisei, second generation men born on the island -- all in their twenties. Will and Molly looked at each other and back at the men. They stepped out of the car.

The men gave away nothing with their faces. They were quiet, as if they expected Will and Molly to know why they were there. They all nodded to the couple and gave a slight bow. Will nodded back.

"Let's go inside," he said to the gathered men.

Will and Molly pulled out what chairs they had, brought in an old fruit box from the back room and pushed two desks in towards the center of the room. They and the young men formed a rough circle in the small room, still cold from the night air. One of the men cleared his throat and spoke to Will.

"Mr. Whitman," Frank Koura said, "we value your opinion. We know the newspaper has a strong voice in our community." He looked around at the others, who sat close together, hands in their coat pockets, looking at Will with worry in their eyes.

"Basically, we are deeply concerned and we want to know what we can do. For one thing, we are afraid of what will happen to our parents. They are Japanese born, as you know, and not legal citizens."

Will was nodding as the clean-cut young man spoke. Frank went on and Will reached for his small tablet and a pen.

"We know that some of us are going to be suspect, no matter what we say. But we are looking for a way—maybe more than one way—to prove our loyalty to our country. Do you have any ideas?"

Molly was watching Frank intently. She heard his voice crack as he spoke. She heard the wind whistling around the small wooden building in the trees. Her eyes were narrowed, her brow furrowed. She turned her head to look at Will, just as he looked at her. They saw in each other's eyes concern, compassion and tenderness for these men they both knew by sight and, with their families, by reputation. Will spoke.

"First, I'm impressed that you're here. That's a sign that you want to do something positive. I don't pretend to know what is going to happen or what you should or shouldn't do," he said. "What I do know is you have my support, and Molly's. I'm not sure how that's going to translate into print right now. We're sort of feeling our way through this, just as a lot of people are. You can be sure, though, that you're going to take some flack. There are people on this island, just as anywhere else, that are going to be upset. There are racists here too, no use mincing words. So you're going to have to have patience and keep your noses clean, absolutely clean. No drinking, no parties, no standing around in big groups, no misbehaving – and stay away from the Japanese language school—in fact, stay away from anything labeled Japanese. I hate to say it, but I think all of you are going to be suspect. I wish it weren't that way but my wishes don't matter for much in this case."

"Yes, we understand," one of the other men said. He was Paul, one of the youngest, and shyest, of the group. "We are grateful for any help you can give us. We are especially afraid of what will happen to our mothers and fathers."

"Yes, I am worried too," Molly chimed in. "Very worried." She smiled at Paul, but it was not returned. He nodded and looked back to Will.

"If you want," Will said, "you can write letters to us, expressing your concerns, expressing your love of this country, this island —whatever it is you want to say. We can only reach our island, but it will affect a thousand people, maybe more."

"Thank you for your openness and support, " Frank said and stood up. The other men stood also, as if signaled. Will glanced out through the small window and saw the ferry to Bremerton gliding silently through Rich Passage. Suddenly he was sad and felt a tingling in his eyes.

CHAPTER FOUR

Later that morning what nearly every American was expecting became official. Will and Molly huddled together in the office with cheese sandwiches and coffee, listening intently to the small wooden radio on Will's desk. President Franklin Roosevelt was addressing Congress and the entire nation was listening.

"Yesterday, December 7, 1941 — a date which will live in infamy — the United States of America was suddenly and deliberately attacked by naval and air forces of the Empire of Japan. The United States was at peace with that nation, and, at the solicitation of Japan, was still in conversation with its government and its Emperor looking toward the maintenance of peace in the Pacific.

"Indeed, one hour after Japanese air squadrons had commenced bombing in the American island of Oahu, the Japanese Ambassador to the United States and his colleague delivered to our Secretary of State a formal reply to a recent American message. And, while this reply stated that it seemed useless to continue the existing diplomatic negotiations, it contained no threat or hint of war or of armed attack.

"It will be recorded that the distance of Hawaii from Japan makes it obvious that the attack was deliberately planned many days, or even weeks, ago. During the intervening time the Japanese Government has deliberately sought to deceive the United States by false statements and expressions of hope for continued peace.

Will looked at Molly and she stared back, her eyes wide open, shining with moisture. Will shook his head slowly.

"The attack yesterday on the Hawaiian Islands has caused severe damage to American naval and military forces. I regret to tell you that very many American lives have been lost. In addition, American ships have been reported torpedoed on the high seas between San Francisco and Honolulu.

"No matter how long it may take us to overcome this premeditated invasion, the American people, in their righteous might, will win through to absolute victory. I believe that I interpret the will of the Congress and of the people when I assert that we will not only defend ourselves to the uttermost but will make it very certain that this form of treachery shall never again endanger us. Hostilities exist. There is no blinking at the fact that our people, our territory and our interests are in grave danger.

"With confidence in our armed forces, with the unbounding determination of our people, we will gain the inevitable triumph, so help us God.

"I ask that the Congress declare that since the unprovoked and dastardly attack by Japan on Sunday, December 7, 1941, a state of war has existed between the United States and the Japanese Empire."

Will reached over and turned the radio down. They could both hear the applause and the shouts from Congressmen and Senators. America was at war.

"That's a strong speech," Will said. "Well, we're in for it now. Batten down the hatches. Looks like Japan is attacking people all over the place."

"I could hear the anger in his voice," Molly said. "I think he feels betrayed."

"I wouldn't doubt it, what with talks still going on back there." He paused and took the last bite of his sandwich. "I think the Japanese have made a serious mistake. They've pissed off America."

The next morning the sun was bright early outside the small house. Light streamed in through the front windows, spotlighting a rocking chair that sat near the window closest to the door. Will sat at the kitchen table reading a handwritten document that he had found wedged in the front door. Someone had copied a statement from the president of the Japanese

American Citizens League that had been wired to President Roosevelt. Will read it over a second time before calling to Molly in the bedroom.

"Mol, come listen to this."

"OK sweetie, on the way."

Will sat down in the kitchen chair and read aloud:

"In this solemn hour we pledge our full cooperation to you, Mr. President, and to our country. There cannot be any question. There must be no doubt. We in our hearts know we are Americans loyal to America. We must prove that to all of you."

Will felt the blood rise in his face as he read the letter aloud. He was again moved. He felt a mix of empathy, compassion and anger all at the same time.

"Where's that from?" Molly watched her husband intently. In the last two days she had felt her love for him grow, as if a tide were rising in her. It was her love for her husband and it was feeling everything around her more deeply. The world had changed. His world had changed and her world was changing too.

"I found it out front this morning. It's from the Japanese American Citizens League, to Roosevelt; wired today and copied by someone on the island."

Molly walked over and sat down at the table across from Will. "I'm impressed. I like the words and I like that they did this so quickly." She paused. "Did you see what the LA Times said?" Molly reached into her purse and grabbed a small piece of newspaper.

"No, am I going to like it?"

"I think not. Here it is, quoting from their editorial of yesterday: 'A viper is nonetheless a viper wherever the egg is hatched — so a Japanese American, born of Japanese parents — grows up to be Japanese, not an American."

"My God. A viper, where do they get these people who write this? Where do they think the rest of the people in this country came from? Do they think they just sprouted here?" Will spoke with obvious disgust, rising up from the table and walking to look out the window over the sink. He stared at the old apple trees, bare, stark and gnarled, almost merging into the gray sky.

Molly walked over and looked at the man she married. His dark straight hair hung down around his eyes. His blue robe opened at the top to reveal a strip of dark hair in the middle of a wide chest. He was not strikingly handsome but his face was smooth and open and most of the time even peaceful. Now, it was tight with outrage and anguish. Two creases ran down from his nose and surrounded his mouth. She smiled at him.

"What?" He said, taken over by his anger.

"Nothing, just appreciating you."

He smiled back, pursed his lips and made a small chirpy sound that imitated a kiss.

"You know what impresses me so far?" Molly asked. Will raised his eyebrows and lifted his chin, urging her to continue. "How quickly the Japanese Americans –at least all that I've seen and heard—have gotten this, have understood the nation's crisis as well as their own, have realized what they need to do and are doing it."

"I agree."

"They're going to need help Will."

"You bet they are."

There was a knock at the front door. Molly, still in her robe, retreated to the bedroom and Will stepped to the door. Through the small window he saw his neighbor Frank.

"Come on in buddy."

"How are you two?"

Frank Viola owned a small auto repair shop near the middle of the island. A handsome 35-year old, Frank had met Colleen in a coffee shop in Seattle and the two of them had moved to Bainbridge Island in the same month Will and Molly had. Fast friends, they shared home-grown vegetables and fresh eggs, played cards every couple of weeks and had long talks in front of the fire. Frank fancied himself a pretty good photographer and occasionally took pictures that he offered to Will for publication in the Review.

"Good. Mol's in the back getting dressed. Want coffee?"

"Sure. You got a minute?"

"Yeah, but not much more," Will said, "we've got a bunch of things to take care of."

"Yeah, I can imagine. I notice you had a visitor this morning."

"Someone dropped off a statement. I think I'll run it."

"Yeah? Is it important?"

"I think so. It's a statement from the Japanese American Citizens League expressing their loyalty."

"Good, but they need to do a lot more than that."

Will turned and became more focused on his neighbor. "Like what?"

"Something more than words. They gotta sign up. They gotta make some sacrifices. They can't just sit here and say they're loyal. That's not gonna cut it."

Will was surprised at Frank's intensity. "I think they know that Frank," he said and watched Frank's face closely.

"Yeah, well. Will, you know as well as I do that not everyone around here loves the Japs."

"I'd much rather hear you call them Japanese Americans or…"

"Pardon me Will. That's too long."

"Or Americans of Japanese descent. Or maybe just Americans."

"But that's the point Will. They're not *just* Americans. They're Japanese. Some of them are here for just a few years. Some of them have served in the Japanese army for god's sake."

"Frank, this is really surprising to hear from you, especially considering that you just became a citizen yourself. Why aren't you out there proclaiming your loyalty to the United States of America? I mean, look what Italy is doing in Europe, teamed up with Hitler!"

There was an awkward silence. They heard Molly's footsteps in the bedroom. They both turned to see if she was coming.

"Yeah, I thought of that Will." Frank paused and looked out the kitchen window. "But Italians are different. Those guys in the army are just some guys following Mussolini. It's not like the whole nation is at war with everybody."

Molly strolled into the kitchen, having heard most of the conversation from the back of the house.

"And you think that's different from Japan?" Will asked, growing more impatient.

"Yes I do Will. And I think most people do. The Japanese, they're different. They're more of… a race. They're more…I can't think of a word. United, maybe. Cut from the same cloth. They worship this Tojo guy. They're different from us. They follow. They have a deep loyalty to family and their country."

"Doesn't sound too bad to me," Molly piped in.

"Morning Molly. I'm trying to get something off my chest here and maybe I'm not doing a very good job of it. I'm just trying to say that Japs

—Japanese Americans—are different than we are. They're kind of mysterious, you know? You never know what they're thinking. You know that word people say about them: descrutable?"

"I think you mean inscrutable," Molly said. Frank was staring into his coffee.

"Yeah, inscrutable. You can't read them. They don't open up to you. And they stay so close to home, they don't really mix with the rest of us. You two gotta know what I mean. I think I'm saying something true and you won't accept it." He looked over at Will and back to Molly, an anguished look on his face, then collapsed into the chair opposite Will.

"Frank," Will said and waited until he had Frank's full attention. "This island, as much as any place I know, is a real mix of people, a mix of nationalities, races, ages, sexes. People have come here from all over the world to work in the shipyard, to grow berries, to open their own businesses. German, Italian, Polish, Australian, English, Irish, Chinese, Austrian, Hawaiian, Japanese – they're all here. Our challenge—all of us—is not to see each other as 'they.' We can't just lump people into a handy little group and say they're the enemy. We're doomed if we do that. The whole, big American dream is doomed if we can't accept the ways that we are all different."

Molly edged over to Will and put her arm across his shoulders. Frank looked a little sad.

"I know you're right Will. I know it. That's the ideal. But there's something in me, I gotta confess. There's just something in me that says they're *too* different."

Will looked up at Molly and saw her bright blue eyes looking back at him.

"Well, I'll tell you one thing Frank. We're all going to learn just how different some of us are in the coming months." He stood up and took Molly's hand. "Right now, we've got a paper to get out."

CHAPTER FIVE

Two days after the attack on Hawaii President Roosevelt scheduled a national radio address. Most people in America, many of whom revered Roosevelt, found their way to a radio that evening and in houses all over America, families and neighbors sat together, drinking coffee or a cold beer, wanting to hear the latest news from their leader. Radios were switched on in bars, meeting halls, living rooms, barbershops, garages and back porches. Molly and Will had made ham sandwiches and settled into their favorite chairs in the living room. Will turned up the wooden floor model receiver and moved his pencil and notepad to the arm of the chair.

"My Fellow Americans," the Presidents deep voice boomed out of the box with his usual confidence.

"The sudden criminal attacks perpetrated by the Japanese in the Pacific provide the climax of a decade of international immorality. Powerful and resourceful gangsters have banded together to make war upon the whole human race. Their challenge has now been flung at the United States of America. The Japanese have treacherously violated the long-standing peace between us. Many American soldiers and sailors have been killed by enemy action. American ships have been sunk; American airplanes have been destroyed. The Congress and the people of the United States have accepted that challenge.

"Together with other free peoples, we are now fighting to maintain our right to live among our world neighbors in freedom, in common decency, without fear of assault. I have prepared the full record of our past relations with Japan, and it will be submitted to the Congress. It begins with the visit of Commodore Perry to Japan eighty-eight years ago. It ends with the visit of two Japanese emissaries to the Secretary of State last Sunday, an hour after Japanese forces had loosed their bombs and machine guns against our flag, our forces and our citizens.

"I can say with utmost confidence that no Americans, today or a thousand years hence, need feel anything but pride in our patience and in our efforts through all the years toward achieving a peace in the Pacific which would be fair and honorable to every nation, large or small. And no honest person, today or a thousand years hence, will be able to suppress a sense of indignation and horror at the treachery committed by the military dictators of Japan, under the very shadow of the flag of peace borne by their special envoys in our midst. The course that Japan has followed for the past ten years in Asia has paralleled the course of Hitler and Mussolini in Europe and in Africa. Today, it has become far more than a parallel. It is actual collaboration, so well calculated that all the continents of the world, and all the oceans, are now considered by the Axis strategists as one gigantic battlefield.

"In 1931, ten years ago, Japan invaded Manchukuo without warning. In 1939, Hitler invaded Czechoslovakia without warning. Later in '39, Hitler invaded Poland without warning. In 1940, Hitler invaded Norway, Denmark, the Netherlands, Belgium and Luxembourg without warning. In 1940, Italy attacked France and later Greece without warning. And this year, in 1941, the Axis Powers attacked Yugoslavia and Greece and they dominated the Balkans without warning. In 1941, also, Hitler invaded Russia without warning.

"And now Japan has attacked Malaya, Thailand and the United States without warning. It is all of one pattern. We are now in this war. We are all in it all the way. Every single man, woman and child is a partner in the most tremendous undertaking of our American history. We must share together the bad news and the good news, the defeats and the victories the changing fortunes of war. So far, the news has been all bad. The casualty lists of these first few days will undoubtedly be large. I deeply feel the anxiety of all of the families of the men in our armed forces and the relatives of people in cities which have been bombed. I can only give them my solemn promise that they will get news just as quickly as possible."

Will stirred in his seat and stopped taking notes. He got up and went into the kitchen. Molly heard the pop and fizz of a beer bottle being opened. She smiled at him as he returned to his chair.

"Many rumors and reports which we now hear originate with enemy sources. For instance, today the Japanese are claiming that as a result of their one action against Hawaii they have gained naval supremacy in the Pacific. This is an old trick of propaganda which has been used innumerable times by the Nazis. The purposes of such fantastic claims are, of course, to spread fear and confusion among us, and to goad us into revealing military information, which our enemies are desperately anxious to obtain. Our government will not be caught in this obvious trap and neither will the people of the United States.

"To all newspapers and radio stations all those who reach the eyes and ears of the American people I say this: You have a most grave responsibility to the nation now and for the duration of this war. If you feel that your government is not disclosing enough of the truth, you have every right to say so. But in the absence of all the facts, as revealed by official sources, you have no right in the ethics of patriotism to deal out unconfirmed reports in such a way as to make people believe that they are gospel truth. Every citizen, in every walk of life, shares this same responsibility. The lives of our soldiers and sailors the whole future of this nation depends upon the manner in which each and every one of us fulfills his obligation to our country."

Will looked at Molly and raised his eyebrows and shook his head in agreement. Molly suspected he was impressed by the President's emphasis on journalists.

"Now a word about the recent past and the future. A year and a half has elapsed since the fall of France, when the whole world first realized the mechanized might which the Axis nations had been building up for so many years. America has used that year and a half to great advantage. Knowing that the attack might reach us in all too short a time, we immediately began greatly to increase our industrial strength and our capacity to meet the demands of modern warfare.

"Precious months were gained by sending vast quantities of our war material to the nations of the world still able to resist Axis aggression. Our policy rested on the fundamental truth that the defense of any country resisting Hitler or Japan was in the long run the defense of our own country. That policy has been justified. It has given us time, invaluable time, to build our American assembly lines of production. Assembly lines are now in operation. Others are being rushed to completion. A steady stream of tanks and planes, of guns and ships and shells and equipment -- that is what these eighteen months have given us. But it is all only a beginning of what still has to be done. We must be set to face a long war against crafty and powerful bandits. The attack at Pearl Harbor can be repeated at any one of many points, points in both oceans and along both our coast lines and against all the rest of the Hemisphere.

"It will not only be a long war, it will be a hard war. That is the basis on which we now lay all our plans. That is the yardstick by which we measure what we shall need and demand; money, materials, doubled and quadrupled production ever increasing. The production must be not only for our own Army and Navy and air forces. It must reinforce the other armies and navies and air forces fighting the Nazis and the warlords of Japan throughout the Americas and throughout the world. I have been working today on the subject of production. Your government has decided on two broad policies.

"The first is to speed up all existing production by working on a seven-day week basis in every war industry, including the production of essential raw materials. The second policy, now being put into form, is to rush additions to the capacity of production by building more new plants, by adding to old plants, and by using the many smaller plants for war needs.

"The fact is that the country now has an organization in Washington built around men and women who are recognized experts in their own fields. I think the country knows that the people who are actually responsible in each and every one of these many fields are pulling together with a teamwork that has never before been excelled. On the road ahead there lies hard work grueling workday and night, every hour and every minute. I was about to add that ahead there lies sacrifice for all of us. But it is not correct to use that word. The United States does not consider it a sacrifice to do all one can, to give one's best to our nation, when the nation is fighting for its existence and its future life. It is not a sacrifice for any man, old or young, to be in the Army or the Navy of the United States. Rather it is a privilege.

"It is not a sacrifice for the industrialist or the wage earner, the farmer or the shopkeeper, the trainman or the doctor, to pay more taxes, to buy more bonds, to forgo extra profits, to work longer or harder at the task for which he is best fitted. Rather it is a privilege. It is not a sacrifice to do without many things to which we are accustomed if the national defense calls for doing without.

"A review this morning leads me to the conclusion that at present we shall not have to curtail the normal use of articles of food. There is enough food today for all of us and enough left over to send to those who are fighting on the same side with us. But there will be a clear and definite shortage of metals for many kinds of civilian use, for the very good reason that in our increased program we shall need for war purposes more than half of that portion of the principal metals which during the past year have gone into articles for civilian use. Yes, we shall have to give up many things entirely. And I am sure that the people in every part of the nation are prepared in their individual living to win this war. I am sure that they will cheerfully help to pay a large part of its financial cost while it goes on. I am sure they will cheerfully give up those material things that they are asked to give up. And I am sure that they will retain all those great spiritual things without which we cannot win through.

"I repeat that the United States can accept no result save victory, final and complete. Not only must the shame of Japanese treachery be wiped out, but the sources of international brutality, wherever they exist, must be absolutely and finally broken. In my message to the Congress yesterday I said that we 'will make very certain that this form of treachery shall never again endanger us.' In order to achieve that certainty, we must begin the great task that is before us by abandoning once and for all the illusion that we can ever again isolate ourselves from the rest of humanity. In these past few years and, most violently, in the past three days we have learned a terrible lesson. It is our obligation to our dead. It is our sacred obligation to their children and to our children that we must never forget what we have learned. And what we have learned is this:

Will leaned forward, notebook and pen in hand.

"There is no such thing as security for any nation or any individual in a world ruled by the principles of gangsterism. There is no such thing as impregnable defense against powerful aggressors who sneak up in the dark and strike without warning. We have learned that our ocean-girt hemisphere is not immune from severe attack and that we cannot measure our safety in terms of miles on any map anymore.

"We may acknowledge that our enemies have performed a brilliant feat of deception, perfectly timed and executed with great skill. It was a thoroughly dishonorable deed, but we must face the fact that modern warfare as conducted in the Nazi manner is a dirty business. We don't like it, we didn't want to get in it, but we are in it and we're going to fight it with everything we've got. I do not think any American has any doubt of our ability to administer proper punishment to the perpetrators of these crimes. Your government knows that for weeks Germany has been telling Japan that if Japan did not attack the United States, Japan would not share in dividing the spoils with Germany when peace came. She was promised by Germany that if she came in she would receive the complete and perpetual control of the whole of the Pacific area and that means not only the Far East, but also all of the Islands in the Pacific, and also a stranglehold on the west coast of North, Central and South America.

"We know also that Germany and Japan are conducting their military and naval operations in accordance with a joint plan. That is their simple and obvious grand strategy. And that is why the American people must realize that it can be matched only with similar grand strategy. We must realize for example that Japanese successes against the United States in the Pacific are helpful to German operations in Libya; that any German success against the Caucasus is inevitably an assistance to Japan in her operations against the Dutch East Indies; that a German attack against Algiers or Morocco opens the way to a German attack against South America and the Canal. On the other side of the picture, we must learn also to know that guerrilla warfare against the Germans in, let us say Serbia or Norway, helps us; that a successful Russian offensive against the Germans helps us; and that British successes on land or sea in any part of the world strengthen our hands.

"Remember always that Germany and Italy, regardless of any formal declaration of war, consider themselves at war with the United States at this moment just as much as they consider themselves at war with Britain or Russia. And Germany puts all the other Republics of the Americas into the same category of enemies. The people of our sister Republics of this hemisphere can be honored by that fact.

"The true goal we seek is far above and beyond the ugly field of battle. When we resort to force, as now we must, we are determined that this force shall be directed toward ultimate good as well as against immediate evil. We Americans are not destroyers; we are builders. We are now in the midst of a war, not for conquest, not for vengeance, but for a world in which this nation, and all that this nation represents, will be safe for our children. We expect to eliminate the danger from Japan, but it would serve us ill if we accomplished that and found that the rest of the world was dominated by Hitler and Mussolini. So we are going to win the war and we are going to win the peace that follows. And in the difficult hours of this day through dark days that may be yet to come we will know that the vast majority of the members of the human race are on our side. Many of them are fighting with us. All of them are praying for us. But, in representing our cause, we represent theirs as well our hope and their hope for liberty under God."

Applause started in Congress and Will got up and turned the radio down.

"I have to say Mol, that he's a great speaker. He nailed this one, I think. It's appropriately scary enough and optimistic enough at the same time." Molly was nodding and her eyes were filled with tears. "I was impressed by how much he conveyed and I liked it that he sat up that whole context at the beginning."

"You know what I didn't know? How closely Germany, Italy and Japan have been collaborating." She ran her hands through her loose auburn hair. "I appreciated his global perspective and the idea that we have to win the whole war, not just defeat the Japanese."

"Yeah, and it sounds like it'll be a long one."

"Honey," Molly said and paused. "I'm scared. Maybe I'm too suggestible, but I just feel the presence of evil in the world in a way I never have before. What happened in Hawaii probably brought it home to me. That was pure evil. What Hitler has done so far in Europe is evil; there's no other word for it. All those people – dead. And there's more to come, more evil. How can we not be afraid?"

Will looked deeply into her electric blue eyes, wet and rimmed with red lids.

"I love you sweetie," he said. She nodded, holding her breath and holding herself against her own fear and negativity. "All we can do is live our lives now to the fullest, to stand up and say the things we need to say, to step into the roles we've chosen, to speak for ourselves and our neighbors, to have those tough conversations with people like Frank. And continue to love each other. We need to act. And live our lives. That will take care of our fear."

He put both his large hands in back of her neck, gently, and pulled her softly toward him. He kissed her forehead, her nose and her lips. She smiled and nodded.

"Thanks honey. That helps. I think you're right."

CHAPTER SIX

In the days following the attack on Pearl Harbor most of the population of the west coast of the United States was living in fear. Nowhere was that more evident than on this small island due west of Seattle. One could draw a circle around Bainbridge Island of about fifteen miles and encompass within it the shipyard on the island itself, employing 3,000 men and women, Bremerton Naval Base, the Boeing aircraft production facilities, the Seattle port and shipyards, Sand Point Naval Station, the submarine/torpedo station at Keyport and the international airport. To those who lived on the island, it felt as if they were the bull's eye of a target that circled the Great Northwest.

Anti-submarine nets were strung across the narrow passages that surrounded the island and could have easily been direct routes to the Bremerton naval base and the Keyport facilities. Large white barrage balloons floated in the cold blue December sky and hundreds of volunteers scanned the western horizon, on the watch for approaching aircraft. Church bells were silenced, to be used only for air raid warnings. Residents were warned not to drive at night and, in while in their homes, were required to pull their shades and otherwise cover their windows so no light could escape. Ever since the reports of the Pearl Harbor attack reached the mainland, men, women and children could imagine Japanese planes flying low over their own homes. And neighbors began to keep watch on neighbors, looking and listening for the slightest indication of a lack of patriotism or allegiance with Japan, Germany or Italy.

Americans clung to any small piece of information, no matter where it came from or what it said. Rumors became fact. Federal restrictions were ordered, freezing the bank accounts of first-generation Japanese Americans. In the Seattle area, as well as much of the West, this paralyzed entire families and slowed the economy of cities and smaller communities.

On Bainbridge, as elsewhere in the West, resentment grew like waves breaking on a beach. Issei, first generation Japanese, were prohibited from traveling off the island, even to Seattle. Government officials began "visiting" homes in late December looking for any kind of contraband. Truckloads of radios, cameras, binoculars, knives, swords and small bore rifles were hauled off the island to a storage building in Port Orchard, the county seat some 20 miles away.

The news from thousands of miles away –the "official news" -- only served to heighten the fear and resentment many Americans along the West Coast felt. Japan systematically attacked Kuala Lumpur, Burma, Hong Kong, Wake Island, the Philippines and was threatening to invade India and Australia.

Most Japanese Americans, especially older people, were left bewildered and confused by it all. Some did not understand the nuances and language of new restrictions and laws imposed on them. They struggled mightily to emotionally adapt to a new world. They were dependent on their children to tell them how to react and what to do. Directives from the federal government changed almost daily. What was true one day was history the next, replaced by a new regulation. Saturday December 6 Japanese Americans—and many other citizens-- lived in one world and beginning on December 7, they lived in another.

Government and Army officials repeatedly denied rumors that a mass evacuation of all Japanese Americans was imminent. But the talk persisted and grew. And in the meantime, the pressure, the resentment, the anger and the fear spread like a virus, reaching into the hearts and minds of men and women, regardless of their race, education or social class.

Henry laid his worn iron axe up against the side of the shed and let out a deep sigh. It was enough. He had split a large pile of firewood after a long day tilling the fields around the house and he could feel his heart beating heavily in his chest. He reached for his crumpled up kerchief in his back pocket and reached around his brown, wrinkled neck to wipe the sweat from his head and neck. Time now for dinner and tonight it would be with his son, Henry Jr., daughter-in-law, Carol, and their two young children. He expected them at any moment.

Instead, a black Ford sedan crept up the long dirt drive that was the approach to his home with his wife, Edna. Immediately, Henry was afraid. He knew that first generation Japanese were now targeted, suspicious, watched. Born in Osaka in 1889, Henry had come to Seattle, then to Bainbridge Island, in 1920. After working for a decade clearing land for other farmers, he settled in at the Port Blakely shipyard and saved enough money to build his own house, two years ago, and buy his own farm. The farm, however, was not in his name. "Alien land laws," passed in the early Twenties, prohibited Issei from owning any land. So his son's name was on the deed, though Henry Jr. –born on Bainbridge--lived two miles away, in a small house near the ferry dock. It was in the family. That was enough.

The black sedan came to a halt some twenty yards away from the house. The doors remained closed. Henry could not see inside the car and his anxiety grew by the minute. He thought of Edna in the house and turned to see if he could see her. Edna was leaning over looking out the front window at the car. He could just see her face close to the glass, worried. He saw her dark brown eyes and graying hair, pulled up over her head. Henry stood still, his worn and cracked fingers absently brushing the legs of his canvas pants.

After a long five minutes, the driver's door opened and a tall white man stood up beside the car. He wore a plain black suit, white shirt, dark tie and a small gray fedora. When he closed his door the other three doors of the sedan opened and three men dressed exactly the same got out and joined the driver at the front of the car. They huddled for a moment and the driver, who wore black-framed glasses, took a folded paper out of his breast pocket. They turned and walked toward the house. Henry walked quickly to meet them at the front steps.

"Mr. Kitano? Mr. Henry Kitano?"

Henry spoke some English, enough to get along at the grocery store and the barbershop, but it was rudimentary and he felt unsure of himself in a conversation with most white men.

"Yes."

"I am Floyd Devereaux and I am an agent of the Federal Bureau of Investigation. These are my colleagues, Mr. Dickerson, Mr. Little and Mr. Johnson." Henry nodded his head. "We are here, Mr. Kitano, under orders from the director of the FBI and the Western Defense Command, to search your house and seize any contraband we may find. I'm sure you realize, it will be in your best interest to give us your full cooperation."

Contraband. The word stuck in Henry's mind. What is contraband? Search your house, he understood, but what was contraband? He turned and looked back at the window. He could not see Edna.

"What do you look for?" Henry asked. The man who seemed in charge adjusted his collar with his finger. The other men stood with their hands folded in front of them. Henry wondered if they had guns. He turned again to look for his wife. He looked at the other three men, unconsciously looking for something that would indicate any kind of kindness or warmth or cooperation. They were mute and unreadable.

"We are entitled to seize any material, tools or equipment you might use to aid the enemy; things such as guns, short wave radios, binoculars, explosives and anything else we may deem dangerous."

Dangerous. Henry thought about that word. How could he be dangerous? Just then he saw Henry Jr. and his family coming up the drive. No, no, no —stay away, he thought. He had to restrain his hands and arms. His face and eyes tightened and he looked yet again to the window for Edna.

The agent Devereaux saw the look on Henry's face and turned to see the car driving up to the house.

"Expecting company?"

"This is my son," Henry said, with resignation and some, he didn't know why, defeat.

The family quickly flowed out of the small car, all with curious and worried expressions. Henry attempted introductions, but the FBI agent quickly interrupted and explained their purpose. Henry Jr. and Carol picked up their children and walked toward the house.

"Come in. I'm sure there will be nothing here you are interested in," Henry Jr. said. The father and son exchanged looks, but said nothing. Henry senior yielded to what he considered the worldly knowledge of his son and his familiarity with the white man's government and laws.

Once in the house, the four men unbuttoned their coats and began to look around the small living room. Edna walked in from the bedroom. She had taken off her apron and brushed her hair. She looked at her husband and saw the great sadness in his face. The small house was simple and clean, wooden floors scrubbed clean, white walls with one family picture prominent on the far wall, behind a green couch. The first agent nodded to her and spoke to the family:

"You may want to wait in the living room while we search the house. I think you will be more comfortable. If you like you may take the children out to the car…if they become upset."

Upset. Why would they be upset, Henry thought. We have nothing to hide. What will you do to upset them? What are you planning? How could that bother my grandchildren? But he remained silent.

Two of the agents headed into the hallway and the back of the house. One headed for the kitchen. The driver, Devereaux, began to look in and around the brick fireplace.

The Kitano family sat on the couch and in two chairs the flanked the fireplace, watching and listening, as their breathing became faster and more and more shallow. They could hear kitchen drawers being opened, silverware shuffling around, doors opened and slammed. Plates clattered as they were moved to the kitchen counter. Edna heard closet doors opened and closed and soft thumps on the floor – clothes? The family heard the footsteps of strange men in their home. The older Henry fought the urge to get up and go into the rooms with these strangers. Edna, who had not spoken, sat twisting her fingers in her lap and staring at the floor.

The agents were thorough. After fifteen minutes, almost in unison, they came back to the living room. Three of the agents looked at the driver and opened their hands in front of them. He nodded.

"See, I told you there would be nothing," Henry Jr. said with some relief.

"I'm afraid we're not finished," Devereaux said. "Ben, check the shed. Rick go out to the car and get some tools."

The agent Ben soon walked back into the living room with a worn paper bag in his hand.

"Take a look at this." He pulled the stained old bag off and revealed four pale red tubes. The three other agents quickly converged at his side.

"Dynamite," one of them said.

Henry Sr. sat in his old padded armchair with sad resignation. His wife sat in the matching chair on the other side of a small table. Her eyes were wide with fear. It was their son that spoke again.

"Yes, dynamite. It's perfectly legal. For years my father has used dynamite, just like everyone else here, to clear farmland. We blow up the old stumps. I'll bet you every farmer –Japanese or not-- on the island has some dynamite somewhere on their property."

"Perhaps," Floyd said. "But what concerns us right now is that you have it. Rick, take a look at the floor."

The man called Rick was back in quickly, carrying two crowbars, a straight iron shaft and two hammers. Floyd took one of the crowbars, stepped over to the fireplace and wedged in between two bricks at edge.

"Wait. What are you doing?" Henry Jr. shouted and stood up from the couch.

"Please, Mr. Kitano. We're only doing our job. We have to search the premises."

"But there is nothing here. Certainly there is nothing in the fireplace. We're just farmers for god's sake." The children, two and three, began to whimper and draw closer to their mother.

The agent Rick took the second crowbar and walked to the back of the house, turning into the bedroom that held the Kitano's steel frame double bed. An old red and white quilt was folded at the foot of the bed, partially covering the chenille spread. He wedged the crowbar into a small gap in the wide pine flooring and pulled back. He moved along the length of the board until he had pried it from the studs beneath. In the living room, the children began to cry. Edna Kitano took the youngest girl in her lap and hugged her, pulling her close to her chest. Henry stared at his only son until he caught his eyes. He shook his head. He held his right hand out, palm facing his son and ever so slightly waved it back and forth. He did not want a fight. They sat listening to the creak and the clunk and the whining of wood that came from the bedroom. The driver, Floyd, was pulling two bricks away from the wall in the living room. In the kitchen, another agent was pulling pots and pans out onto the kitchen floor. Carol, eyes filled with tears, moved to take her children out to the car.

"I'd like you to stay on the premises," Floyd turned to say. Carol nodded to him but could not find her voice. She took the boy and girl out to their car.

The fourth agent, who had gone to the second bedroom, came back to the living room with a large folded paper. He huddled with Floyd at the fireplace, talking in hushed voices. Henry and his son looked at one another.

"Mr. Kitano."

"Yes?" the older man answered.

"This appears to be a drawing of the Panama Canal."

"I don't know. What is it you have?" The old man was visibly flustered and bewildered.

His son said: "Yes, its mine. It's something I did in junior high school, a drawing of the canal. It was an assignment in seventh grade. My mother kept it because she was very proud of it."

"So, it is a rather detailed drawing of the Panama Canal?"

"Yes, it is. It was done years ago. I was twelve."

"Take this out to the car. Then help Rick in the bedroom."

"But, it's a child's drawing. From the seventh grade."

"Sorry sir." He went back to his work on the fireplace. The creak and whine in the bedroom continued. Henry Jr. looked into the kitchen, where the agent was removing the siding on the wall opposite the kitchen sink.

An hour later, the four agents came together at the front door. Carol was in the car with the children. Edna sat on the couch with her face in her hands, quietly crying. Henry Kitano sat in his chair. His face sagged with the weight of what was happening to his family and his home. Henry Jr. sat on the couch next to his mother, drumming his fingers on the padded green arm. After a short conversation with the three other agents, Floyd spoke. He referred to a small blue notebook in his left hand.

"We have four sticks of dynamite, a drawing of the Panama Canal, a radio, a pair of binoculars and three books written in Japanese," he said. "We will have to take these things."

"The books have been in our family for three generations. They are books about Buddhism," Henry Jr. said.

"That only serves to demonstrate your loyalty to your native country."

"It is not my native country." The young man spoke deliberately and loudly. "I was born here. I am an American citizen."

Floyd met Henry junior's eyes with an unexpected hardness. "That may be, but your father is not. We are going to have to take Mr. Kitano with us."

"What? Where? This is absurd."

"I'm afraid I can't tell you that."

"This man is my father, a loyal American. He has lived here and worked here for nearly 30 years. He is proud to be an American. He has <u>never</u> done anything to anyone. You can't just <u>*take*</u> him."

"I can, Mr. Kitano. And I will."

Edna lifted her face. Here eyes were swollen and her cheeks flushed with blood. She moved to her husband's chair and knelt in front of him, hugging his legs. She spoke to him in Japanese. Floyd scribbled something in his notebook. Two of the agents moved to the side of Henry Kitano's chair. The other man opened the front door.

Edna stood and watched the black sedan roll up dust as it left the farm.

CHAPTER SEVEN

Will was a saver. He grew up in a family tradition of saving and conserving. Even though his family was middle class and his father a physician, his father and grandfather, close as he could remember, saved just about everything. He had distinct memories of his grandfather saving tin foil, washing it if necessary, folding it and putting it back into a kitchen drawer to be used again. His grandfather on his father's side, Robert F. Whitman, who worked for the railroad all of his life, saved string, tying it end to end and rolling it into a ball. Will had clear pictures to this day of the string, tied to stakes around a section of the garden, some white, some brown, some thin, some thick, all from Grandpa Bob's roll. Everything, he used to say, can be reused. His voice echoed in Will's memory: "No use throwing that away. We'll find a use for it."

His father, Robert E. Whitman, carried on that value, that way of living. If something was a quality product, it could last a lifetime; in fact, it should last a lifetime. Shoes were re-heeled and resoled. Socks were darned. Pants were mended, much to Will's embarrassment when he went to school. Any piece of clothing, a shirt, say, that had seen its long life come to an end was put into service as a rag, first a "clean" rag and when that phase ended, a dirty rag, for outdoors. Will's father had three suits, a blue one, a gray one and, for formal occasions such as funerals, a black one. Will still remembered him in his gray suit, a dark blue tie and his worn black shoes, leaving for the office in the morning. "My patients don't care if I have a new suit," he told Will; "in fact, I think they like it that I don't."

For her part, Will's mother Bea made use of every ounce of food that came into her kitchen. Roasts became stews after they had been sliced at the table once. Chicken bones became soup. Fish bones became fish stock and any thing left over became fertilizer for the garden. She was so good at using food again, that a teenage Will crowned her the "queen of leftovers," a title she accepted but did not exactly relish.

Conservation as a family value spilled over to the use of words. Will's grandfather was laconic and pithy. His father carried the gene. "Why waste words," he often said to Will, who grew up inured to the practice of watching for signs, paying attention to body language and studying facial expressions. Almost as a dog might, he watched his parents carefully and learned to know what they wanted and how they felt. This was sometimes hard for Molly. More accustomed to a lively sisterly exchange in her own farm family, she expected more conversation from Will.

"God, you're a writer. Words are your business," she would say in moments of frustration. Will had no good rejoinder. Molly, on the other end of the spectrum, would talk about almost anything, the smallest thing, the details of her life, that Will would never think of sharing. But through her expressions, he slowly came to know the joy of talking about details. He could, now, in their relationship, go with Molly when she talked about the beauty of the moth's wings on the kitchen window or the path the black beetle took across the old wooden floor.

Will realized his own lack of verbosity. His only excuse, which he rarely said out loud, was that he saved it all for the printed page. After the first couple of years of their marriage, she came to accept his silence and, in fact, came to appreciate it. He had a way of condensing the truth down to a few words, sifting through the unnecessary and keeping the core of meaning. She trusted that if something needed to be said, Will would say it and in the moments that he felt like talking, he delivered. He said things that mattered, things that moved her, made her think of the world in a new way, words that touched her heart. His words were few, but clear and usually carried deep meaning.

Will stretched out his full six feet under the covers, touching the black steel frame of the double bed with the soles of his feet and his long toes. Molly joined him in bed, hiking up her pink and blue flannel nightgown to her waist and rolling over into Will, draping her leg over his legs.

"Still love me?" Will asked with a slight smile.

"Maybe." She paused and looked into his eyes. "What have you done?" Molly rubbed the three-day-old stubble on his chin with her knuckles.

"Nothing. You know. I think I'm just feeling a little unsure tonight." Molly realized he wasn't kidding around.

"Unsure?"

"Maybe. It just seems we're pretty much alone in this, as far as the press goes anyway. Everything else I read sounds pretty crazy, just laced with hatred. Do you think we're right?" He rolled his head over quickly and looked into her eyes, looking for a response in her face. Molly whisked her rust-colored curls off her forehead and looked into his eyes.

"Look, this is fear and racism, pure and simple," she said. "This is a story as old as we are, we human beings. People look different. Their eyes are different, they speak funny, their skin is a different color, they think differently, they have a different religion—and we are afraid of them and we find all kinds of rationalizations to not trust them and cast them out. It's happened over and over again and it's happening again now. It's fear, Will. We're afraid they're going to take our jobs, marry our children, overwhelm us with their growing families, work cheaper than we do and worship a different god. You know this. I know this. And if we can't say what we believe in our own paper and stand behind it in the face of so-called popular opinion, what good is it to have this little newspaper at all?"

Will smiled at her.

"Yeah, you're right. We're right."

"Beware of the righteous," Molly said and laughed her girlish high-pitched laugh in her throat. "Seriously, Will. I don't put much weight into right or wrong. I think that believing you are right is the beginning of a downfall. If we get up on a horse that's too high, we risk losing touch with the people who read our stuff. I think we have to stick to the law, stick to the things we've agreed on in our society."

"Agreed on?"

"Yes, the agreements we've made in our constitution and in our law books...the covenants, the moral agreements. If we don't have those to fall back on, we're in for chaos."

"Babe, what happens to progress then? What happens to social change? Was it right that half our nation had slaves? Was it the law? Was it right that women did not get to vote? Was that the law?"

He rolled up on his elbow and looked into her eyes.

"I understand your point Will. But I'm afraid of getting too strident, too righteous about this. After all, isn't that what we're criticizing others for?"

"Yes, but..."

"And what *if* the whole rest of the island, maybe the whole state of Washington is against us? Is that what's important?"

Will was quiet for a moment, shaken by her point of view. He shook his head.

"It wouldn't matter to me that much," he said. "It matters that I think what I think and feel what I feel and that you're with me."

Molly reached over and took his chin her in hand. She could smell his breath and relished it.

"I am with you 100 percent. Listen to what I just said. I think we can stand against racism and against fear. I think we can look at what it means to be a citizen of this country. I think we can support the families on this island in their pain and time of need. We just need to name what we see, call things as we see them and not claim that we –you and I—have some moral high ground." She paused and put her finger up in front of Will's face and went on:

"But maybe war changes things. *Maybe* there are gray areas that we don't know so much about and don't have a good feel for. I just don't think we can be so certain that we think we know everything; that's all. We know what we know and we can also say we don't know, that we doubt, that we have misgivings. That's part of our truth too."

Will rolled over and turned out the bedside lamp, an ornate glass table lamp that was a gift from Molly's grandmother. He rolled back to Molly and took her in his arms, burying his face in her curls.

"I love you peanut," he whispered. "Just stay connected to me." Molly slowly nodded her head and held him even more tightly. The rain on the roof and Will's breathing was all she heard.

After Molly drifted off to sleep Will looked over at her face. Sweet, innocent, he thought. Sleeps like a baby, peaceful. All seems right with the world when I see her like this. He looked out the bedroom window at the shape of the big Doug firs swaying back and forth in the night breeze. They seemed peaceful too. Then the war came to mind – he pictured explosions, bombs dropping, men running for their lives. Fear. What was it? What made a man run for his life? His face contorted, his body tight as a drum and his stomach twisting in on itself? Was it as simple as death? Were we all just afraid of death? And how was that fear, the fear on the battlefield, different from the fear that drove men to hate other races? Were we human beings wired to hate other human beings if we didn't know who they were, because they were darker, or lighter, or their eyes looked different than ours did? Was this somehow an evolutionary programming?

He rolled over on his back and put both hands behind his head.

What was the essence of fear? He'd never really thought about it before, just kind of accepted it as a word that described part of the human condition. Fear, love, hate, anger, sadness, joy…we all experience all of those things at one time or another. But what are they, really? He knew the standard fight or flight stuff, that we had certain reactions that moved us to run or attack the other. But what was that made up of? Reaction, that's an interesting word. What are we reacting to? Something we see or hear, I guess. But then we sometimes get afraid when there's nothing in front of us, nothing right there threatening us. What's that about? It's got to be our thoughts. Our own thoughts scare us. Is that right? Not many of us, despite this war, are directly face to face with someone who's going to kill us or even hurt us, yet we still have fears. All of us who are home safe in our cozy little houses are still afraid of the Japanese and the Germans. It's got to be our thoughts, the things we make up in our heads.

Predictions! We are busy predicting that something is going to happen to us. It hasn't happened yet and it may never happen, but we hang on to the prediction. That's got to be it. Based on what we hear from our neighbor, read in the paper or hear on our radios, we get afraid that something is going to hurt us. But some of us are afraid of things—and people—that others are not. That's got to be training. We're trained into fear. We're trained into the things we're afraid of. We learn, from our parents no doubt, to be afraid of certain things, certain kinds of things.

Wow. I'm really tempted to wake Molly up and talk to her about this. He smiled. But it might scare her.

CHAPTER EIGHT

Christmas was clearly going to be different in the Sugimoto household this year. "Mutt" Sugimoto and his wife Suki had already resigned themselves to the fact that they would have little to give each other or their children. In fact, they felt, as the days of December reeled past them, that this Christmas was going to be a season of loss.

Mutikano Sugimoto had come to America in 1926 when he fully realized, that as the number three son in his family, he would inherit none of his father's clothing shop in Tokyo. As in most Japanese families, the wealth and the power in the family went directly to the firstborn son. Mutt's two older brothers were determined to continue their father's business and the young boy saw the handwriting on the wall by the time he was in high school. Mutt left his island home with a heavy heart, determined to make his own way in the world.

With a small cash investment, he decided to try beet farming in this small Puget Sound community and in his first year sold the entire crop to a wholesaler from Oregon. Beets were easy to grow and there were plenty of canning operations and sugar producers within 100 miles. Alone in America and not having a very good way with English, Mutt sent a carefully worded advertisement back to Japan for a "picture bride." He sought a woman who could help him on the farm, keep an orderly house, keep him warm on cold winter nights and, hopefully, they would come to love one another. After two months he got his first letter from Suki. She seemed bright, optimistic and ready for an adventure in America. The picture she sent showed a thin but well muscled young woman with short black hair, dressed in Western clothes. He had a good feeling about the look on her face. He believed that infatuation was not necessary for a good marriage. Love would grow between them. The deal was made and, in the spring of 1928, Mutt met Suki in Seattle and took her on the ferry to his modest island home. Now, after thirteen years of successful farming, their future, as two Tokyo-born Japanese, was cloudy.

After a couple of long talks late at night, they had decided to rid themselves of anything Japanese that could be used against them. They had read the words of the US Army and the FBI and heard about their neighbors. Anything could be suspicious. Anything could be a reason to take away all they owned.

Mutt, Suki and Amy, their 11-year-old daughter, gathered in their back yard on a cool December night just after it turned dark. They had not yet had dinner. They heard the wind blowing through the fir trees adjoining their farm to the east. Mutt had built a small fire in a steel barrel he used to burn trash.

For a few moments the three of them stood around the fire, staring into the flames. Amy stood next to her mother, hugging her around the waist. Mutt reached into his side pocket and pulled out a handful of white papers, letters he had received from uncles and aunts in Tokyo, written in Japanese. He took a step forward and tossed them into the barrel. They flared up, illuminating the faces of the three. Next he pushed in a text on Buddhism, open faced to easily catch fire. Tears ran down Amy's face. She reached over the barrel and dropped in a small doll, dressed in a kimono. Suki wrapped her arm around her daughter's shoulders. She dropped in an umbrella painted with cherry blossoms. Another doll, this one with a black bobbed haircut and Japanese facial features, went into the fire. Amy choked back a sob. Mutt threw an aged photograph into the fire, of his father, standing ramrod straight in a Japanese army uniform, glaring at the camera. He followed the picture with a small sword encased in wood, a red tassel on the hilt, a red-and-white scroll on the scabbard. Suki had the last item, a dark red obi, a sash to be worn around her waist when she dressed in her Japanese dress. She held the obi to her face and breathed deeply, taking in the rich jasmine odor, then quickly tossed the sash into the flames.

"We must be totally American now," Mutt said. "We must leave everything that is Japanese. That is behind us now." Suki and Amy were silent. The three of them stood watching the fire burn down, the December sky large around them.

CHAPTER NINE

The Andrew Sisters singing "Boogie Woogie Bugle Boy" rang through the small kitchen as Molly fried four bright yellow eggs.

"Hey, did you see that coffee went up to 29 cents a pound this week?" she sounded just a little outraged.

"I guess it's not that bad, considering some folks can't even get it," Will yelled back from the other room.

"Yeah, yeah. But 29 cents a pound!"

"Yeah, that's bad but I don't think it's the end of it," Will said. "Hey, let's have Frank and Colleen over this week. I think we need to finish up that conversation we were having."

"OK, I'll call them."

Frank and Colleen arrived that evening with a six-pack of Schlitz and a new deck of cards. Over the past six months the couples had been playing Setback, a partners bidding game they all had grown fond of. Will and Colleen usually played against Frank and Molly, as it was tonight.

"You know," Molly said after two hands, "I think this game is a lot like life. You don't really score any points unless you take a risk. The bigger the risk, the more points you can make."

"And the more you can lose," Will chimed in.

"Oh, thanks for that, Mr. Sunnyside up. I'll bid three."

"Atta girl," Frank said. "Go for it." Molly led with the ace of diamonds.

"Did you here what happened at Gerry Tanaka's grocery?" Will looked around the table. Heads shook no.

"He was stacking some canned goods yesterday late, you know lining up the cans so they're at the front of the shelf, and he found a handwritten note. Will paused for emphasis. "Don't shop here. This is a Jap store." It upset him, understandably. He goes over to his produce manager and the produce guy says, "Yeah, I found one too, in the potatoes. It said: 'Japs go back home.'"

"Geez," Colleen said. "That's ugly."

"You ain't heard nothin' yet," Frank said, slapping down a queen of diamonds to take the second trick. "Over in Seattle this young Japanese couple comes home from a trip downtown with their two kids and someone had painted the side of their house with yellow paint: 'Yellow peril,' it said. And down in Fresno, two young Japanese guys were just walking down the street and a gang of white men beat the you-know-what out of them." He took a swig of his beer. And, you know what, I don't think this is going to get any better any time soon."

"Yeah, I heard that Japanese people are being fired in Seattle, for no reason at all," Colleen said. "And that banks and even some businesses like stores and gas stations won't do business with them. They won't let them come in and buy anything -- can you believe that?"

Will shook his head. "This is getting hysterical. We're just lumping everyone with tan skin into the same pot. It really turns my stomach."

"Will, I hesitate to say this," Frank said, "because I know how you feel, but we lost 2,400 American men and women at Pearl Harbor. They were undefended, just sitting there on deck, on the ground, in their beds. Two thousand four hundred people."

Will sat his beer down and clasped his hands in front of his chest. He took a deep breath.

"I fully understand that Frank." Colleen watched Will with a worried look on her face. Molly was looking at Frank. "But we've got to be able to make some distinctions. We can't arrest all the Germans in this country. We can't round up all the Italians and send them home. It's just pure racism. Think of the hundreds of thousands of people who streamed through Ellis Island and made their homes here. Think of their children, who are now legitimate US citizens. Hell, we're made up of people who came here from somewhere else. We can't just pick out one race and put them all away somewhere. They get to live their lives too."

Frank hung his head, discouraged and, for the moment, yielding to his friend's point of view. Colleen touched his arm.

"You know Will, the funny thing is I think you're right. You're right in your head and in what you believe. But there's something else here that I'm not proud of, in myself or any of my fellow citizens, and it's in my gut. I just can't forget that some sneaky bastards attacked an American base and killed a couple thousand people and that some of those bastards' relatives live in my town." He reached a hand out toward Will and left it on the table between them. "I'm sorry. Hell, I don't even know why I'm apologizing. I just feel this way. I can't help it. Call me a racist if you want to, but there are some generalities that are just true."

"And which generalities would those be," Will asked in a low voice. Frank sat up in his chair, elbows on the table.

"That there are Japanese people in Seattle, Los Angeles and San Francisco that are sons, daughters, brothers, uncles and nieces of people in Japan and they can't help but feel some tie, some loyalty to each other. I mean if push came to shove, isn't blood thicker than water?"

"That would mean that if we were at war with Italy," Will paused and looked hard at Frank, as if to say 'we are, dummy,' "that you would feel some ties with the folks who support Mussolini."

"You know Will, you're my good friend and I don't want this to ruin our friendship. That said, I do think about my cousins and my grandparents in the old country and what they must be going through."

"So does that mean I should dump paint on your house? Does that mean I should stop taking my car to your shop?"

"Will, you know I'm not a danger to this country. I love it. I'm an individual. I don't think and feel just as an Italian."

"Exactly."

CHAPTER TEN

The next morning Will sat in his small office, feet propped up on his old wooden desk, reading the editorial page in the San Francisco Chronicle:

"It is our view that all enemy aliens be evacuated from California, Oregon and Washington as soon as possible. All Japanese, including American born, must be able to prove actual severance of any allegiance to the Japanese government and, if they cannot, they must be classified as enemy aliens. No passes or temporary permits should be issued to any enemy aliens.

"The industrial, communications and military installations in these states are so vital to our war effort that _any_ hostile activities in these states will be a serious embarrassment to our Armed Services and to our country as a whole.

"The reputed operations of Axis spies and Fifth Columnists in Europe and the known activities of such elements during the recent Japanese attack on Hawaii clearly indicate the danger of temporizing with such a menace. It is deemed to be a certainty that any hostile operations in these states will be characterized by a similar treacherous activity. From what we know of the Japanese character and mentality, it is also dangerous to rely on the loyalty of native-born persons of Japanese blood unless such loyalty can be affirmatively demonstrated.

"In this horrible war racial affinities are not severed by migration. The Japanese race is an enemy race and, while many second and third generation Japanese have become United States citizens and have become 'Americanized,' the racial strains are undiluted. To conclude otherwise is to expect that children born of white parents on Japanese soil to sever all racial affinity and become loyal Japanese subjects, ready to fight and, if necessary, die for Japan in a war against the nation of their parents.

"That Japan is allied with Germany and Italy in this struggle for world dominance is not ground for assuming that any Japanese, barred from assimilation by convention as he is, though born and raised in the Unites States, will not turn against this nation when the final test of loyalty comes. It therefore follows, that along the vital Pacific Coast, over 112,000 potential enemies of Japanese extraction are at large today."

Wow, Will thought to himself. There it is in black and white. Just like Molly said, just like Frank said, racism pure and simple. It got Will's blood going again; something started in his stomach, wound around and climbed up his chest and into his throat. He felt like yelling, something, anything, just yelling. The phone rang. It was Molly.

"Hey babe, I've got this publication called *The Golden Bear*. It's the official publication of a group called The Native Sons and Daughters of the Golden West."

"Yes, I've heard of them. Pretty conservative."

"Right, you said it. I've got it in front of me; let me summarize what they said.

"Let's see…if the state and federal governments had only used the Exclusion Law and the Alien Land Law, if the quote Jap propaganda agencies unquote in this country had been silenced, if we had we denied citizenship to those Japs born here—they go on like this for awhile – if quote Jap dollars not been so sought after by landowners and businesses, if the quote white-Jap and the yellow-Jap fifth columnists been properly disposed of, if the Japs had been denied—get this—a breeding ground for dual-citizenship…then the treacherous Japs probably would not have bombed Pearl Harbor and this nation would not be at war with Japan today."

"Dammit. That's just hateful."

"And, Will, I just heard on the radio that the American Legion has called for the evacuation of all Japanese to places at least 300 miles inland. And they added something like: this is no time to worry about hurting the feelings of our enemy."

As 1941 became 1942 it seemed as if the sluice gates had been opened and a full flow of frustration, prejudice, fear and hatred was loosed on the West Coast. Feeding the fear was the aggression of the Japanese Army throughout the Pacific Rim in Asia. In early January the Japanese conquered Kuala Lumpur. A week later they invaded Burma. Singapore, Bali and Sumatra followed. In mid-February they loosed aerial attacks on Australia. Clearly they intended to dominate the Pacific.

In February in Washington State, thirty eight American Legion posts passed resolutions urging the evacuation of all persons of Japanese descent, proclaiming that "this is no time for namby-pamby pussyfooting or consideration of minute constitutional rights."

The West Coast agricultural community turned against the Japanese Americans too. In a newsletter published that spring, "The Grower-Shipper Vegetable Association" wrote:

"We're charged with wanting to get rid of the Japs for selfish reasons. We might as well be honest. We do. It's a question of whether the white man lives on the Pacific Coast or the brown man. They came to this valley to work and they stayed to take over. If all the Japs were removed tomorrow, we'd never miss them because white farmers can take over and produce everything the Jap grows. And we don't want them back when the war ends either."

The Western Growers Protective Association and the California Farm Bureau Federation joined in demanding harsh measures against all Japanese, assuring politicians and the public that their removal would in no way diminish agricultural production or supply. State and federal officials were concerned that the imprisonment of Japanese field workers would slow the flow of fruits and vegetables to the American public.

Politicians were quick to join the growing tide. The mayor of Los Angeles came out in favor of mass evacuation. The Los Angeles County Board of Supervisors fired all of county Japanese employees and adopted a resolution asking for the federal government to ship all Japanese aliens away from the West Coast. Sixteen county governments in California adopted like resolutions.

The City of San Francisco demanded suppression of all Japanese language newspapers. The City of Portland revoked business licenses of all Japanese nationals. The California State Personnel Board ordered "all descendants of enemy aliens" barred from civil service positions. The California State Department of Agriculture was authorized to revoke the produce-handling licenses of enemy aliens.

California Congressman Leland Ford, apparently responding to constituents and his own sense of what was right, was a leader in the assault on Japanese Americans early on. He informed the director of the FBI, the Secretary of War and the Secretary of the Navy of his plan in January, 1942: "All Japanese, whether citizens or not, (should) be placed in inland concentration camps. As justification for this, I submit that if an American born Japanese who is a citizen is really patriotic and wishes to make his contribution to the safety and welfare of this country, right here is his opportunity to do so; namely, that by permitting himself to be placed in a concentration camp, he would be making his sacrifice and he should be wiling to do it if he is patriotic and is working for us. As against his sacrifice, millions of other native born citizens are willing to lay down their lives, which is a far greater sacrifice, of course, than being placed in a concentration camp."

Not all Americans were taken up with the hysteria. Shortly after the attack on Hawaii, Congress commissioned a study of Japanese American communities in the Western United States. The report, which Congress and the President had full access to, found that "ninety to ninety eight percent of Japanese Americans are loyal to the United States. The Nisei are pathetically eager to show this loyalty. They are not Japanese in culture. They are foreigners to Japan. Though American citizens, they are not accepted by Americans, largely because they look differently and can be easily recognized. The Japanese American Citizens League should be encouraged -- while an eye is kept open -- to see that Tokyo does not get its finger in this pie, which it has in a few cases attempted to do. The loyal Nisei hardly knows where to turn. Some gesture of protection or wholehearted acceptance of this group would go a long way to swinging them away from any last romantic hankering after old Japan. They are not oriental or mysterious. They are very American and are of a proud, self-respecting race suffering from a little inferiority complex and a lack of contact with the white boys they went to school with. They are eager for this contact and to work alongside them."

The report went unheeded.

Newspaper and radio journalists, much to Will's disappointment and shame, fell right into line.

The young cartoonist Theodor Geisel (Dr. Seuss) penned an editorial cartoon depicting a line of Japanese men, dressed all the same, in black suits and black bowler hats, glasses and thin mustaches. The line stretched over three states, Washington, Oregon and California, lined up waiting to receive TNT from a booth manned by other Japanese. A Japanese man was on top of the booth with a spyglass. The caption: "Waiting for a signal from home."

Geisel would write: "... right now, when the Japs are planting their hatchets in our skulls, it seems like a hell of a time for us to smile and warble: 'Brothers!' It is a rather flabby battle cry. If we want to win, we've got to kill Japs, whether it depresses John Haynes Holmes or not. We can get palsy-walsy afterward with those that are left."

Conservative columnist Westbrook Pegler wrote in his February, 1942 column:

"...the enemy has been scouting our coast. The Japs ashore are communicating with the enemy offshore and...on the basis of 'what is known to be taking place' there are signs that a well-organized blow is being withheld only until it can do the most damage...We are so dumb and considerate of the minute constitutional rights and even the political feelings and influence of people whom we have every reason to anticipate with preventive action!"

In just a month's time, the Constitutional rights of thousands of Americans had become inconsequential..."minute."

A columnist for the Hearst newspapers, Henry McLemore, wrote in late January:

"The only Japanese apprehended have been the ones the FBI actually had something on. The rest of them, so help me, are free as birds. There isn't an airport in California that isn't flanked by Japanese farms. There is hardly an airfield where the same situation doesn't exist.

"I know this is the melting pot of the world and all men are created equal and there must be no such thing as race or creed hatred, but do those things go when a country is fighting for its life? Not in my book. No country has ever won a war because of courtesy and I trust and pray we won't be the first because of a lovely, gracious spirit...

"I am for the immediate removal of every Japanese on the West Coast to a point deep in the interior. I don't mean a nice part of the interior. Herd 'em up, pack 'em off and give 'em the inside room in the badlands. Let 'em be pinched, hurt, hungry and dead up against it...

"Personally, I hate the Japanese. And that goes for all of them."

Will read this column in the Seattle Times and he could hardly contain his disgust. He sat down with a heaviness of body and spirit. He felt the accumulation of all that had gone on in the past week. As he has done for so many years of his life, he looked down at his old Royal; the black keys, ringed in silver faded on the T, H, J, I, E, where he hit them the hardest. ASDFGHJKL: He typed: the quick brown fox jumped over the lazy brown dog. No errors. Hmmm. He was able to think more clearly when he sat down at the typewriter. Words came when his fingers touched the keys. His brain started working in a different way. The contact his fingertips made with the keys started an expectation that something meaningful was going to be said. No, not said, written. The familiar whack of the flying key head on the paper, once twice, over and over again, started his juices going. He liked the imprint the steel key head made on the soft, bone-colored typing paper and the way the ribbon popped up for capital letters, the way it poked along through the narrow gap between the paper and the ribbon guide. Some of the paper itself and the ink were retained on the key head, on the letter 'W' or the number 4. Writing like this, having this intimate contact with his typewriter gave him a sense of power, an illusion perhaps. He could write something that might change the world he lived in. He could write something that would impact one, or two, of his readers. Words...symbols of something else. He often thought that words weren't real, just fingers that pointed to something else that was real. But they did carry meaning. They were weighted with impact on those who heard or read them. Danger. Hope. Optimism. Fear. Love. Just words. Beware. Watch your neighbor. Spend your money. Aren't we swell? Buy my book. Dress well. God is real. Butter is good for you. He made his living with words, small words in type that ran together on the page and large black words in headlines that drew people to the page. JAPS BOMB PEARL HARBOR. ISLAND DEFENSES SET. TWO TEENS KILLED IN CRASH. SPARTANS WIN BIG. TOURISM OUTLOOK GOOD. NEW HARDWARE OPENS. Of all the words he had written in his life, he had the feeling that what he was about to write would mean more than all of the words before this. Maybe not tonight, maybe not tomorrow, but soon. Was he up to it? Could he say what he wanted to say? Would he choose the right words? Was he good enough? Strong enough? Could he get it out and on paper?

He slowly placed his fingers on the keys and typed the first word. Shift, caps, shift down, three whacks: "The"

The time has come to bear out the truth in our words, written two months ago in our extra edition of The Review. We spoke of the danger of a blind, wild hysterical hatred of all persons who can trace ancestry to Japan.

Will pursed his lips and squeezed his lower lip together with his fingers.

Up and down the Pacific coast, in the newspapers and in the halls of Congress are words of hatred now for all Japanese, whether they be citizens of America or not. These words reached a shrieking crescendo when Henry McLemore, with all the intelligence of a blind pig, wrote in the Seattle Times: 'Personally I hate the Japanese. And that goes for all of them.'

That may be patriotism of a hysterical degree, but it certainly isn't the kind of patriotism that will win this war. Let us think, for a moment, what would happen if the government should adopt Mr. McLemore's fervid pleas for the 'immediate removal of every Japanese on the West Coast to a point deep in the interior. I don't mean a nice part of the interior either."

To say nothing of the economic impact this would have on the entire West, consider the wreckage that it would bring to the lives of thousands and thousands of loyal American citizens who can't avoid Japanese ancestry. For who—besides those so blind as Mr. McLemore - can say that the large majority of our American Japanese citizens are not loyal to the land of their birth - this United States? Their record bespeaks nothing but loyalty. Their sons are in the Army; they are heavy contributors to the Red Cross and the defense bond drive. Even in Hawaii, was there any record of any Japanese-American citizen being other than intensely loyal to our country?

The Review argues only with Mr. McLemore and his ilk. It will not dispute the federal government if it, in its considered wisdom, calls for removal from the coast of all Japanese. Such orders—which we hope will not come—will be based on military necessities and not on hatred.

Will sat back in his chair and shook his head. He was troubled. What difference does it make what it's based on, military necessity or hatred? The effect will be the same. Thousands of lives will be wrecked. Millions of dollars in crops and closed businesses will be lost. Families will be torn apart. And think of the shame our Japanese friends will suffer. He pictured some of the men and women he knew on the island, saw their faces as they heard the news and fully realized the implications. That shame will stick with them forever.

Should I change that sentence? 'We will not dispute the federal government'...why the hell not? The government can be wrong, dead wrong. Sure we've been attacked, sure lives have been lost – and many more to come I'm afraid, but these people I know had nothing whatsoever to do with that. They are innocent. They are American citizens. They love this country as much as Molly and I do. I'm damn sure of that.

God, I need a drink.

CHAPTER ELEVEN

Will liked his alone time. He liked to recharge his batteries by reading a newspaper in the evening or listening to music, Glenn Miller preferably. He wasn't much for parties or public occasions. Molly led the way in their social life, such as it was, arranging for dinners with other couples or day trips to the city for a movie or music. But mostly the couple stayed in their island home.

Tonight he was listening to Artie Shaw and thinking about his father. A country doctor, Robert Whitman had married Will's mother late in life, at 35, and they had lived out their lives in a small Wisconsin town, serving the small, tight-knit population as care givers and informal counselors. Helping others seemed to come naturally to his dad, as did honesty and directness. He rarely said more than he needed to, especially when he was talking to Will or his younger brother, and his tongue could be sharp when one of the boys stepped outside the lines "Dr. Bob" had drawn for his sons. Will admired most the quality of attention his father gave him. When he sat down to talk to Will, or when Will would ask a question—a good question, one that presented an opportunity to learn something, for he was not tolerant of what he called "self-serving frivolity"—his father would put down whatever he was doing and look Will in the eye. He would inevitably say, at some point,

"What do *you* think Will?" He could hear his voice now...and what do you think Will? His mind reeled with what had happened in his world and in the world of all the people he cared about just a month. His only peace, it seemed, was when he talked to Molly, or pictured her face, as he did now.

An island gives people an opportunity for a distinct sense of place. This island, laying at the edge of a large undersea valley eight miles west of Seattle, offered a rich and varied landscape to take advantage of. The Suquamish tribe had lived here peacefully for hundreds of years, harvesting salmon and clams, hunting deer, rabbits, pheasant and quail and using the Western red cedars that are here in abundance for everything from long house building to baskets. When the Europeans came they saw the opportunities for harvesting the cedars and the 120-foot Douglas firs that took so well to the wet, moderate climate. Scandinavians, Germans, Poles, English, Slavs and Serbs flocked here at the turn of the century in order to harvest the giant trees and turn them into the long wooden sailing ships that dominated trade on the West Coast until the steel ships took over.

Chinese, Filipino and Japanese joined them from the other side of the globe, searching for opportunities that did not exist at home. For the most part the ethnic groups kept to themselves, huddled in wooden houses in various neighborhoods on the island. Eventually, working together at the shipyard at Port Blakely and the want to do business together, brought families in close contact and relationships were formed. The Asians maintained a sense of distance from the rest, staying in their own houses and working their farms, once they moved there, holding on to bits and pieces of the homeland's culture by studying Buddhism, the Japanese language and martial arts and getting together to watch Japanese films. Rice bowls, sake cups, scrolls and traditional dress were lovingly stored and brought out on special occasions.

By the end of the 1930's many first generation Japanese had saved enough money to start their own business or own their own farms. They raised strawberries that were shipped and eaten all over the world. In 1940 island farmers produced two million pounds of strawberries. They grew beets, cucumbers, lettuce and flowers and kept bees for honey. Cutting lumber in the early part of the century opened up farmland and the moderate winters and warm summers were ideal for many crops.

The island was, as yet, unconnected to the mainland to the west, separated by a quarter-mile passage from the large, arrow-shaped Kitsap Peninsula. A fleet of privately owned small ferries, dubbed the Mosquito Fleet for the way they flitted around the island and back and forth to Seattle, served to get islanders back and forth when they needed. But for the most part people stayed on the island. There was a strong sense of community and there was plenty of work to be done at home. A trip away from the farm and into the big city was indeed a special occasion.

Like the Native Americans before them, the Japanese took what nature gave them, hunting and fishing, gathering seaweed and clams, scooping out small octopi from the tide pools at the shore, combing the woods for mushrooms and eating fresh eggs from their chickens. In addition to farming, they opened grocery stores, plant nurseries, barbershops, photo studios, bathhouses and gas stations. The small, ethnic neighborhoods often had their own small post offices.

The island was only four miles wide and twelve miles long. To the people who moved here, worked hard, saved their money, put down roots and built their homes here, it was indeed a special place to build a life, diverse, peaceful and generous.

Molly's own personal history fit this place like her hand in a velvet glove. Raised on a farm in eastern Washington, Molly was the oldest of three girls and bore the responsibilities of an oldest child in a hard-working family. For three generations, the family had maintained a summer home on Bainbridge Island, making the trek over the Cascade Mountains to enjoy the cool breeze off Puget Sound and take a break from the dry, hot wheat fields. As her grandmother aged and slowed down she began to stay in the island cottage for more and more of the year. Molly often lingered with her, despite the pressure to go back home and work with the rest of the family. School brought her home in early September the year she was twelve. That fall her grandmother fell ill and died within a week.

Molly's love for Grandma Kate and her time with her on the island cemented her desire to return and live in that small wooden house. It was primitive, as were many homes there. In the old days, there was no electricity, no indoor toilet and the heat came exclusively from old wood stoves in the living room and the kitchen. Will and Molly had added some modern conveniences – electric service, a bathroom and a phone – but the cottage retained the feel it had had for generations before. Molly remembered with fondness getting her baths in the kitchen, standing in a galvanized steel tub half full of warm water while her mother washed her, then hugged her with a big white towel. In the summer the family would shower outside, under a fifty-gallon drum her father had put on the roof of the shed, filled with rainwater and rigged with a showerhead. She and her sisters would often shower and run around the yard nude to dry off. Then they would slip into cotton shorts and warm sweaters and go inside for dinner, their hair still wet and cool on their young necks.

Sometimes now, Molly would sit in the house alone, while Will was out at a meeting or putting the paper to bed at the office and she would picture herself and her sisters, sitting on the couch together reading, running around the house in the dark or out at the old henhouse collecting eggs. She carried those moments in her heart.

That night, a rather mild night for February, Will came home late. He was agitated. Molly smiled at him and hugged him in the living room. She could smell the sweat on his cheeks and neck.

"What is it dear?"

"Well, he's gone and done it."

"Who?"

"Roosevelt. He's declared the whole West Coast a military zone and given the Army the authority to move whoever they want out of here."

"Anyone?"

Will was taking off his coat, dropping his folder of papers on the low table in front of the couch. "Yeah, anyone. The order is not aimed specifically, by name, at Japanese Americans, but it gives the generals the power to pick up anyone they want and move them wherever they want. We need to get a copy of it Mol. It's called executive order 9066."

Executive Order 9066 was a broad and ambiguous initiative that handed over complete authority to the Secretary of War and "military commanders he may from time to time designate" to decide who may live where, when, how and why. The order made no distinctions in ethnic background or nationality, but it soon became clear by the way it was carried out that it was aimed at the Japanese population along the West Coast. Roosevelt had given in to the enormous pressure from Congress, the public and the military that had built up since the attack on Hawaii. The legal community was not at all sure the order was constitutional, but it too eventually gave in. The "all we have to fear is fear itself" President had yielded to the fear of the enemy within.

Will got a copy off the AP wire the next day.

Executive Order No. 9066
The President   Executive Order
Authorizing the Secretary of War to Prescribe Military Areas

Whereas the successful prosecution of the war requires every possible protection against espionage and against sabotage to national-defense material, national-defense premises, and national-defense utilities as defined in Section 4, Act of April 20, 1918, 40 Stat. 533, as amended by the Act of November 30, 1940, 54 Stat. 1220, and the Act of August 21, 1941, 55 Stat. 655 (U.S.C., Title 50, Sec. 104);

Now, therefore, by virtue of the authority vested in me as President of the United States, and Commander in Chief of the Army and Navy, I hereby authorize and direct the Secretary of War, and the Military Commanders whom he may from time to time designate, whenever he or any designated Commander deems such action necessary or desirable, to prescribe military areas in such places and of such extent as he or the appropriate Military Commander may determine, from which any or all persons may be excluded, and with respect to which, the right of any person to enter, remain in, or leave shall be subject to whatever restrictions the Secretary of War or the appropriate Military Commander may impose in his discretion. The Secretary of War is hereby authorized to provide for residents of any such area who are excluded there from, such transportation, food, shelter, and other accommodations as may be necessary, in the judgment of the Secretary of War or the said Military Commander, and until other arrangements are made, to accomplish the purpose of this order. The designation of military areas in any region or locality shall supersede designations of prohibited and restricted areas by the Attorney General under the Proclamations of December 7 and 8, 1941, and shall supersede the responsibility and authority of the Attorney General under the said Proclamations in respect of such prohibited and restricted areas.

I hereby further authorize and direct the Secretary of War and the said Military Commanders to take such other steps as he or the appropriate Military Commander may deem advisable to enforce compliance with the restrictions applicable to each Military area hereinabove authorized to be designated, including the use of Federal troops and other Federal Agencies, with authority to accept assistance of state and local agencies.

I hereby further authorize and direct all Executive Departments, independent establishments and other Federal Agencies, to assist the Secretary of War or the said Military Commanders in carrying out this Executive Order, including the furnishing of medical aid, hospitalization, food, clothing, transportation, use of land, shelter, and other supplies, equipment, utilities, facilities, and services.

This order shall not be construed as modifying or limiting in any way the authority heretofore granted under Executive Order No. 8972, dated December 12, 1941, nor shall it be construed as limiting or modifying the duty and responsibility of the Federal Bureau of Investigation, with respect to the investigation of alleged acts of sabotage or the duty and responsibility of the Attorney General and the Department of Justice under the Proclamations of December 7 and 8, 1941, prescribing regulations for the conduct and control of alien enemies, except as such duty and responsibility is superseded by the designation of military areas hereunder.

Franklin D. Roosevelt
The White House,
February 19, 1942

At first blush, Will and Molly, like much of the rest of the nation, thought the order broad and open enough that it would be used only if necessary and would not be used exclusively against Japanese Americans. In fact, patriots that they both were and after much discussion, they cautiously lined up in favor of the order and that week wrote in The Review:

NOT ANOTHER ARCADIA

Not since the Arcadia of which Longfellow wrote in "Evangeline" has a minority group been faced with the forced evacuation which the American-Japanese residents of this Coast feared as late as last Saturday.

That fear has gone now, paradoxically enough, in the President's decree that any citizen, anywhere, may be forced by the Army to move from his home.

That decree—one of the broadest assumptions of power by any President—comes as a welcome answer, The Review feels, to the bigots who have shouted for the evacuation of Japanese only.

The President didn't aim his order at Japanese or at those American-Japanese citizens so mistakenly called "Japanese" by the unthinking. He was not moved by an unreasoning passion in his desire to protect military establishments when he directed the Army to move any persons – Japanese, Germans, Italians and American citizens whether white, yellow or black – believed to be dangerous to the safety of any military post.

This order perhaps will mean the removal of Japanese, Germans and Italians from Bainbridge Island. It probably will strike mercilessly at many persons who have failed to complete their citizenship papers. It will ruin businesses and tear apart homes. Chiefly affected will be the Japanese homes here.

The Review hopes that the order will not mean the removal of American-Japanese citizens, for we still believe they have the right of every citizen to be held innocent until proven guilty.

But whatever the President's order may mean for the island's residents, The Review is glad that it will strike all fairly without bigotry and without malice.

Our President acted with all the finality of a dictator in making that order, but there isn't a right-thinking American who questions his act. It was necessary, for we are in an all-out war. It is a thrill to note, though, that the very order itself was fair and equal to all. Dictatorship-like though it was, its very content bespoke this nation's continued fair treatment of all who reside within its borders.

The Whitman's idealism and loyalty—and the "thrill" that the order was fair and equal-- were badly misplaced and it would not take them, or the rest of the nation, long to discover that Executive Order 9066 was only about the Japanese – Japanese born and American born -- citizens of the United States. The disenchantment, for those few who suffered it, would not take long to sink in.

Sixty-one-year-old Army Lt. General John L. DeWitt was the hardnosed veteran to whom the defense of the American West Coast fell. A medal-winning officer in World War I, the Nebraska native had a reputation for toughness, a quick temper and harsh words. He had worked since December, not so quietly, but out of the public eye, to persuade Congress, Roosevelt's cabinet and the President to grant sweeping powers to the Army.

As commander of the Fourth Army and the Western Defense Command, he urged that the 1942 Rose Bowl be moved from Pasadena, fearful that the large crowd would be vulnerable to sabotage. The game was played in North Carolina. Later that year he enacted a ban on deer hunting on the West Coast.

In early February DeWitt reported to the President that no sabotage by Japanese Americans on the West Coast had been confirmed, before, during or since the attack on Pearl Harbor. This, he wrote, only proved "a disturbing and confirming indication that such action *will* be taken." Following this strange bit of logic, he recommended the evacuation of all Japanese from the coastal areas of California, Oregon, and Washington.

At first, a "voluntary" evacuation plan was in place and, given certain provisos –proof of employment and a place to live-- Japanese Americans could leave the West Coast on their own. As February came to a close, the Army issued a press release that, while confusing, further tightened the noose for all "aliens."

"ASSURANCES GIVEN ALIENS --Restraint Will Be Kept to a Minimum Enemy aliens and Japanese-Americans, who must get out of the vast military area extending across the entire Pacific Coast and the southern half of Arizona, today were assured they will be "allowed to lead their lives with a minimum of restraint" in areas in which they will be resettled. When definite dates for evacuation are ordered, "all will be in readiness for orderly, humane handling of the people affected," it was announced at Lieut. Gen. John L. DeWitt's Western Defense Command headquarters here."

General DeWitt again cautioned the aliens and Japanese-Americans against too hasty disposition of farms, shops, residences and other property, pointing out that federal officials are being appointed to assist them in handling and transfer of their property. Until they have an opportunity to turn their properties over to an official custodian, such persons should not dispose of their possessions unless they receive full value in return, the general said.

Exclusion has not been ordered, it was pointed out, and when it is ordered 'there will be no mass movement of law-abiding persons on a moment's notice.' The Army suggested, however, that aliens who are able to leave strategic military areas now without economic loss or extreme personal inconvenience "would probably gain advantages through being pioneers in new resettlement districts." Those unable to leave at once were urged to continue their farming operations " as the best possible evidence of their loyalty to this country."

DeWitt had won a sweeping victory that granted him unprecedented power for controlling thousands of peoples' lives.

CHAPTER TWELVE

Two weeks after the issuance of Executive Order 9066, DeWitt began implementing a plan for classifying, rounding up, and removing "undesirables." On March 2, 1942, DeWitt issued "Military Proclamation No. 1" which designated the western-most parts of California, Oregon and Washington as "a military area." A provision was included directing that "any person of Japanese ancestry, now resident in Military Area No. 1, who changes his place of habitual residence must file a 'change of residence notice' at his local post office not more than five days nor less than one day prior to moving."

Within a week, DeWitt announced that the Army had acquired nearly 6,000 acres of land near Manzanar, California, for construction of a "reception center." The land, he said, was "to be used principally as a clearing house for the more permanent resettlement elsewhere for persons excluded from military areas."

Later that month General DeWitt would issue new orders applying to Japanese Americans, setting an 8 p.m. to 6 a.m. curfew and banning ownership of firearms, radios, cameras, and other contraband. In the order he said: "Let me warn the affected aliens and Japanese Americans that anything but strict compliance with this proclamation's provisions will bring immediate punishment. We plan to increase the tempo of the evacuation as fast as possible."

Citizens in specific areas were required to report to their designated "Civil Control Station," where they would then be taken to an "Assembly Center" for relocation. Ancestry, citizenship, employment or education carried no weight. DeWitt's view, expressed openly, was "A Jap is a Jap" whether a citizen or not.

The handwriting was on the wall, many walls in fact. On the morning of March 24, armed US Army soldiers, from towns in rural New Jersey, marched off the ferry from Seattle and into the island town of Winslow, carrying scores of official posters. They were met by a large group of young men, Nisei, second generation Japanese Americans. The young Japanese Americans welcomed the soldiers to their island, extended their hands to the soldiers and offered their help.

"We'll help," one said. "We'll show you the best places to post these and we'll take some ourselves."

Within two hours the official notices were distributed in key locations and the immediate fate of 274 Japanese Americans on the island —70 percent of them born in the United States-- was known.

WESTERN DEFENSE COMMAND AND FOURTH ARMY WARTIME CIVIL CONTROL ADMINISTRATION

INSTRUCTIONS TO ALL

JAPANESE

Living on Bainbridge Island

All Japanese persons, both alien and non-alien, will be evacuated from this designated area by 12:00 o'clock noon Monday, March 30, 1942 without obtaining special permission from the Civil Control Office established on the island near the ferry boat landing at the Anderson Dock Store in Winslow.

The Civil Control Station is equipped to assist the Japanese population affected by this evacuation in the following ways:

1. Give advice and instructions on the evacuation.

2. Provide services with respect to the management, leasing, sale, storage or other disposition of most kinds of property including real estate, business and professional equipment, household goods, boats, automobiles, livestock, etc.
3. Provide temporary residence elsewhere for all Japanese in family groups.
4. Transport persons and a limited amount of clothing and equipment to their new residence as specified below.

The Following Instructions Must Be Observed:

1. A responsible member of each family, preferably the head of the family, or the person in whose name most of the property is held, and each individual living alone must report to the Civil Control Station to receive further instructions. This must be done between 8:00 a.m. and 5:00 p.m., Wednesday, March 25, 1942
2. Before leaving the area, all persons will be given a medical examination. For this purpose, all members of the family should be present at the same time, when directed by the Civil Control Office.
3. Under special conditions individuals and families will be permitted to leave the area prior to this date for complete evacuation listed above. In general, the conditions imposed on voluntary evacuation are as follows: (a) that the destination be outside Military No. 1 prescribed by Proclamation No. 1 of the Commanding General, Western Defense Command and Fourth Army, March 2, 1942. (b) that arrangements have been made for employment and shelter at the destination.
4. Provisions have been made to give temporary residence in a reception center elsewhere. Evacuees who do not go to an approved destination of their own choice, but who go to a reception center under Government supervision, must carry with them the following property, not exceeding that which can be carried by the family or the individual:

   a. Blankets and linens (no mattress) for each member of the family.
   b. Toilet articles for each member of the family.

c. Clothing for each member of the family.
  d. Sufficient knives, forks, spoons, plates, bowls and cups for each member of the family.
  e. All items carried will be securely packaged, tied and plainly marked with the name of the owner and numbered in accordance with instructions received at the Civil Control Station.
  f. No contraband items may be carried.

5. The United States Government through its agencies will provide for the storage at the sole risk of the owner of the more substantial household items, such as iceboxes, washing machines, pianos and other heavy furniture. Cooking utensils and other small items will be accepted if crated, packed and plainly marked with the name and address of the owner. Only one name and address will be used by a given family.
6. Each family, and individual living alone, who goes to a reception center will be furnished transportation and food for the trip. Private means of transportation will not be permitted. Instructions will be given by the Civil Control Office as to which evacuees must be fully prepared to travel.

Go to the Civil Control Office at the Anderson Dock Store in Winslow between 8 a.m. and 5 p.m. on March 25, 1942, to receive further instructions.

J. L. DeWITT
Lieutenant General, U. S. Army
Commanding

Will was seething with anger, frustration and betrayal. This was <u>all</u> about the Japanese. He had been duped. Or let his idealism fool him. He brought home a poster-sized copy of the "instructions" to the "Japanese persons, both alien and non-alien."

Molly saw right away the pressure that had built up in her husband. She consciously decided to put her fear, her own feelings of disgust and sadness aside, and let him vent.

"Listen to this," he began, dropping his coat and worn leather briefcase to the floor. The feds are going to quote assist the Japanese population affected by this evacuation in the following ways. How kind of them! They yank them out of their homes with so little notice it's pathetic and now they're putting themselves in the role of helpers. And it goes on in that vein: "Provide services, I like that, provide services with respect to management, sale, etc. Now they're going to help them sell off everything they own. Their generosity is more than I can bear."

Will stomped into the kitchen, opened the little fridge and grabbed a cold beer.

"They're going to provide temporary residences for them and, get this, when they go they're going to transport a limited amount of clothing and equipment for them, <u>to their new residence</u>. God, I wonder what that will be like."

He fully looked at Molly for the first time since he entered, such was his rage.

"Molly, I'm sorry, I just need to vent."

"Go ahead honey. It's OK."

"And do you know," he continued after a deep breath, "what they can take? You won't believe it. I heard they're allowed two suitcases. Two suitcases! Hell, these are adults who have lived their life here, who have *made* a life here. And they talk like they're going to camp. Hell, they are going to camp, a concentration camp. Let's call it what it is."

Molly didn't say a word. She walked over to Will, put her arms around him and drew him to her. She could feel his hot face on her forehead, hear and feel him breathing heavily. She continued to hold him and felt his breath, sour now with anger, on her face. Then she felt the tears drop on her neck and shoulder.

The forty three families of Japanese descent on the island now had six days to try to protect their land, their homes, their furniture and appliances and the choose the things they would carry with them to…they did not know where. The Army had held out the hope of voluntary evacuation, but that turned out to be a short, vague dream. Very few people could meet the requirements of a job and place to live elsewhere. Who among them knew someone in Atlanta, Chicago or Denver? Even this slim hope was quickly dashed when the governors and congressman from the states immediately east of the "military zone" made it clear that these "undesirables" were not welcome in their communities and, further, openly challenged the location of "reception areas" and internment camps in their states. No one wanted the Japanese.

And the Army promise--"there will be no mass movement of law-abiding persons on a moment's notice"—was false.

"Mol, have you read this?"

"Yes Will. They're all over the place."

"I feel sick. I feel like a fool. We sort of knew it was coming, but not this bad, not this total, this complete. They mean to take everyone – women, kids, farmers, professors, business owners--everyone ." Will was pacing the living room floor and speaking loudly, even though Molly was close by. He was somewhat settled from his outburst.

"I mean we got behind this, you and I. We were duped just like everyone else. The racists got what they wanted and the Constitution means nothing. What a jerk I've been." He kept striding around the small cottage and talking loudly.

"Did you hear what they did with the soldiers?"

"You mean helped them put the notices up?"

"Yes. You know these people. They are brought up to respect authority, listen to their government, not cause any trouble, be polite – it's just who they are." He ran both his hands through his long black hair. "They will just submit and be taken away."

"Will, what do you want them to do? A couple hundred people can't take on the Army."

"I know sweetie, I know. I just feel so… hopeless, so powerless. I'm just no use at all."

"I understand. And you're Caucasian Will. You're free. You get to stay here. Think how they must feel. I say, let's just do what we do. Let's write about it."

Because of a cruel war in which they have no part nor parcel, there are many heartsick people on this island today, including the Whitmans. Many are sad because of the dark news that, daily, is shadowing hopes for their nation's victory. Some weep for the loved ones lost in battle.

Still more are heavy hearted because they have been told that they must prepare to move from this island – move inland to places they have never seen and amidst people who will not welcome them.

For this latter group, The Review has done what little it could do to keep them here, for we trust them and believe they are good residents of this nation. Others, in the majority, have ruled otherwise. We have a real sense of loss, not only a loss of friends and neighbors, but of rights and the democracy we are fighting so fiercely to defend.

These citizens we all know and thousands more in other Washington communities, Oregon and California will be taken away without any kind of investigation or due process, much less a trial. Nothing has been proven. They have not been judged by their peers.

We are talking about American citizens! Where, in the face of their fine record since December 7, in the face of their rights, in the face of their own families being drafted and enlisting in the US Army, in the face of American decency, is there any excuse for this high-handed, much-too-short evacuation order?

On this day, three months into this horrible war, our heart is heavy and our faith in some of the principles we believed in is shaken.

Will handed the page to Molly with a heavy sigh. "Let's run it on page one."

CHAPTER THIRTEEN

The Whitman's sadness and outrage was not shared nor accepted by everyone on the island, to say the least. In the next issue, Will ran some of many letters he would receive that spring.

"The President of the United States has seen fit to give the high command of our Army permission to use their best judgment to protect the Pacific Coast from sabotage and/or fifth column activities. Under these circumstances, I fail to see that it is within the province of The Bainbridge Review to question either the evacuation, or the time element involved. Please cancel my subscription immediately." **Irma M. Wright**

Others were more venomous.

"These Japs have worked here for years, taking less money for work that others could have. They keep to themselves and hold on to their old ways. There's no question in my mind that they remain Japanese, first and foremost, and if the chance came up they would side with their Army. I say take them all somewhere where they can't do us any harm. And, as for you Mr. Editor, you can take this little rag of yours and wrap some fish in it. Cancel my subscription so I don't have to read this unpatriotic rot any longer." **Carl Wolfson**

"You're wrong on this one, Whitman. You're going against your country at a time when it needs you. You're lucky you're here instead of headed for the islands in the Pacific. There are a couple of thousand men, one of them the son of my friend, who are now lying on the bottom of the ocean and the Japanese took their young lives. Think about that in the next editorial you write." **Eddy Vector, Seattle.**

Will steered the black Pontiac north on Miller Road, past the plant nursery and gas station at the bottom of the hill, and pulled off the road on a small patch of dirt at the edge of the forest. Here the magnificent Douglas fir and Western red cedar reached up more than 100 feet and blocked the sun. Alder, hemlock and big leafed maple filled in a lower canopy and Oregon grape and sword ferns carpeted the forest floor. A series of streams made their way down from the watershed to the east. Molly and Will liked to walk here. He stuffed the car keys into his jacket pocket and the two of them quickly merged into the trees and the light mist that hung in the morning air, walking through sun and shadow, alone in the woods. They were silent for a few minutes, striding easily down the worn dirt path and soon Will was ready to talk about what had been rolling though his mind since early in the morning.

"I've been thinking about just what it means to be a man, or a woman, in this world that we find ourselves in. It seems that everything has changed so quickly, that so many lives have been disrupted. I think we are in danger of losing our way, individuals and as a people."

Molly was always ready to listen to Will. Day-to-day he didn't talk a lot, saving his verbal output, she often thought, for his old Royal. She usually wanted to hear more.

"Well, you're right that our world has changed. Tell me what you've been pondering."

"How is a man with any principles or integrity supposed to act? Is it better to fight against a government you think is in the wrong? Or is it better to be what most people call 'patriotic' and quote join the team unquote? I'm not quite sure."

"Yeah; it's a great question. Is this a personal dilemma for you, or one you're posing for the rest of us, the ordinary citizens?"

Will quickly glanced at Molly to see if she was completely serious. Deciding that she was, he went on.

"Well, I think it's for everybody, me included. I'm not a great student of history or philosophy, but it seems to me a human dilemma, two different ways of thinking about society and individualism. I mean one way of thinking is that we should, as loyal citizens, accept what our government decides and go along with the policies and rules that we mutually arrive to together. Or, at least, some of us have decided at some point that there are hard and fast rules."

"Yeah, and the other?"

"Well, to be an advocate for change. Maybe it's a battle, an ongoing tension between accepting things as they are and changing things for the better. It seems like most people just want to take what's given them, what their leaders have decided, and follow. While others, and I must be in that category, don't necessarily want to follow, just because a president or a governor says it's the thing to do. You know me Mol, I'm not some kind of impulsive rebel who likes to go against the grain just for the sake of it. But I do reserve the right to say 'Wait a minute, this just doesn't seem right.'"

"Well, maybe that's why you're a journalist. There is a slight—maybe more than slight—iconoclastic tendency in you." She smiled to herself. "Isn't that the old adage about journalists, that they comfort the afflicted and afflict the comfortable? Doesn't that describe the wanting to change things for the better, as you put it, and not just accept what others think is the truth?"

"Yeah. That's a good connection." Will shifted so he could see Molly's face.

"There's a little more to it, for me and I'm not sure how to say it," he said. She remained quiet and they took long steps across a small streambed. The sun streaked down through the big cedars and formed spotlights on the forest floor.

"I remember my dad, a doctor all of his life, constantly talking to me about tolerance of human beings --all kinds of human beings --acceptance really," he went on. "I can hear him now: 'When you cut through that thin layer of skin on the outside of a person, you see how alike we all are. All of us have got pretty much the same things inside and they're the same colors too.' I'll never forget that lesson."

She heard his voice catch in his throat before he continued.

"Dad was a man that extended himself to every kind of person he encountered. It didn't matter how much money he made, what color he was, how smart he was, where he was from or the family that raised him. He accepted him. I never saw him turn anyone away. And my mom too. I never heard her say a bad word about anybody."

"Those are wonderful lessons Will."

"I think so too. I learned a lot about acceptance. But does that mean we just take everything that's directed our way without complaining or fighting back? It seems to me that acceptance has its limits."

"So you're thinking that this kind of acceptance –and I might say compassion too—that your mom and dad stood for can go too far?"

"Yes. And I don't think compassion is what's troubling me." Will adjusted his jacket and zipped open the front to let in some cooler air. "It's tolerance, or maybe passivity. What worries me about the Japanese Americans is that they will just roll over and take this –whatever you call it – incarceration, evacuation, relocation – that they will just go along with it in their polite, mild mannered way."

"And if they do that, that will trouble you?"

"You're a damn good listener Mol and when I eventually shut up, I'd like to hear what you'd say." She squeezed his arm. "Yes, it will bother me. I want them to fight for what they believe in. I want them to cry out against the injustice and inhumanity of this mass criminal conviction of thousands of citizens without a trial. I don't want them to just hold their hands out for the handcuffs and say 'Take me, I'm sorry for who I am. I'm sorry I'm Japanese."

"Well, that's a little overstated, wouldn't you say?"

Yeah, but you get my point."

"I think there's more to it," Molly said. She took his hand as they took a long stride across a puddle. "I think there is a strong cultural thing with the Japanese and it's about honoring the group—society and the family—over the individual. Most of the people I've talked to, and what I've read, say that a Japanese hesitates to act if he or she is not sure what the consequences will be for their family or the larger group. They just have this consciousness that they want to act with the good of the whole in mind. I think Americans act as individuals first. We've grown up with the idea of individual freedom pounded into us from first grade for goodness sakes."

"Yeah, but does that mean they can't stand up for what they think is right?"

"Well, we're dealing in great, glittering generalities here. But for an individual Japanese man to stand up and say he's angry and go against his society, or his sub-culture here on the island, would be seen as disrespectful. It would take an enormous amount of courage."

"So you're saying there's a huge pressure to conform."

"Yes, conform maybe, but stay a part of the group. Don't get alienated. Don't stand out in a way that will draw attention to yourself."

"You don't think that's what I'm doing, do you?"

"No. You're being who you have to be and maybe they're being who they have to be. I understand you Will and I'm glad you're getting this off your chest, but I think that any violence or strong resistance will make things worse for them, maybe for all of us. Maybe the way they are 'taking things' as you put it, is a kind of wisdom, a way of going with things, taking the river downstream as it were and realizing the inevitability of it."

"Well, that's the crux of it, isn't it? Do we go with the river and float downstream to wherever it takes us, or do we swim against the current because we know the current is wrong, that it's going to a place that will harm all of us? Or do we get out of the river altogether and stand on the bank and shout at the rest of the people in the river?" Will chuckled out loud at the picture he'd made in his head.

"And I suppose that's who I'm married to, the guy who's pulled himself out of the river and is standing on the bank in his skivvies, yelling at the folks floating downstream."

"I think you're right. And god help you."

Molly shoved her arm inside of his and put her cheek up against his shoulder and they turned to walk back to the car.

CHAPTER FOURTEEN

In the office the next day there was a sense of urgency as Molly and Will worked together on the final issue of the month. Will was reading through the notice to the Japanese American evacuees for the fourth or fifth time. Molly was at the second desk going over advertising income for the last several months.

"Mol, see if you can make a story out of this. I got it in the mail last night." Will walked over and handed a couple of news releases on coarse yellow paper, mixed with notes in Will's handwriting. Molly read through them quickly.

"OK, here's what I get," she said: "Sugar rationing is coming soon, but we're not sure when or how tight it will be." Molly read a little more. "And there is a limited number of tires available for us islanders —eight tires available for cars and sixteen for trucks. But, you've got to get an inspection and a certificate in order to buy them."

"Yep."

"And you know there will be no new license plates, not metal ones anyway. We're going to get paper plates. Finally, if you want a new car in the next three months, you better apply now and the odds are against you. There are only 50 new cars assigned to all of Kitsap County between now and June."

"That's the gist of it. Knock that out tonight will ya, just kind of a roundup of what's being rationed. I'm working on how much an evacuation would cost the island, you know in the berry harvest, and there's also a loss to the school district from per capita money they would not get from the state."

"Good. I'll read it when you're finished."

Will swiveled in his old desk chair and faced Molly. "I love you sweetie."

"Thanks babe, me too." She smiled. "What else you got?"

"You know this island pumped out a few million pounds of strawberries last year. This year's crop is just as big and we will have virtually no one to bring in the berries."

"Geez, that's a big deal."

"You're darn tooten. The school picture is not so bad -- the state won't pay the high school its 25 cents per day for each student if they don't attend. I'm not sure yet how many students that will be." Will leaned over the desk, grabbed another envelope and opened it. "Hey, get this. The war production board has banned a whole boat load of stuff, mostly appliances."

"Like what?"

"Let's see...nobody can make toasters, waffle irons, irons, grills, cigarette lighters, shavers, portable mixers, hair clippers, dishwashers...the list goes on. Apparently it's anything that has a lot of metal in it, or even a little, and anything that has a substantial electric motor. Wow, that's a lot."

The phone rang. Molly picked up the black handpiece and listened. She turned to look at Will as she listened to the caller.

"Yes, I see. I understand. You have every right to your point of view." She paused. "Well, we regret your decision but we understand it. Goodbye."

She laid the phone back in the cradle.

"That's another cancellation. That's five this week and it's only Wednesday," she said shaking her head.

"Ouch. Let's see, that's ten bucks. I guess you'll have to work without pay next week.

"You mean again next week."

"This worries me a little Mol. I hope this isn't a trend."

"Sweetie don't worry. Eagledale Grocery is still with us, so is the Lynwood Theater and the theater in Bremerton, and Walberg Motors. Just yesterday, the hardware store, the drug store in Winslow and the tackle and bait store called and wanted more copies. They ran out."

"That's a good sign. Why didn't you tell me?"

"I don't know sweetie. I guess your distribution manager is not the best communicator," Molly said and smiled at her husband. Will shook his head and smiled.

"Well, at least the bastards are still reading us, even if they don't agree with us."

The cancellations and the advertisers that dropped away seemed to add fuel to the fire that burned in Will's belly. At home that night, he read the Seattle Post-Intelligencer editorial headlined: "The Japanese Must Move – the problem of the Japanese in our midst."

"Dammit," he shouted and flung down the paper. "These people are not the quote problem, Mol, they are fine decent people who happen to have different skin than we do. Why the Japanese? And why not the Italians, German, Poles, Russians, Chinese—hell, why not the Chinese? They have dark skin and funny eyes. Why don't we just take all the immigrants and all the immigrants' children and ship 'em home? It'd be a pretty lonely country wouldn't it?"

"Take it easy honey," Mol said and continued to dry the dishes. Just continue to say what you believe in...in slightly different language, I hope."

Two days later Will ran a front-page editorial titled:

NOT TIME ENOUGH

The time element of the evacuation of Bainbridge Island's Japanese alien and Japanese-American citizen population is an outrage!

The Review long has contended that the evacuation of Japanese American citizens (not aliens) would be an outrage, itself, against all the precious rights of citizenship guaranteed by our constitution. The time to argue that point has long passed however.

We cry out now, not against the evacuation, but against its modus operandi. To us it is pointless and merciless in its speed.

From December 7 -when Japanese bombers roared against Pearl Harbor—until now is a period of more than three months. During that lengthy time we have heard of no overt act by any Japanese resident—alien or citizen—against our government or its many military and naval establishments. In the meantime, The Federal Bureau of Investigation has investigated all Japanese here thoroughly and has arrested those few it found suspicious. The FBI seems to have the situation well in hand.

Yet with sudden awfulness our Japanese neighbors were told Tuesday that by next Monday they must be gone, bag and not much baggage. That is only six days notice.

Why such haste, in view of the peaceful three-month record of these people? Why could not a two-week notice, or three weeks, been given to them? Why could not time have been given them so that they could have taken advantage of the Army's "voluntary evacuation" order and avoided being herded like so many sheep? In the short days given, that "voluntary" opportunity is just a piece of irony.

Perhaps we wouldn't make this protest (which we realize will not be at all popular with those who do not know our Japanese neighbors) if only aliens were concerned. They, certainly, must be ready to face harsh wartime measures. But we are talking here about 191 AMERICAN CITIZENS! Where, in the face of their fine record since December 7, in the face of their rights as citizens, in the face of their own relatives being drafted and enlisting in our Army, in the face of American decency, is there any excuse for this high-handed, much-too-short evacuation order?

We hope this statement of ours doesn't embarrass them. We say this on our own accord. It is not an echo of anything we have heard a single Japanese person say. They are taking this treatment without a single bitter word. At least we have heard none.

Who to blame for this is a pointless thing on which to speculate. An Army General named DeWitt actually signed the order, based on a proclamation by President Roosevelt. A jittery Navy undoubtedly had a part in it.

A fine group of Army officers and men, each apparently trying to make this ordeal as painless as possible, is here handling the situation. Of course, they can't be blamed for they are merely obeying orders. Their splendid attitude has won for them the admiration and thanks of the whole island.

There probably would be no justification for this outburst if we didn't think it would do some good. It won't help Island Japanese; that's true. But it may make those responsible for future evacuations aware of the fact that six days is not sufficient time in which to ask a large community to move itself. We can see no valid excuse for such undue speed.

Will's frustration was boiling up inside him. One rock after another seemed to drop on the Japanese community's head and it might as well of dropped on his too. He paced. He mumbled. That night at home he had two drinks, Dewar's neat, and didn't talk much to Molly.

The next morning Molly found three letters pinned to the door of the Review's small office, stuck there overnight. She carefully opened the damp envelopes and removed all three letters before reading them. One by one she looked them over and tears formed in her blue eyes. She reluctantly called Will at home to read them, her heart thumping in her chest the whole time.

"Shut up Whitman. Stop your whining about something that is already decided and is a military necessity. The Japs are taking this a whole lot better than you are. I would demand that you two cancel my subscription, but I've never signed up for your liberal rag."

"No signature?" Will asked.

"Not on this one, but this next one is from an old friend."

"You guys are swimming upstream on this one. The evacuation needs to happen, to protect us and to protect the Japanese. I've read your ranting for the last couple of months and I don't think I can take it any more. Further, I don't think Carl's Tire and Battery Garage can be associated with the Review for any longer. I'll be pulling my ads, at least until you return to your senses. Sincerely, Carl"

"Well, at least he was fairly polite."

"There's another one, unsigned."

Will sighed. "Read it."

"So we imported you from Seattle and you took over our little hometown paper. I think it's time you two left Bainbridge and stopped this traitorous activity. There is no room here for someone who continually challenges our government in a time when our young men are being killed by foreign powers. I will no longer read your rag and will have to look for something else to start my fires with."

"Ouch."

"Yeah. But this is only three people Will and I know that there are hundreds out there who are on our side and on the side of the Japanese community."

"Well, that's great. I just wish they'd poke their heads up."

The weight of what was happening around him bore down on Will like a large, rain-soaked cape that seemed impossible to take off or change. He was, in his bones and muscles, without energy, without courage and feeling absolutely powerless. All that he had thought, talked about and written seemed to make no difference to the world. Who had heard him? Who had heeded his warnings? Who had given the least significance to what he had written about race, hatred, stereotyping and rush to judgment? What damn bit of difference did it make to anyone? The world just seemed to keep spinning in its mad, uncontrollable way, full of greed, murder and a relentless drive to have power over other people. Not only were people being killed by the thousands, American families were being torn apart and scattered across the world like bushels of fruit thrown across the landscape, never to be together again. Because of the mere color of their skin, men, women and children were about to be carted away and isolated from the rest of the world behind barbed wire, like cattle.

And me, he thought, pompous, arrogant Will, big deal editor who was going to set the world right with his trusty old typewriter; what has that come to? How could I have thought I could sit in a room on Bainbridge Island, population 3,000, and write something that would change a country, that would change human nature? For God's sake, Whitman, get your head on straight. Get a real job.

CHAPTER FIFTEEN

Six days -- five really, if you didn't count Monday. The Sugimotos were nearly panicked. Their house, their five acres, their farming equipment, their stove, dishes, couch, chairs, the Model A Mutt had built a wooden bed on to serve as a pickup – they would have to find a place for all of this. Or sell it. He thought first of his neighbor, Milton Baker, a man he did not know too well, but was friendly with. Baker owned 20 acres that adjoined Mutt's place. He raised pigs, grew blueberries and made most of his money fishing. Maybe Milt would help.

Mutt stood in the kitchen by himself, his hands limp at his side, his face passive. His tan, long sleeved shirt smelled of the earth and of sweat. His shoes were scuffed and dirty. He wore a ragged straw hat, the brim folded down all around. He stared at the kitchen sink. The faucet was dripping slowly, the water drops hitting an old brown stain at the edge of the sink trap. He thought about his years in the house, the years unfolding like pages of a weathered magazine. He saw himself clearing the land, bent over the cedar and fir stumps that dotted the hillside, swinging a pick, pulling at roots, dragging the stumps away with a young gray mare that he borrowed from his friend.

The beets, every year, every spring, the seeds went in the ground in the same rows. Beets were such simple plants, from the crinkled tan seeds to the intense maroon, bulbous root and the thick green leaves, all edible, all sweet. He saw the color of the cut beets as his wife Suki cut them under running water, such deep red color running out and down the drain. He thought of taking his own life. What am I now, he asked. Who will I become? What will happen to Suki and Amy? Who am I, being uprooted like this, pulled off this ground, pulled out like a beet and tossed on to the dry earth somewhere else, just to dry out and rot? I will wilt, he thought. I will lie on the ground and all the life will pass out of me, all the water will leave me and I will be limp and useless.

He stepped through the front door and ran his hand along the gray board-and-batten fir that made up the outside of the small house. His hand, rough and dry, scraped along the wood with reverence and appreciation for the walls that had held him and his wife and his daughter. His eyes welled up with water. His heart began to hurt, a slow, dull hurt that he knew would last for a long time.

His neighbor Milt Baker was a crusty loner who kept mostly to himself. He had been born in Seattle and found his way to Bainbridge when he was in his twenties, anxious to make his own way in the world, determined to be self-sufficient. He had taken a small nest egg, earned in the construction business since high school and purchased a piece of land near the center of the island. He fished and crabbed in the Sound and sold to the stores on the island. Most of the rest of his money came from his blueberry crops.

Milt was unmarried and seemed to be in no hurry to find a mate. He worked hard and found some pleasure having a beer with the loggers and mill workers who were plentiful and more than willing to slake their thirst with their friends. He liked Mutt, from a distance. He respected his work ethic and the way he was with his small family.

On the morning of March 25 Milt was well aware of the events unfolding around him and welcomed the chance to talk to Mutt when he saw him walking up the dirt road to his house.

"Morning Mutt," he shouted out when Mutt was about twenty yards from the house.

"Mr. Baker, good morning to you. Though I am afraid it is not so pleasant for me today."

"Yep, I've heard. I'm sorry. And please call me Milt. Mr. Baker makes me uncomfortable."

"Yes, thank you." Mutt looked down at the dirt and moved a small stone with his foot. "You can help me, I think."

Milt, as much as he liked Mutt, was cautious. He wanted to avoid what he thought of as politics. He didn't want to get into a scrape with the feds. And he surely did not want to put his farm at risk. He liked most of the Nips, as he called them in private, but kept them at a distance. He folded his hands in front of his body and studied Mutt's face.

"What can I do?"

Mutt looked up into the taller man's face. Milt could see the pain and sadness in his eyes.

"I think you can buy my farm. Buy my farm from me and keep it for me and my family. Just until we get back. Please." These were the most words Mutt could manage and Milt could see the effort it took to say them. Neither man spoke for a moment.

"I can't afford to buy your farm Mutt." Both men looked down at the ground between them.

"Oh, yes, not for the real price. Just for a few dollars, a hundred dollars maybe, and I can have some money to spend and you can have the farm until I get back. Then I can give you a hundred dollars, maybe more, and have my land back."

"A hundred dollars."

"Yes, and you can harvest the berries and make some money and do what you want after that. You can get some help from the Filipinos and others. It should not be hard. And you can use all my machinery, everything. It will be yours."

Milt rubbed his chin. He had not expected this. He thought about the position Mutt was in. He thought about the trust it took, the desperation he must feel. He wondered if the sale was legal. He had the money. He had $300 in a Mason jar under his bed.

"And that will help you and Suki?"

"Oh yes. It will save us."

"And I guess you're in a hurry."

"Yes. We must act fast. You must, please, write a paper that says what our agreement is and we both will sign it. Are you in agreement?"

"Well, Mutt, I guess so. This is awful sudden." He paused and looked out over the fields, his and Mutt's property next to it. "I guess it won't hurt me any to do this. And it will help you a lot." Mutt nodded vigorously.

Milt wiped his hand on his pant leg and reached out to Mutt, who took it in both his hands and shook it hard.

"When we get back, I can buy this back, you will see. And you can make some money while we are gone. It will work out. Thank you Mr. Baker, Milt. Thank you from me and Suki and Amy. Thank you very, very much."

Neither man had any idea how long it would be, of course, but they both had the sense that it would end soon, that the killing and the aggression would stop and that Mutt and thousands of other Japanese Americans would come home eventually. Milton would care for, and use, all the Sugimotos owned outside of the house. Suki, in the meantime, had made an arrangement with the Kuzuo family to take what was inside, the furniture, some clothes and appliances. The Kuzuos were one of two families on the island that had agreed to leave the island right away to live with cousins in Idaho. They were to leave tomorrow. No money had changed hands, but there was the understanding that somehow, sometime Suki and Mutt could recover their belongings.

Mutt walked back to his house, anxious to share the good news with Suki and Amy.

CHAPTER SIXTEEN

Will and Molly sat in their favorite chairs, two light green armchairs that flanked the stove in the living room, each with a floor lamp behind it. It was evening, just before dinner. Molly was reading the Seattle Times and Will was staring at the fire, sipping on a small glass of Scotch. The wind had picked up and was rattling the lilac bush against the front window.

"You know these times are going to define us," he said, out of the blue. After a moment, Molly put the paper down and responded.

"Yes, and a hell of a lot of other people too."

"Yeah, sure. But tonight I just have the sense that this time and this place is some kind of pivotal point for our lives, you and me. This island, this evacuation, what we do, what we write…I know that we are witnesses—and participants—in one of the most important events to happen in a lifetime, hell, maybe this century. My dad used to tell me that a person has one really good idea in his life, one theme maybe or one way of looking at the world and that idea, if it's good enough, will define him. It's kind of like what will be written in one's obit, you know?"

"Yes. And what might that be for you and me?"

"Geez, I don't know yet, Mol, I just know that we are in the middle of it and it's not going away and how we respond to all this is going to define Will and Molly Whitman."

"What would you like that obit to say?" Molly pressed him.

"Something like: 'They kept their heads and held onto democracy and the Bill of Rights when most other people were sorta going crazy."

"That would be worthwhile," Molly said. "That would be worthwhile."

Molly was endlessly, boundlessly curious. She never seemed to run out of questions. She wanted to know what Will thought about, what he saw, heard, felt and wanted. In the morning, waking early and rolling over next to Will, she would ask: "Are you going back to sleep?" "What did you dream about?" And in the evening, as they sat by the fire reading, she would look at Will and ask: "How much longer are you going to read?" Or "Are you going to bed early tonight?" "Who did you talk to today?"

Ordinary questions, one might say, yet to Will the ongoing drumbeat of the inquiries into his nature or his behavior sometimes seemed invasive. Some of the time the questions seemed to him unanswerable. It was like asking him if he was going to burp in five minutes, probing some natural function that might happen or just as well might not happen. How did he know if he was going to sleep? If sleep came, it rolled over him when it was ready. He didn't <u>decide</u> to sleep, he <u>fell</u> asleep, and falling was not something you planned to do. Asking him about things like that only brought a sense of encirclement to Will, as if someone was building a corral around him. The questions, but maybe more the answers, forced him to decide something; more, they forced him to be something, something he was not entirely sure he wanted to be. Living in an 1,100- square-foot house in the winter was confining enough, to say nothing of the regimented schedule of putting out a weekly newspaper. Give me a little breathing room, he would say to himself when the pressure got to him, just let me be, without deciding anything or saying who I am in a given moment.

Molly, of course, did not see her questions in this light. If she had, she surely would have stopped asking. She would have trained herself to stop asking any kind of question at all if she got the sense it corralled her husband. She would have watched him even more intently, but she would not have asked. Her questions came from a deep curiosity about human beings, and in a way her husband was The Human Being beside her, and the questions came from a need to be included. She wanted to be brought into his life, escorted in, as it were, to the life of the man she married, so she could be part of him. He was so important to her that she wanted—not just to be in the circle of his arms, though that was sorely the case—but in the circle of his brain and his heart and his consciousness. To be included in his life meant that she would mean more to him, that she would be significant. This was, perhaps, her deepest hunger.

Could she be significant by herself? Surely she was a strong enough woman to say yes to that question. But was she sure? Could she know how she would be important in the world? And what was wrong with wanting to be significant? It seemed to Molly that everyone wanted that, especially when one thought of the opposite, of living out one's life and having no significance to anyone.

"Mol, have you seen the letter from Todi? The one about his farm and equipment?" Will stepped briskly into the kitchen where Molly was fixing lunch, grilled tuna and cheese sandwiches.

"Nope," don't know anything about it." She turned to smile at Will, who was taking off his rumpled tweed coat and sitting at the kitchen table.

"I'll read it to you. I think it sums up a lot of what these folks are going through."

"Where did you get it?"

"Todi dropped it off this morning. He was taking it over to Seattle." Molly wiped her hands on a kitchen towel and sat down opposite Will.

"It's addressed to the John H. Tolan Committee, whatever that is; must have something to do with the War Relocation Authority."

"Dear Sirs: I am one of the Japanese-Americans being evacuated from this area and desire information as to the disposition of property we own. Would your committee kindly help me or refer me to the proper authorities that may be able to help?"

"Our family has a greenhouse business here, in which we have planted tomato and cucumber crops and have tended and cared for these crops right up to the present time. We did so in the hope that Japanese, if citizens of the United States, would be permitted to remain, if approved by the authorities to be loyal to this country. However, we find we may be evacuated also. These crops will be ready to harvest beginning next month, and, in the event I have to leave, I want very much that someone handle it rather than lose the crops."

"I have tried to contact parties who might be interested and able to take over this business and the crops on a rental or purchase basis. My contacts are limited so I would very much appreciate some help in finding a trustworthy man who is capable of handling this business and also the proper procedure to safeguard my interests here in my absence. I have attached a copy of the description of the property and the condition of the business."

"Thanking you for the favor, I am Yours very sincerely, T. Nakamura"

"He then tells the committee exactly what he has." Will, shaking his head with resentment and sadness, continued reading:

For Sale or Rent

At Poulsbo, Washington, Kitsap County: Three greenhouses, 15,000 square feet under glass. Packing house and garage for two cars or trucks. Acre and half land on waterfront, on main highway only 13 miles from ferry to Seattle, Wash.

Truck and all equipment for operation of this business. Principal crops, tomatoes and cucumbers in spring and summer; and chrysanthemums in fall and winter. Potted plants. Tomatoes and cucumbers are now planted and cared for, and everything ready for some experienced and responsible party to carry on. Estimated income from this crop coming in, $5,000. From chrysanthemums, $2,000.

A new residence, seven rooms, now under construction, will be finished and ready to move into this month. Also, small four-room residence on this property.

No encumbrances. Sell, $22,000, terms. Rent, $3,000 cash for crop now planted and $100 month for duration.

Will looked up and Molly was looking him directly in the eyes. Her blue eyes were filled with tears.

"God, Will, that just lays it right out there, what he has, the cost to him and his family, what he expects in the future. And he's just walking away from it."

"Well, I wouldn't say 'walking away' exactly."

"Yeah, you're right. He's being taken away from it. What a mess, what a royal mess."

"And Mol, he just finished building his new home. I don't know how these people bear it."

After lunch Will went into the spare bedroom, the room the couple used for keeping books and papers. A table was stacked high with copies of the Seattle Times and the Review. The walls were lined with reference books, magazines and family photos. Sitting on a small table near the window was a black typewriter and Will pulled an old maple dining room chair up to it and put his fingers on the keys.

The decision to evacuate persons of Japanese ancestry from the West Coast was made on the basis of military necessity, according to the US Army. The Review takes a different view.

While we acknowledge the terrible war the nation of Japan is waging in the Pacific and the fear that some have of an invasion of our coast, we cannot help but point to other forces that drive our politicians and military officers to forcefully remove US citizens from their homes without due process.

First of all, the Army and President Roosevelt seemed to have decided that race equals loyalty. There seems to be the belief that one's ethnic background unequivocally determines his or her allegiance to a political or military position or action by their home nation. We need look no further than the Italians, the Germans or our own history books in this nation to see that we are capable of serious disagreements regarding national policies.

Further, the opinions and reports of the FBI, Naval Intelligence and the Army General Staff itself have been ignored; those reports state that no sustained Japanese attack on our shores was possible and that they only needed to keep watch on a relatively small number of suspicious individuals.

General John DeWitt seems to have relied heavily on the opinions of a part of the public and politicians as opposed to sound military reasoning. People with their own axes to grind have spoken the loudest and appealed to our fears. Our leaders, including the President, have taken no measures to calm the public down or refute the ugly rumors of sabotage and fifth column activities. In fact the politicians have chosen to listen to the pleas for security and heeded the racial slurs instead of basing their logic on sound military reasoning. This, at the expense of our liberty.

Our Attorney General, saying that this massive evacuation was unnecessary, did not make a strong case to his President that failure to make out a case of dire military necessity would render the evacuation unconstitutional. Where are those who speak for our civil rights in Congress? Where are the "special interest groups" for our liberties? Where is the courageous fourth estate, our magnificent press, to convince us to act out of sanity and compassion?

Finally, where is our leadership? In this national crisis are we so intent in carrying out a war against other nations that we give up our rights, our freedom and our reasoning? Have we lost sight of our basic principles and allowed ourselves to deprive a group identified by race (it might as well be by age or sex) of its right to have a home, property and freedom of movement?

Perhaps the enemy is more entrenched in our social fabric than we think. Perhaps there is more to defeat here than Hitler and Tojo.

CHAPTER SEVENTEEN

Friday, three days before the evacuation was to take place, Mutt Sugimoto went to the Old Anderson Dock Store, one of two buildings the federal government had rented to expedite the exodus from Bainbridge Island. The one-story wooden building, recently abandoned, sat on a large lot on the south side of Eagle Harbor. Mutt was following orders on a posted notice to register his family with authorities. He stood in the doorway with his faded, sweat-stained hat in his hands in front of him and surveyed the dimly lit room. Dust motes floated in the morning air and he could only make out silhouettes of men and women standing near tables and desks. He felt afraid and ashamed. He was also angry, but determined not to show anyone. He kept his weather-tanned face as calm as possible, but inside he was shaking.

"Come in sir," a young woman called to him. She was pleasant and matter of fact. "Have you come to register?" Mutt nodded his head.

"Over here, sir, have a seat."

The woman, young enough to be his daughter, was clean and crisp in a blue and yellow flowered dress. Sara Jeffries was a senior at the University of Washington, a bright, caring young woman who was the daughter of a fisherman from Ballard. She was hired temporarily as a clerk to process paperwork for those families about to leave. Her long brown hair was pulled up in the back and curled around the top of her head. She was pleasant to Mutt and seemed to have been instructed that she should be as businesslike as possible, nothing personal.

In the fifteen minutes he was in the room, Mutt would learn that the federal government had agreed to transport his family's furniture and other belongings to a storage site, where it would be safely kept, along with other families' belongings, for the duration of their stay in a relocation center.

"Yes, Mr. Sugimoto, the government will put everything you list in storage. It will all be safe and ready for you when all this ugliness is over," Sara told him.

"I see. And this is true for all of us?"

"Yes, we have a large storage facility not far from the island where all the furniture and other belongings will be stored." She smiled at Mutt.

This information lit a small spark in Mutt's chest. It was something, the smallest thing, to hang onto. They could have their furniture in safekeeping. There was no need to sell anything from the house at all. He would not need to impose on the Kuzuos. Suki could keep her kitchen utensils. They could keep their bed. He hurried back home.

That afternoon, he, Suki and Amy raced in separate directions to recover their goods, to bring them back together in one place so the government could take them to storage. It was an embarrassment, yes, but they would have something to return to with no obligations. It would be some degree of certainty. Mutt went to find Milton Baker to tell him. Suki and Amy raced to see the Kuzuos.

Suki discovered that the Kuzuos had left for Idaho early that morning. They had taken everything they could stuff into their truck. She drove back to the grocery store on Miller Road and saw friends of hers. They were scrambling to buy back furniture and personal belongings they had sold. There was some sense of relief, something to hold onto that represented home, some idea that the war would not last that long. Otherwise it felt as if they were being cast adrift on an open sea, destination unknown and not much to return to. She and Amy made their way back to the house, disappointed. They could only hope now that they would get their things back from Idaho when the Kuzuos returned.

Mutt approached the house and saw Suki with tears in her eyes.

"It's gone. We are too late."

Twenty four hours later, Saturday afternoon, the Federal Reserve Bank, through Army personnel on the island, announced to a small crowd in downtown Winslow that, no, the government would not transport and store any property owned by evacuees. Costs for transportation would not be paid for any equipment, household belongings or furniture. Families could make arrangements themselves for storage, but the responsibility was not that of the federal government. Further, evacuees would be allowed to take with them only what they could carry...two suitcases.

The fragile control Mutt had maintained on his emotions broke. His round, ruddy face was contorted, wrinkled with pain and anger. He walked with heavy footsteps throughout the small house, now empty. He was speaking in Japanese, unintelligible to Amy and Suki it was so garbled. He slapped the doors with an open hand. He kicked the walls. He seemed to be looking for something to throw but there was nothing. He stopped and looked up at the ceiling, shaking. Tears began to flow.

"I am nothing. I am not important. I have nothing. The world is caving in." He blew out a long breath.

Suki did the only thing she knew. She went to her husband and put her arms around his broad shoulders.

All over the island Japanese American families were scrambling to adjust to a new cruel reality: they had hours left before they would be taken from their homes. Houses, furniture, household goods, books, pictures, toys, and many clothes would have to be left behind. What would happen to "things," many of which had deep meaning to men, women and children who were leaving, was not known. They were to pack what they could in two suitcases and be taken to a place they did not know, to begin a life that would last...how long? Who would they live with? How would they live? What would they eat? What was to happen to their children? The only thing they knew for certain: they were leaving.

When Will was needy, he was a little unsure of how to say what he needed directly and plainly. When he wanted to make love to Molly, he was even more unsteady. Their physical relationship was a good one and had been since the beginning. Both were at ease with their bodies, unashamed and had not made up any reason to be self-conscious or defensive. And yet there were occasional times when Will was not sure how to initiate sex. In those moments when he wanted her, words were almost too blatant, too direct and harsh sounding when he thought about them. It seemed like what he wanted should be able to be communicated non-verbally, without having it "out there" between them in words. His recourse was to communicate physically. He would rub the small of her back as she was standing at the kitchen sink. He would hug her from behind as she was sweeping the living room floor and ease his loins up against her cheeks. He would toy with the hair on the back of her neck as she sat on the bed or grab her buttocks as she washed at the bathroom sink. More times than not, but not always, these were invitations to climb into bed together.

And so it was this night, this unseasonably warm March night, in the midst of all the change, tension and stress going on in their world, that he hugged her from behind as she stacked dishes on the sink and kissed the nape of her neck.

"Hmmm. That's nice."

"Uh huh."

He ran his large hands along the muscles that ran from her neck to her shoulders and gently squeezed along their length. He ran his nose and mouth up the length of her neck and into her rust-colored curls, her hair fine and wispy and smelling of the heat in the kitchen. She carefully put a dish in the sink and began to dry her hands on the faded blue dishcloth. He drew her body closer to his.

"Shall we head for the bedroom?" she asked.

"That's my vote," Will mumbled into her hair and started to walk backwards, slowly pulling her with him.

In the bedroom, Molly lit a candle on the dresser and sat on the edge of the black frame bed and slowly, deliberately removed her clothes. Will did the same on the other side of the bed. They rolled together under the down comforter and their bodies joined in sweet relief. They were in no hurry. They relished in the dim light, the smell of each other and the feel of one another's skin. This was their haven. This was their retreat, their cave of peace, total relaxation and safety. Here, with each other, no one would find them, speak to them, argue with them – no one would even see them. Here they were apart from being publishers, writers, public figures – they were only man and woman, stripped of any kind of role other than what they were to each other in that moment: lovers.

They wound around each other and kissed and tasted each other. They took in one another's breath. Will left part of himself deep within Molly and they both broke open some seal of tension and desire. Both bodies, spent and sweaty, relaxed and rolled to the side. Will's chest rose and fell with his breath and he stared at the ceiling.

"Wow."

"Yeah."

Slowly, their minds eyes replayed the last half hour, running over the touches, the smells, the movements, the sounds they had made. Then, regrettably, their thoughts drifted back to their other world, to the newspaper, ad income, the impending departure of their neighbors and to the fear and injustice around them.

CHAPTER EIGHTEEN

Will and Molly talked for a long time after dinner. Molly had not been sleeping well and her fatigue and the sadness she felt for these island residents were wearing on her. Will was trying to be sympathetic but the anger he felt was sitting atop any other feelings he could muster. He was angry with President Roosevelt, other politicians in Washington, the Army, General DeWitt and the islanders who were in favor of the evacuation.

"It's as if we have reverted to some primitive state," he said loudly to Molly. "We have become some kind of animals and forgotten our laws, forgotten the Constitution and lost our common sense." He looked at her face. "I'm sorry old girl, you're tired and bummed out. And probably tired of listening to me rant. I don't blame you."

"I just feel like a good cry."

"Well go ahead."

"I think I will, but one more thing Will. I think we need to figure out a way to stay in touch with our neighbors, a way to let people here know what's going on with them while they're away. We could ask some people to write to us, or write for us. What d'ya think?"

"I think you're brilliant, Molly dear. Why the hell didn't I think of that? And I think I know just the guy."

"Paul?"

"Exactly."

Paul Hamada was an 18-year-old senior at Bainbridge High School. Born and raised on the island, Paul helped Will and Molly with the paper from time to time, cleaning up around the press, running errands and distributing copies around Bainbridge. He had an open, helpful attitude, was a good student and liked the Whitmans. His parents, John and Elaine, did not own land but worked in the fields for several farmers to make ends meet.

"We don't have a lot of time, Molly said. "You better talk to him tonight."

"Right. I'm on my way." Will pulled on his tan corduroy jacket and stepped out into the cool March night. Three beats later he was back in the front door.

"Mol, are you OK? Do you want me to stay?"

"I'm OK babe. Go. Go." She smiled and waved him out the door.

The Hamadas lived in a small wooden house near the downtown area, Winslow, which had grown up around Eagle Harbor. A dirt road ran down the center of the town flanked with homes, small stores, a barbershop, a bathhouse and a grocery. The lights were on at Paul's house and Will could hear the family moving around in the house as he got out of the car. John came to the door.

John Hamada was a short, stooped-over man with salt and pepper hair that stood in spikes around his head and he wore simple rimless glasses. Behind him Will could see Elaine and Paul sorting through clothes, books and items from their bathroom.

"Will. Good evening. What a nice surprise," John said.

"Hello, John. Sorry to disturb you this late." Will was unprepared for the feeling that ran through him just then. Without any provocation he noticed a chill ran quickly up his spine. His neck and arms shuddered, as if a cold wind had blown through him, but the night was still. Tears welled up in his eyes. His throat caught. Seeing them together in their small home, moving together, the way the light fell on their faces…he was shaken with feeling for these three people.

"Would you like to come in?"

"Uh." Will hesitated, reluctant to enter their world at that moment. "Thanks, no, John. I'd like to talk to Paul."

"Certainly." He turned and called to his son. Then he looked at Will with curiosity but said nothing.

Paul agreed to write for The Review, but only after he fully understood what Will and Molly were looking for -- not professional journalism, just a short, regular story from the relocation center, something that said how people were doing, how they were adapting, what kinds of things they did for entertainment and what the conditions were like, wherever they were going.

"I know you're smart. I think you're a keen observer and I can edit whatever you send. I know it will work," Will said.

"OK, Mr. Whitman. I'll give it a shot. At least it'll give me something to do."

"Be sure and tell your parents. They can help if they want to."

"Right."

Will reached out and took Paul's hand. He shook it vigorously and held on to it for a few seconds longer. "I'm really sorry all this is happening Paul. We'll just have to make the best of it."

A tired smile grew on Paul's face and he nodded his head, turned and went back inside. Will stood on the porch for a moment, struggling with his feelings, turned and made his way back to the car in the dying light.

"That was pathetic," Will said to himself on the drive home. "We'll just have to make the best of it. We! Who is we? I sound like some Sunday school teacher. These people are having their lives ripped apart and I'm telling them to make the best of it. Jesus, is that all I can say, all I can do?"

He bounced up the long dirt road that led to his cottage, going a little faster than usual. There was a lamp on near the front window. After he parked he got out of the car and looked up at the tall trees around the house. The stars were out, not all that usual for a March night. He sighed. He went through the front door quietly, shut off the lamp and walked into the bedroom. The old floor creaked under his weight. He slipped out of his clothes, keeping his eyes on the curve of Molly's hip under the covers. He slid carefully into bed, inching up behind her and pulling her hips and buttocks into his loins. His right arm was draped over her and his hand found her breasts.

"Hi sweetie," she said. "How'd it go?"

"Just fine, Mol. He'll do it." He pulled her even closer. "I love you Mol."

"Me too sweetie."

CHAPTER NINETEEN

In the Kobiyashi house the lights were on late. A light breeze wrapped around the little red and gray farmhouse, rattling the bamboo wind chime as Bert and Linda sat at the kitchen table talking. She was playing with the wax from a candle she had lit on the table between them. His dark eyes reflected the wavering candlelight.

They had come to a painful decision. Linda, who was white and grew up on Bainbridge Island, would stay here. Her parents lived three miles away and worked for the State of Washington. Her family and home was here. For some days she had tried to persuade Bert that she should go with him and adjust to whatever life awaited them in the camp. Bert was adamant. His wife would not go to such a place. He would not have his wife humiliated and dragged off to some camp in conditions that no one yet knew about. He would write. She would write. The time would be short. She could take care of the place. She could give him something to come home to.

Bert's parents had come to this island from Osaka near the turn of the century, worked in the Port Blakely shipyard, like so many of their countrymen, and lived up on the hillside above the bay in a small Japanese community called Yama. Bert was born there in 1916. Bert worked hard and stayed close to his parents. He met Linda, a slim, quiet blonde, in their junior year at Bainbridge High School and they had been inseparable ever since. An only child, he graduated near the top of his class and inherited the small farm when his mother and father died, within three months of each other, four years ago. Bert and Linda had no children, just a small dog, "Toto," and were known in the Japanese American community for their devotion to each other and to their home and land. The farm – five acres of lettuce, beans, carnations and strawberries-- was clean and organized and one of the most profitable on the island.

"This has to work," he said to Linda. "In a way we have an advantage over some other families. They have to walk away from their house and land with no one here to take care of it. They have no guarantees about what will be here when they come back. This way, we can have our life back."

"Yes, that's true, but at what cost?" Linda was teary and tense as she talked. She had her fingers in the warm wax, mindlessly shaping it into small balls. "We have no idea where you are going or what will be there when you get there. Who knows how they will treat you? What if you don't come back at all? Bert, You know I couldn't stand that."

"Honey!" he took her hands in his. "Calm down. I have to go. You don't. It's that simple."

"It's not fair!"

"You're right. But it's happening. I'll go. You'll take care of the place, with your friends and parents. Toto will be with you. We'll write. And, as soon as possible, I'll be back. We can do this. We have to do this."

"Bert, how did it get to be like this? I don't understand. How could our lives be completely at the mercy of some men in Washington who don't even know us, know this community and know how we feel, how we live? How could that happen?"

Bert took a deep breath and sighed. "Honey, it's war. It's a world war. People lose their good sense when it's a war. We're just caught up in it. It's like a whirlpool and I'm not sure anyone has control over it. That's all I can say."

Linda got out her chair abruptly and moved onto Bert's lap. "Please honey, just put your arms around me and hold me. Hold me for a long time."

US Army PFC Sal Palatino, 20 years old and two months out of boot camp, snapped awake, clear headed and energetic. He had slept through the night and was grateful for a good night's sleep. He thought immediately of what was ahead. The middle son of three boys from an Italian family in Trenton, Sal had an easy way about him and more compassion than most young men. His instructor in boot camp, an 18-year veteran everyone called Snake, had seen this "soft inside like tapioca puddin'" and had ridden Sal hard. Sally, as his buddies called him, had given in when he needed to give in and stood fast when he had to. He and Snake came out with a mutual respect. Now, right out of the box, he knew he and his platoon had a demanding and thankless job ahead of them.

He strapped on his leggings, shoved his feet into his big black shoes, tied them tight, and strode out into the morning.

The morning of March 30 was cloudy and cool, a very typical spring day in the Northwest. All the soldiers were up early. Half a dozen scrambled up into a large flatbed truck with high walls. They were, at the same time, eager and hesitant. Sal and his friends had talked about their task for a long time yesterday. A natural leader in his platoon, he urged efficiency and patience.

They were to make systematic rounds of the Japanese American homes on the island. At each stop they were to load families and individuals into the trucks with as little trouble as possible.

The soldiers stood in the back of the truck, armed with rifles with fixed bayonets. In twos and threes, they knocked on doors and escorted families into the truck. They met no resistance, although the men, women and children moved slowly and were often crying. The soldiers lifted small children up into the truck bed and helped with the luggage the families carried out of their homes. When the truck was full, they would drive to the ferry dock on the south side of Eagle Harbor, where the specially chartered ferry Keholoken sat waiting. They would unload, hand over their cargo to officers, and drive back to another part of the island for more passengers.

Bert picked up his suitcase, his father's old leather case he had to tie together, and a cardboard box wrapped in twine. He wore his best overcoat and a gray felt hat he had worn for some years, a little dirty, a little frayed, but comfortable. Linda was holding her self in check, making her self busy in the house, until Bert was helped up into the back of the truck and then she openly sobbed. She tried to say something but she had no breath. Everything was in a tight knot in her chest. Bert managed a small wave and watched his young wife as the truck pulled away. Linda waved back and watched the truck until it was out of sight.

At a small Japanese church near the center of the island, the Rev. Kiro Hayakawa was holding a final service for about thirty parishioners. Just as he was finishing – "may peace be with you and with those you love"-- a large moving van pulled up outside the church, ready to load the piano, chairs and church supplies off for storage. Everyone in the church turned toward the door when they heard the truck's loud engine.

"What has to be has to be," Rev. Hayakawa said to the assembled Japanese Americans. "I am grateful for the fact that we can all go together. These will be hard times, I know, but we will have each other. I have faith that most of us will return to this island together. We will all wait for that day when we come home. If this is what has to be, then we will do it. If this evacuation will help our country, we are proud to obey this order." He stood in the doorway and shook each person's hand as they walked out of the church and headed back to their houses.

Suki, Mutt and Amy were waiting for the truck when it pulled in. Amy had been crying since they came outside. Suki was calm and stood hugging her daughter. Mutt, drained of his anger, stood as still as a post, watching the truck pull in. He then turned to look at the house and the cherry tree in the front yard, full now of light pink blossoms. He watched the breeze stir the leaves and blossoms. He took Suki's hand, then Amy's and walked toward the large, loud Army truck idling in his driveway.

Henry Kitano Jr., his wife, Carol, and their two girls were scrambling to get ready. Living near the harbor they figured to be among the last picked up. The girls – Kate, 6, and Eileen, 4—were walking slowly around their living room as if in a daze. Eileen carried her stuffed pony by the neck. They remember their grandfather being taken away in a big black car only days before. They had plenty of questions for their mother and father but got little satisfaction from their parents' answers. Now they seemed nearly hypnotized, their large black eyes blank and dull. Finally, their father stumbled into the large front room with two brown suitcases and put them down by the door.

"What's most important -- Kate and Eileen -- listen to daddy: what's most important is that we stay together." He waited to see if they were listening. The two girls looked into his eyes. "Where's mommy?" Eileen said.

"She is getting her things in a bag. She'll be right here." Eileen stuck her thumb in her mouth and looked behind her father's legs.

"Just remember that. We'll be OK if we stay together. You must always know where mom and dad are, OK?" The two girls nodded slowly, lacking any kind of brightness. Carol walked into the room, hurried and tense. And they all turned to the door as they heard the sound of a large truck outside.

Private Palatino jumped off the bed of the truck and trotted up to the door.

"Come on girls," he said, as the door opened wide, revealing the family in the morning light, reflected off the water of the Sound onto the front of the building. He slung his rifle on his back, adjusted the strap and reached out with both arms. "I'll carry you."

The girls retreated and looked up at their father.

"It's all right," Henry said. "Kate you go with the soldier. I'll take Eileen."

Carol closed the door and the latch snapped shut. She could barely breathe.

By 11 o'clock, two hundred and seventy four Japanese Americans were assembled on the road and in a small parking lot near the water. Some yards away from those families were an equal number of island residents who had come to see them off. There were tears, hugs and handshakes. The soldiers, in their dark heavy overcoats and steel soup-bowl helmets, were efficient and friendly. Some carried small children. Others helped with the makeshift luggage and boxes. The green and white ferry pushed up against the dock, its props turning slowly to keep it in place.

Seen from the air, it could have been a morning commute, a few hundred people boarding a ferry to Seattle--except for the luggage, and the emotion. The men, for the most part, were somber and stoic, fighting not to reveal anything to the soldiers and wanting to keep their families intact. The women, most holding small white handkerchiefs, cried openly as they said goodbye to neighbors or herded their children like mother hens.

Many women, dressed in some kind of fashionable hats and long coats to protect them from the morning chill, carried babies. Most people had a paper tag affixed to a button or pinned on, numbered by hand, which identified them and their families. The gray morning, the clouds, the steely water seemed to mute any sounds. People moved slowly, reverently almost, as they said goodbye in soft voices.

The Japanese Americans were dressed as if going to church; calf-length dresses, suits, brightly colored ties, felt hats and their best overcoats. Periodically another Army truck would pull up and unload yet another family. Subdued greetings would follow and the arriving families would tend to their luggage, some leather suitcases, some cardboard boxes, some cloth bags and a few small wooden chests carrying personal family treasures. Mothers and fathers kept busy, checking on children, making sure belongings were gathered together, checking to see if they could help other families.

All pets had to be left behind and many children were still teary from goodbyes to their dogs, cats and birds. Children talked to their white friends who were staying behind about caring for their precious pets. A four-year-old girl was crying for her little white kitten, being held in the crook of one arm of a tall soldier. At the last moment the kitten had been discovered in a small box the girl carried. The parents were tugging her away from the soldier, their own eyes filled with tears.

A few feet away, an older Japanese woman suddenly collapsed, her large overcoat folding itself into a pile over her petite body. Her small brown suitcase fell to the ground beside her and popped open, scattering her clothes on the dirt road. Several people around her dropped to their knees. A man felt her forehead. Another man began gathering the clothes together and putting them back into the suitcase.

"I think she's fainted."

"Maybe. Maybe it's a stroke."

Two soldiers arrived and quickly scooped up the woman and carried her away. The suitcase lay on the ground. Two women close to her starting crying. Then several more cried out and sobbed. Several men, watching their wives and friends, broke through the crusty shield they had been holding over their feelings and tears ran down their cheeks. A ripple ran through the crowd, as if a wind were blowing through a wheat field.

Will and Molly had arrived early and had talked to nearly everyone there as they arrived. They were writing down names and numbers -- husbands, wives, girls, boys, uncles and aunts, addresses, phone numbers -- making connections in their minds, reassuring, soothing. Will was taking a few pictures, but had left most of that up to Frank so he could have his hands free and could eliminate any barrier between him and the people he talked to. Molly was talking mostly to women and their children, trying to remain upbeat. She hugged some of the women and children she knew, fighting back her own feelings.

A Filipino man the Whitmans knew, Felix Arota, was particularly upset, wringing his hands, pacing, hugging his Japanese wife Miki, then continuing to pace. Miki stood stoically, hands at her side, helpless. Earlier in the week Felix and Miki had accepted the fact that they would be going, despite the Army policy that exempted Filipinos from evacuation. They prepared themselves and were fully packed. Then, just 24 hours ago, the Army had ruled that Miki would have to be evacuated and that Felix could not go with her. The decision broadsided the couple. Now they were to be separated. Felix walked in near panic, wanting to do something, to say something that would change the madness. He kept raising his hands in the air, palms up, and slapping them down on his thighs. He was helpless.

Suddenly, the ferry whistle sounded, a loud, startling, mournful moan into the spring air. A spell was broken, a page was about to turn, lives were changing irrevocably. There were more hasty goodbyes. People were giving small hand waves now and trying to smile.

Slowly the families turned away from their friends who had come to say goodbye and faced the green and white ferry. They began to walk down a narrow wooden ramp, slowly, in measured paces, lugging their suitcases and boxes, holding their small children in their arms and walked onto the deck of the ferry. Two hundred and seventy four men, women and children moving in a column, in a sad march off of their island home.

At 11:20 the ferry revved up its two diesel engines, churning the green water of Puget Sound and pulled away from the dock.

CHAPTER TWENTY

On the Seattle side of the water, the families, gathered together their suitcases, boxes and bags and walked slowly off the ferry and into an unknown future. Under the eyes of and instructions from government personnel and soldiers they began walking toward the downtown train station. Through Pioneer Square and up the hill to the King Street station they trudged with their belongings, their heads down and eyes averting others, concentrating on their children and keeping their baggage together. A few soldiers accompanied the rag-tag caravan. Seattleites looked down out of office building windows and passersby stopped to stare, saying little if anything to the irregular line of short, dark people.

Once at the train station, Army personnel at long wooden tables registered men, women and children by name and number and gave them two dollars for food for the day. Six black passenger cars stood like large, living beasts waiting silently on the rails headed southeast. A hundred yards down the track the locomotive breathed heavily in the cool spring air, vibrating slightly, restless, anxious to lurch forward and move down the rails.

The walk from the ferry and the interior of the station had warmed the adults and they started to unbutton their overcoats, urging their children to do the same as they walked down the cement walkway and entered the dark, sterile cars.

Above the evacuees, on a pedestrian bridge that arched over the tracks, hundreds of people lined a low cement wall watching, witnesses to the beginning of the largest government evacuation of American citizens in the history of the nation. They watched the figures of mothers and fathers anxiously herding their children and their belongings up the three iron steps of the railroad cars into the slim doorway.

Paul Hamada was standing on the platform waiting for his parents to board ahead of him when he heard a shout. Then another. He heard his name. "Paul." It rang out and echoed in the cavernous station. He looked back down the tracks and saw faces he recognized—Dick Parsons, Henry Lawless, Wayne Longfellow and Billy Taylor—all Bainbridge High School seniors, running toward him. He dropped his suitcase and waved. He looked, seeking permission, at the soldier nearby, who shrugged his shoulders and looked away.

"Hey. Dick, Billy, what's up?"

The four students, in front of a larger group that was walking quickly, stopped and each in turn grabbed Paul's hand.

"We wanted to come and say goodbye," Wayne said. "We cut the rest of the day. We thought it was important." Other students and a few adults from the island joined them and began waving to people on the train. Faces lit up as the Japanese already putting their luggage up into racks inside the cars, recognized friends and friends of their children. Henry Lawless, a tall bony blond boy who sat next to Paul in history class, took out a bound notebook and handed it to him. The nearby soldier watched closely.

"It's a journal," Henry said, turning to the soldier and then to Paul. Henry's face was lit up with feeling. "We thought maybe you could write down some of what goes on while you're gone." Paul looked at each of them, one by one, and smiled shyly. His eyes were wet.

"Thanks guys. You're swell."

The soldier took a step forward. "OK boys, I'm afraid that's it. We've got to get this train loaded." Henry, Billy, Wayne and Dick stepped back and not knowing what more to say, weakly raised a hand to say goodbye. Paul tucked the notebook under his arm and took the three steel steps up into the passenger car.

Minutes later the train jerked forward, the steam engine hissed and groaned and the cars began to pull away. The small crowd on the platform walked forward alongside the cars, waving to friends inside. Smiles had sunk on faces now and hearts had picked up speed. As the train gathered its momentum, some of the students outside the cars began to run, still waving hands in the air. It was 12:40 in the afternoon. Henry, breathing hard and sweating, stopped running and raised both arms in the air. He stood like that until the train rounded a curve and disappeared.

After about an hour, Paul found a seat by himself, away from his parents. He slouched down in the seat and looked out the window at the green Washington countryside. The Evergreen State, he said to himself, the only place I've ever been. He thought about growing up on the island, spending 18 years in one small place, knowing just about everybody in his senior class. What would his friends be doing next week? They'd be out on the baseball field, fielding grounders and listening to Coach Bennett yelling at them to get their bodies behind the ball. They'd be walking home with their friends, listening to records, having a nice dinner with their parents. And me? I'll be in a strange old building somewhere or a big tent maybe, sleeping on the ground or a cot or who knows where? I can do it. I can take it. It's mom and dad I'm worried about it. They are so used to being home and home is so important to them, I don't know how they'll take it. How can we do this to each other? We? Who's the we? The American people? The Army? The government? Who, exactly, is <u>we</u> at this point? They say it's a national emergency. That's for sure, but we —my family and the rest of us from Bainbridge —are not a national emergency. We're just people, some of whom have been born in Japan. My folks can't help that. And I was born here, right on the island, in my own house, on US soil. I'm a citizen. Supposedly I'm protected by the constitution. What happened to that? It just doesn't make any sense. But then here I am, on this long black train headed south to California, I guess. I've got some clothes, a few books and I'm in good health. I can be thankful for those things I suppose. And I've got a job. Well, sort of. I'm a reporter. I suppose I can write about anything I want.

Others were settled into their seats, staring out the windows or tending to their children. Some were opening Mason jars filled with tea and bringing out sandwiches. The car was eerily quiet and all Paul could hear was the clackety-clack, clackety-clack, clackety-clack of the steel wheels on the rails.

Three days later, The Review ran a frontpage account from Paul Hamada, "Review Staff Correspondent" on the trip. It was datelined April 1, Camp Manzanar, California.

"Bainbridge Island's evacuated Japanese residents, well and cheerful, arrived here at 12:30 this afternoon.

"The last stage of the trip—which began in Seattle Monday morning—was accomplished by a fleet of busses that met the train at Mojave early this morning. Islanders were greeted by warm sunshine. They found the Owens Valley region to be level land, with high mountains nearby.

"Everyone enjoyed the trip but missed his island friends.

"On the train there was group singing, card playing and chatting with the soldiers who accompanied the evacuees. Islanders were treated swell by the Army and, in return, cooperated fully because the soldiers were so courteous.

Inside the same issue, on page two, Will ran the following letter. A young Japanese American man had pressed it into his hand on the dock Monday morning:

"Dear lifetime buddies and friends:

"With the greatest regrets we leave you for the duration, knowing deep in our hearts that when we return we will again be neighbors. There will be no trace of bitterness within our group or any show of disrespect toward our government. We accept the military orders with good grace. We write this letter to thank our community – the only community we have known – for its past favors shown to us, the spirit of sportsmanship showered upon us and the wholesome companionship afforded us.

Respectfully, Glenn Hashimoto"

The "relocation" of 120,000 Japanese Americans into camps had begun.

CHAPTER TWENTY-ONE

The Owens Valley is the deepest large valley in the continental United States. It lies between the Sierra Nevada range to the west and the Inyo Mountains to the east, 230 miles northeast of Los Angeles. The valley floor is between 3,000 and 4,000 feet above sea level. Mt. Williams and Mt. Whitney, at 14,500 feet, are visible to the west. Death Valley is over the mountains to the southeast.

The weather conditions in the valley are as extreme as the mountains' jagged peaks. On the valley floor the temperature may drop to zero on a January night and climb to one hundred degrees on an August afternoon. The average swing from hot to cold during the year is near sixty degrees, from twenty-seven to ninety eight degrees. The wind barreling down off the slopes is a constant companion to whoever calls this home.

The Native Americans who settled in the valley called it "the land of little rain," and for good reason; it averages about five inches a year. The water under the ground, however, was abundant and the Owens River and Owens Lake provided plenty of water. Around the turn of the century, from the 1890's to 1920, farmers trickled into the valley to make their homes and their livings. To stand anywhere in the valley was to be awed by its rugged beauty -- snow capped mountains on both sides, a large clear lake and a fast river, fed by the runoff from the mountains. In just a few years farmers who settled in the valley had planted nearly 20,000 apple trees and begun raising chickens and cattle. The apples, grow in ideal conditions for the fruit, were of the highest quality and were regularly trucked to the markets in greater Los Angeles area and sold at farmers markets and grocery stores. Three small towns were situated in the valley, south to north: Bishop, Manzanar and Independence. Manzanar, in the middle of the three, took its name from the Spanish word *manzana,* for apple.

As it turns out, the fast-growing City of Los Angeles wanted much more than apples from the farmers and other citizens nestled into this roughly hewn valley. The first thirty years of the 20th century in Owens Valley stands out as one of the starkest examples of man's exploitation of nature. And of other men.

Politicians and developers in the city of angels saw that, without water from outside sources, their fair city would dry up and blow away. People would not move to Los Angeles, Hollywood, Glendale, Pasadena or the San Fernando Valley without a ready supply of fresh water. By 1900 officials in The Los Angeles Department of Water and Power had turned their eyes to the northeast and they saw Owens Valley. City officials made a number of visits to the valley and could see little through their eyes except the river and the lake. Without much fanfare and in some underhanded ways, the LADWP began buying up land and water rights in the long valley along US 395. The water department eventually began to negotiate with farmers, after it had purchased sufficient water rights so that farmers could see the handwriting on the wall. The five-member water and power board, one of which was a land developer in San Fernando Valley, ended up owning 6,020 acres along the river, including all of Owens Lake.

The farmers eventually, begrudgingly, sold out, abandoned their orchards and moved into the surrounding towns or back to the coast. The LADWP, over the course of eight years, from 1905 to 1913, built a 233-mile aqueduct running southwest and carrying water from Owens Lake to the Los Angeles basin. By 1925, Owens Lake was a silt-filled depression, drained of all its fresh water, and the Owens Valley was a dust bowl. It was as if someone had taken a very large straw and, in a relatively short period of time, gulped all of the water out of the valley.

The towns of Bishop and Independence shrunk but survived. Manzanar was abandoned, its once thriving apple trees left to shrivel in the dust and wind. Sagebrush, mesquite and rabbit brush now dominated the landscape. Day after day after day there was the dust – dust and more dust, a very fine alkaline dust with a touch of arsenic in it, dust so small it blew and settled into every nook and cranny in buildings, cars and human beings, dust with particles so tiny it went right into one's lungs.

In the summer of 1941, the Inyo County Board of Supervisors officially abandoned the buildings, roads, and any remaining infrastructure in Manzanar. The beautiful and rugged mountain valley that was once called "the Switzerland of California" was officially dead.

Just months after that official abandonment, the US Army, hungry for land to use as "relocation centers" for Japanese Americans, also set its eyes on the Owens Valley. The War Relocation Authority, under the direction of Milton Eisenhower, was scrambling to grab land and build buildings in various locations in the West. The WRA, in a very short period of time, was charged with finding and/or building new homes for 120,000 people—houses, laundries, bathrooms, kitchens, sewers, power, water, fences, guard towers and recreation fields, and with little real direction or planning. It was a massive undertaking.

On March 7, 1942 the Army announced that Manzanar, the empty, desolate abandoned land of orchards, would be the first of such camps. It ended up being one of ten camps, most all of them in the interior West, and at the end of the first year it would house 10,000 Japanese Americans from the edges of the west coast, 7,000 of them American born citizens.

The building of the camps, the locations, the design, what the internees would do while they were there -- even what to call the camps – were all subjects of heated debates in the press and state, local and federal agencies. Would they be "relocation camps," "temporary housing camps," "concentration camps," or "internment camps?" At some point all these terms were used. President Roosevelt referred to them as concentration camps in a public address. But in the end most people settled on "internment," as the most accurate word, meaning to confine someone as a prisoner for political or military reasons.

Early on, Milton Eisenhower had announced a five-point program that would find paying jobs for as many of the evacuees as possible. They would work, outside of the camps, in public works programs such as land development, agricultural production, and manufacturing within relocation areas.

However, the limited experience anyone had with this kind of mass, forced exodus meant that, if the program had any chance of succeeding, the governors, and the people, of neighboring states would have to cooperate. State and local governments, as well as private enterprise in selected communities would have to give their blessing to the plans and they would have to hire the Japanese American evacuees. The Governors of Utah, Arizona, Nevada, Montana, Idaho, Colorado, New Mexico, Washington, Oregon, and Wyoming, and a host of other officials, were called together in the spring of 1942 to hear about and work on such a program. They met in Salt Lake City.

Eisenhower and others made lengthy presentations, stuffed with statistics and graphs, and answered questions. The governors of the mountain states were unimpressed with any of the ideas proposed by the WRA officials. The governors opposed any land purchases for evacuees or settlement in their states. They wanted written guarantees that the federal government would forbid evacuees to buy land and that the government would remove evacuees at the end of the war. They objected to the federal government using the interior states as a "dumping ground for a California problem."

The people in these western states were so bitter abut the whole relocation, the governors said, that evacuees, if left on their own would face physical harm. The most extreme viewpoint was expressed by Utah Gov. Herbert Maw, who suggested a plan whereby the states would operate the relocation program with federal money, setting up camps where Japanese could be detained while working on federally approved projects. He felt strongly that evacuees should not be allowed to "roam at large." Gov. Maw suggested that the WRA was too concerned about the rights and liberties of Japanese American citizens and suggested that the Constitution be amended to allow for his plan. The governors of Idaho and Wyoming agreed, the latter urging that evacuees be placed in "concentration camps." Most of the state government officials present agreed in general and even the farm owners in attendance, who had some hope of using the Japanese Americans for agricultural work, eventually agreed.

At the end of the meeting it was clear that the plan for reception centers would be accepted only as long as the evacuees remained under guard within the camps. Eisenhower, discouraged and facing rigid, unified opposition, had to admit that his plan for resettlement and employment in private industries would have to be abandoned.

Even before any more humane and mutually beneficial program could be adopted, Eisenhower and the WRA were forced by political realities to abandon "resettlement" and plan for evacuee "confinement." The choice of words was telling and the lives of thousands of people had been changed. Politicians, the press and the public on the West Coast had achieved, earlier that spring, their goal of exclusion and now political leaders of the interior states had achieved their goal of detention. The War "Relocation" Authority had now become the jailer, leaning on the paper-thin logic that confinement was for the benefit of the evacuees and that controls on any kind of outside freedom were designed to prevent mistreatment by other Americans.

The noose had grown even tighter.

CHAPTER TWENTY-TWO

"I get along without you very well, of course I do…" Terry Allen's voice reverberated in the small office as Will sat reading. The afternoon sun shone through the south window, warming his back. He was reading a letter from one of the evacuees he didn't know, a young man who knew Paul and said Paul had encouraged him to write.

As he turned to the second page, the phone rang. Will stretched out his long frame and turned the radio down.

"Hello, Bainbridge Review."

"Hi sweetie, it's me."

"Hi Mol, how's my girl?"

"I'm fine. I have some news."

"Yeah?"

"I'm late."

"Were you supposed to be here now?"

"No. I mean, you know -- late. I haven't had my monthly friend."

"Oh! Holy Moley. You're late. Um, how late?" Will was fidgeting in his well-worn wooden chair.

"Well, I, uh, it's been two months."

"Does that mean we're gonna be parents?"

"Sweetie, I don't know. It could. And it could mean something else too. I think I need to go see Doc Martin and see what's up."

"OK. Can I go? Should I go? Do you want me to go?"

"You're sweet. But there's not much you could do. I'll just get an appointment as soon as I can."

"OK babe." He paused. "I'm not sure what to say here."

"I know. It's OK. I just wanted to tell you and since you have that meeting tonight, I probably won't see you 'til the morning."

"OK Mol. I love you. Don't know what I'd do without you."

"Me too Will. Me too."

Will leaned back in his chair and took a deep breath. "Wow," he whispered. The letter he was reading fell to the floor.

Dear Mr. Whitman:

I am writing just to tell someone my thoughts about our evacuation and the trip here. Paul said you would be a good person to write to. I am not suggesting you run this in your newspaper. I'm not a very good writer. But I do want someone to know the truth.

I saw what Paul wrote for you. It is true, but I think it was only part of the story. The trip here was long and hot and the rail cars were very crowded. The older people made the most of it, playing cards, talking, even singing, as Paul said. But many of us are full of anger and have many mixed feelings about our government. We cannot understand how we are treated this way.

On the way here the train made a couple of stops for breaks, I think, or because the track ahead was blocked by another train. The soldiers got out first and then we were allowed to step outside the train. The soldiers had set up three or four machine guns along the length of the train and they were pointed at us! We couldn't believe it. It was like a bucket of cold water in my face. All that we have been through and they were going to shoot us instead of letting us run away in the desert! The soldiers, as individuals, have been nice to us, especially back on Bainbridge, but I am afraid that things are going to get worse.

As you know, we are here in Manzanar now. I am writing you from a wooden building, just four walls, a window at each end and nothing more. Nothing! (I am using my old suitcase as a desk, so this may look kind of messy. Sorry.) We are supposed to get dinner tonight but no one knows where it's coming from. There is no bathroom in here. There are no beds. Maybe those things are here somewhere but none of us have seen them.

We are in a very large square camp, surrounded by fences and barbed wire. Guess what. There are guard towers and soldiers with machine guns. Is this what our "evacuation" means? This is a concentration camp!

I can't write anymore right now. I have to go see how my parents are doing. If you don't mind I will write you from time to time, in the hopes that you will keep my letters and the American public may someday know the truth about this whole disgusting evacuation of Americans.

Thank you for "listening."

Rick Kobori
American Citizen

Linda sat at the same kitchen table Bert and her had huddled over two nights ago. Toto curled himself up at her feet. She absent-mindedly twisted her blonde hair in the fingers of her left hand. In her right hand she held a treasured black fountain pen, poised over creamy white stationery.

My dearest Bert:

This is night number two away from you. The first night was strange, empty and weird somehow. It just didn't seem right that you were so far away and somewhere else without me. Today and tonight are a little different. The strangeness is gone and it is replaced by a big void, a big emptiness, as it settles into me that you are really gone and won't be back for a while.

There have been lots of rumors on the island today, about where you all are. The best we can figure, it's somewhere in the middle of California in the mountains. That may be pretty, but they say it also could be very cold.

People here are already pulling together to harvest the berries and vegetables this month and in the early summer. I got two calls yesterday from a guy who's organizing a cooperative effort. It helps that all of you left things so clean and in such good order. Mom and Dad will help me, of course, and I think we'll be OK.

Toto knows you are gone. You know how dogs are; they know these things. I suppose we'll be good company for each other.

Bert, I don't want to burden you with my feelings too much, but you have to know how much I miss you and how much I love you. This is a terrible, terrible thing for me. At the same time, I know that you and the others there are going through something much worse. I promise that I will stay as strong as possible and take good care of things here.

I was listening to Arthur Godfrey this morning – you know I like him—and he was talking about the war effort and the sacrifices we will need to make, trying to make all his listeners feel like they were in this together, I think. That's all well and good, I said out loud, but I couldn't help being a little angry at all the talk of patriotism after what has happened to you and me and many others.

OK, that's enough. I miss so many things about you... just one: being in bed together. We don't have to be doing anything, just lying there, our bodies touching and talking softly before we get up.

Please write. I don't know if I can stand it if I don't hear from you.

All my love, Lin

Linda folded the letter carefully, raised it to her cheek and slowly rubbed the folded paper up and down on her cheek and along her hair. Maybe he'll be able to smell me, she thought.

CHAPTER TWENTY-THREE

A thousand miles to the south, Bert was waiting in line just outside one of the long wooden buildings, awkwardly cradling his suitcase under one arm. Twenty or so men stood in front of him, going slowly up some wooden steps and into the front door. The spring wind was strong enough to move his hair around. The man behind him was telling him the story of three young men who had brought some bourbon with them and spent the night finishing the bottle amongst the three of them. Staggering back to their room, one of them stumbled into the latrine, a long open ditch some 30 yards from the building they were waiting to enter. The other two men were just drunk enough to begin laughing, but not drunk enough to go into the latrine after their friend. Their laughter attracted two nearby MP's, who extended their rifles to the man in the ditch, tugged him out and sent him on his way.

The man talking to Bert was chuckling as he told the story. Bert was not amused. He tried to ignore the stranger and turned to walk up the steps. He could feel the heat of the man as he spoke and smell his sour breath.

"It's a good thing it's only our second night here," the man said. "Or that thing would have been more full. As it was, the guy had to sleep like that, all wet and covered with shit."

"You know, I don't find it funny. I don't find much of anything funny right now," Bert said and turned away.

Once inside the building, the men received a cursory physical exam, were assigned a registration number that would identify them for the length of their stay and assigned to quarters. For the bachelors, and Bert was registered as a bachelor, that meant a long wooden building full of folding cots; no interior walls, no barriers, no privacy. Just before they left the building, men and women –white government workers-- seated behind a wooden table asked them to volunteer for a job. Cooks, dishwashers, carpenters and gardeners were all needed. Bert volunteered to work in a vegetable garden.

He stepped out into the harsh April light, carrying his suitcase and the papers he'd received. The wind had picked up. On the other side of the camp, he could see a white cloud stirring up. At first it looked like smoke from a fire, but as he watched the white cloud moved toward him. Soon a mist of fine dust was on top of him, swallowing him and the others still in line. A fine white grit covered his face, coating his eyebrows and eyelashes and sticking in his lips. He pulled his hat down but it didn't help. He could feel it in his nose and began to breathe harder. The corners of his mouth were quickly accumulating the dust. He looked down to see his coat and pants covered with what looked like bakery sugar.

He ran. He headed for an empty building just ten yards away and leaped up on the front steps. Just as he was opening the front door, the wind stopped. Bert spit and spit again and blew his nose as he did some days on his own farm, closing one nostril with his thumb and blowing, then the other. He took his hat off and beat it on his leg. He rubbed his face with his other hand but discovered it only made a mess on his cheeks and forehead. He moved inside the empty building, dropped his suitcase on the floor and sat on it, trying to breathe.

There was nothing in the building, just a long, narrow emptiness with a wooden floor that still smelled green and somehow fresh. He spit again on the floor. He eased himself down on the wood and laid his head back on his old leather suitcase. He raised himself back up to spit once again. His breathing got slower and softer. He lay there for a long time, waiting for his body to recover. Soon he began to think of what Linda would be doing at home.

"I'm beginning to wonder about journalists," Will shouted from the kitchen.

"What? Just now?" Molly countered from the living room.

"Ha ha, but really Mol, I can't find a single paper or columnist on the West Coast who stands behind the Japanese citizens. It's kind of frightening when you think about it, not one newspaper, that I can find, has been against the mass evacuation of a hundred thousand people – 70 percent of them American citizens."

Molly, sensing that this was going to be a longer conversation, walked into the kitchen and took a seat at the table. Will poured her a cup of hot water over a peppermint tea bag and took a seat opposite her.

"I know what you mean sweetie," she said. "I don't think I really expected anything one way or the other, but the longer this has gone on and thinking about what has happened, it's surprising. "

"Damn right it's surprising. I think of journalists as probably the most cynical people in America, more than cops, but they – we – are supposed to be cynical about big oil, or the bankers, or politicians, or the military. But in this case the entire Fourth Estate, or as far as we know, has come down on the side of the feds and the Army and abandoned the ordinary citizen. It makes me sick."

Molly was quiet for a moment and looked at her husband. She looked in his eyes. She saw the idealism, the stubbornness and the courage in him and loved it. She also sensed the sadness he felt and rarely talked about, the sense of shame in his own profession, and she didn't want it to get him down.

"What?" Will said, seeing her look at him.

"I just want you to know I love you. It must be tough for you to think you're the only one in this fight. I mean we're not a very big force in the whole big picture, are we?" Molly drew her hair back with both hands. "A small newspaper with a small audience; it's not like we're going to change the whole world. And yet Will -- and yet -- we still have to keep saying what we think and feel. There's no way around that. Otherwise, why are we in this business? I'm not one to roll over and neither are you. It doesn't matter to me how many newspapers from Seattle, San Francisco or Los Angeles agree with us. What matters is that we do what we believe in and I believe in this."

"Yep, you're right, as usual. I agree with you. _And_ I'd like to be able to change some minds, to persuade some of my colleagues, the gentlemen of the Fourth Estate, to come to their senses."

"Well, maybe we've got enough to do without taking on the American press. Isn't the battlefield big enough for you as it is?"

"Yeah, yeah, right again."

CHAPTER TWENTY-FOUR

The builders of the Manzanar relocation camp faced a daunting, nearly impossible task: build a small city for 10,000 people on a one-square-mile plot in the middle of the high desert and do it in under three weeks. Nearly a thousand framers, carpenters and other construction workers were hired by the federal government and bussed in to erect identical wooden buildings, all 120 feet by 20 feet in straight rows. Green pine, Douglas fir and hemlock were brought in from nearby foothills and hired crews threw up frames and siding at the rate of one building an hour. Additional buildings—for administration, laundry, toilets, recreation and showers –were built last. The men worked at a near frantic pace, getting paid twice as much as they would earn at home, and all were anxious to finish what they were doing and leave the valley.

As each bus arrived with new evacuees, those already in camp stood and watched. Every family had made the arduous trip over the mountains in trains and chartered busses. Each person was faced with an entirely new reality: a strange landscape, rows of ugly plain buildings and strangers waiting for them to get off the busses. The climate was nearly the opposite of what they had lived in and the landscape seemed, to them, dead. Worried, fearful faces were pressed up against the glass of the bus windows, searching for a familiar face perhaps, or a comfortable new home, or even a tree, something that would not say "desolation."

They were hustled off the bus and lined up for the intake process, a series of interviews, lectures and instructions for volunteers. There were hundreds of people waiting in line for these gatherings and the spring sun burned down on each one of them. Army personnel handed out water in paper cups and salt tablets. The evacuees were holding onto each other, or to a baby, or clutching a worn paper bag full of clothing, sweating in their coats and topcoats, turning their heads this way and that, looking for something or someone familiar. They got inoculations. They were handed numbered and signed mess cards, in order to get food. They were questioned about their skills and work history. Then they were shown the back door and led to their new homes.

People who were finished with the intake process were funneled out into the dirt pathways and guided by soldiers down a dusty road and into a bare wooden building. When one building was full, the line moved on to the next building, as if bottles are being filled one after another; one full, move onto the next one, that one full, fill the next. Soon after leading the evacuees into the barracks, soldiers came around in twos and threes and handed out dark blue pea coats and goggles.

Mutt, Suki and Ami looked at each other in wonderment. They held the goggles up to their eyes and looked at each other and laughed. Then they looked around the bare interior and saw the white, fine dust.

The new "homes" for the Japanese Americans were wooden shells, the wood still wet and cracking, barely cut and milled from nearby forests. There were no shelves, no storage spaces and no furniture. Six bare droplights hung from the ceilings, one per living space. Each person was given an Army cot, a blanket and an empty pillow case that they could fill as they wished. There were shells of mattresses on the cots that most people eventually filled with straw. Families divided up the living spaces, six areas to a building. Each family would have a twenty-by-twenty area they would call home. Often two families with three or four members shared a space. For a modicum of privacy, people hung sheets, cardboard or blankets and stacked luggage at the edge of their spaces. There were no sinks, no toilets and no bathing facilities, all those being in the common buildings. In the two large common buildings seventy-two families would share twelve showers, twelve lavatories, ten toilets, four urinals and one sink. There was nearly always a waiting line for the toilets, which were lined up against one wall with no partitions between them. The men in the camp would end up escorting women and children to the toilets, standing outside to ensure their privacy.

The first two nights in camp all the drinking water froze. Men, women and children slept on the wooden floor, or at least lay on the floor all night, while the wind whistled around their ears and a fine coat of dust settled on their blankets. Throughout the night, soft crying and sobbing punctuated the cold night air. Each soul in the hollow wooden building knew and felt the sorrow and loss the others felt.

Bert, in a corner by himself in a bachelor building, laid himself down on the bare wooden floor, covered himself with an Army blanket, tucked his coat under his head and tried to talk himself into sleeping. He was shivering, from the cold and from the emotion that had run through his body in the last 24 hours. His thoughts turned to home and, to his surprise, to high school. He remembered watching Linda walking down a hallway toward him, blonde hair bouncing behind her, that spring in her step that he came to know and love. He felt his love for her in that moment on the floor, cold and alone, and he wondered if he had done the right thing to marry her and make her a part of this whole ordeal.

The next morning it seemed as if everyone in camp was in line for food. Men, women and children stood in front of the mess halls and the line snaked around the side of the building and down the central corridor of the camp. They were given powdered eggs, white bread and coffee. Later that morning soldiers announced that some food was available for each family to keep on its own. They received two cans each of small wieners, spinach and bread pudding.

Gradually a sense of optimism and a small ray of hope began to sprout in the dust and wind of Manzanar. On April 11, just as a seedling pops through the crusty earth into the sun, a newspaper appeared in camp. The Manzanar Free Press, mimeographed in the camp administration building, was placed on the front doors of the barracks and "apartments" of camp residents. Written in English, with a masthead featuring the camp's wooden buildings and mountains in the distance, the Free Press was breezy and upbeat. Half a dozen evacuees had organized and produced the first issue. The lead story read:

PRESENT POPULATION ANNOUNCED TO BE 3,302

Pushing aside the sagebrush and literally growing from the desert sand, Manzanar has mushroomed into a bonanza town of '42, boasting today a population of 3,302. In three weeks this magic town has boomed ahead to become the largest city in Owens Valley - the largest California city east of the Sierras.

From the time when 85 hardy pioneers, including eight girls, came from Los Angeles to stake out their new homes in skeleton buildings, additions and improvements have been constantly speeded.

Today 575 buildings are occupied by the following additions:
March 23- 800 from Los Angeles.
March 25- 9 from Palo Alto; 500 from Los Angeles.
April 1- 274 from Bainbridge Island.
April 3- 1,000 from Los Angeles.
April 4 - 900 from Terminal Island.

Hot water is already running in some of the showers and laundries and work is being rushed on the others. As additional blocks are completed, more contingents are anticipated to swell Manzanar town.

Mutt Sugimoto fell asleep just before dawn, after turning over and over, listening to the crying women and children in the wooden frame building. He, Suki and Amy had been assigned to the second building in the second row and occupied the space at one end, desirable because it held one of the two windows in the building. At least most people thought it was desirable, until the wind had blown steadily through the spaces around the window frames one night and painted the ends of the building with a fine coating of white dust.

Mutt was in a sour mood, not just because of his little sleep but also because of news that had been filtering into the camp about the war. Early in the month the Japanese army had captured Java. A week later Rangoon fell and now was coming news that Japanese forces had badly beaten US-Filipino troops at Bataan and had summarily executed four hundred Filipino officers.

Mutt and Suki had good friends on Bainbridge Island who were Filipino and he could only imagine what they felt this morning. He had a longing to leave the camp and reunite with his friends. And in Mutt's mind, each Japanese victory meant the war would last longer, or worse Japan would win, neither of which bode well for his country, himself or his family. He walked, mumbling under his breath with his head down, over to the office in the administration building. There an Army officer assembled the men who had volunteered to work on the new recreation building.

Amy and Suki stayed behind, cleaning the space they shared with an older couple from Santa Monica, both Issei, who spoke broken English and who were being polite and accommodating to Mutt and his family. Precocious at 11, Amy was holding up well, better than her father so far, and she was worried about his health in the cold and dusty environment. She spoke quietly to her mother as they cleaned and arranged their belongings. Amy folded her clothes carefully, anxious to maintain some kind of order and neatness, and stacked them in a cardboard box.

"Is dad going to be OK? You know, his lungs, in all this dust?"

"I hope so dear."

"Isn't there anything we can do?"

"We can make this window as airtight as possible, for one thing. And you know Amy, like I've always said, worry is not going to get us anywhere. We just have to do the best with what we have. There are doctors here if he gets in trouble. And maybe we can find a mask or a handkerchief."

"If he'll wear it."

Suki, whose fine black hair was cut just below her ears, smiled at her daughter.

"Yes. If he'll wear it. Now, why don't you take that corner for your things and you can use the suitcase to put things in that you don't want to get dusty. Then maybe we can take a little walk."

Amy and Suki walked along the second row of buildings to the east, until they came to a spot where just a frame of a new building stood. Carpenters were up on ladders tying together the joists that would hold up the roof. As Amy and Suki passed they heard a shout.

"Hey, mama-san. Good morning. How are you and your daughter? You look pretty good this morning."

Suki kept her head down and kept walking. Amy looked up to see one of the men smiling at her. He smiled and nodded his head, spitting off to the side. Without raising her head, Suki grabbed Amy's hand and tugged her closer.

"Shush. Don't look. Don't acknowledge them." They turned and walked briskly over to the next row of buildings and headed back to Row Two, Number Two.

"Hey, don't go away mad," the man's voice trailed behind them.

That night as Amy and Suki were settling down to sleep, Mutt was sitting on the front steps, holding himself against the cool night, tugging at his overcoat. He pulled a small notebook out of his pocket, a blue spiral notebook he had been carrying since he left his island home. He pulled out a short wooden pencil and wrote:

In our hearts we weep
Despite the face we show to the white man
In our hearts we weep

We are taken from our homes
We are taken from the people we love
And in our hearts we weep

We are showered with the white sand
It is in our hair
It is in our eyes
It is in our lungs
And in our hearts we weep

I think I am nothing
I blow in the wind
I have no shape
I own nothing
Perhaps I am the sand
In my heart I weep

CHAPTER TWENTY-FIVE

The Manzanar camp residents quickly felt the need to organize themselves and establish a sense of community as soon as they could. By the middle of April 1942, there were twelve blocks of buildings finished and each block had an individual evacuee as an organizer. The organizers were elected in an open, democratic poll of the adults in the camp. It was the first time that Issei and Nisei together participated in an election in America. As the population grew, block leaders were added and by the latter part of May there would be thirty-six people in "The Town Hall Block Leaders Council," representing 10,000 constituents. They had a "congress," of sorts.

The people in the camps were determined to have their voices heard, despite the fact that most of them thought of themselves being in a "concentration camp." Early on, the block leaders council polled its members and other camp residents and listed their major areas of concern. Each of these would be communicated to the Army and the War Relocation Authority:

How are evacuees adjusting to life in the camp?
Is some kind of counseling necessary?
What changes would make adjustment easier?

Is a more thorough orientation necessary?

The issues surrounding housing were the most numerous...there were long lists of complaints about the living conditions: the cold, the dust (each worsened by the spaces in the siding), the lack of privacy, the number of sinks and toilets and the small space assigned each family.

The use and abuse of the latrine came up in the meeting on a regular basis. The odor was sometimes overwhelming. There were not enough toilets for the population. Women and children were often afraid to use the facilities. And the toilets were cleaned infrequently.

Financial worries were high on the list. What happened to my savings account at home? What will happen to the money from the harvests on our farms? How much money can we expect to have when we get out? How can I keep what money I have safe in the camp?

The council would, over the months and years to follow, continually push the Army and the WRA for improvements in their daily life, including employment practices and earning a fair wage while they did the work asked of them in the camp. The councils and other small groups within the camp population did not just complain. They used what power they had to purposefully build a sense of community and get as much of the population involved in activities that resembled life back home.

Soon a camp baseball league was organized. Women formed flower garden groups. Sewing groups, reading groups, a children's book group, a women's softball team, an orchestra, a library, a beauty contest-- all blossomed in these first spring months in the camp.

Nearly all of the 10,000 evacuees were pulling together to make the best of a very trying situation.

CHAPTER TWENTY–SIX

Molly was pregnant. She waited until after the trip to Seattle and the visit to Doc Martin's to tell Will. Riding back home on the ferry she sat quietly by herself, her hands folded in her lap. Occasionally she cradled her hands back onto her abdomen and patted her belly, comforting herself and the life that was beginning inside her body. This was her first pregnancy and Doc Martin had said that everything seemed fine so far. Close as they could figure, she had conceived around the first of March, which meant the baby would be born in late November. A Sagittarius, she said to herself, a bit of a wanderer, curious, philosophical, maybe even deeply spiritual. That should fit in this family, she thought.

When she got home Will was waiting for her, perched in the living room with a glass of Scotch in his hand, his eyes as big as the rim of the glass. Molly just smiled at him.

"Well?"

"Let's just say, I can't be having a drink with you Will Whitman."

"I'm gonna be a father?"

"You're gonna be a father. Doc says probably late November."

"I'm gonna be a father. I'm gonna be a father." Will sat his glass down on a small table and started to dance. He opened his arms for Molly to join him and the two of them twirled slowly around the living room to a beat that only they heard, Molly's royal blue dress cutting an arc in the air behind them.

Paul Hamada did not know what to write. Since the long ferry, train and bus trip from Bainbridge Island, he had been overwhelmed with change, acclimating to the camp, to the weather and the social dynamics of thousands of people clamoring for space and forming relationships. Paul and his parents were assigned building three, space four. He was able to scrounge some scrap lumber from the construction of the other buildings and build a small table for the family. But so much was going on, he found it difficult to choose what to write about. A week went by and Paul had not checked in with Associated Press to file a report for the Review. After another three days, Paul gave up and simply mailed a copy of the Manzanar Free Press to Walt with the note: "This will keep you up to date."

By return mail Paul got the following letter:

"Dear Lazybones:

"Come, come my good man. I find the Manzanar Free Press to be very fine reading, but where the hell has my Manzanar correspondent gone?

"Seriously butch, you'll be doing your own people a great harm if you stop sending us all the local gossip down there. Here's what I mean. When this mess is all over you people are going to want to come home. You'll be welcomed with open arms by the vast majority of us, but also by those who don't or won't understand and will not feel that way. They may actually try to stir up trouble.

"But they'll have a hell of a hard time of it, if, in the meantime, you've been creating the impression every week, week in and week out, that the Japanese are just down there for a short while and that—by being in The Review every week—they still consider the island as their home. Any and every scrap of stuff you can gather and send about how they miss the island is fuel for that fire. See what I mean?

"So…enough of this lazy man's reporting. Let's have Hamada back on the firing line, and soon.

"Sincerely, Will"

The next day Paul, with new enthusiasm, filed a report. Thirty-two internees from Bainbridge were aiding the war effort by working on the camouflage net project. Eight of them were young girls. The Toshigo family had all caught the chicken pox. Many people were complaining of the dust and of headaches. A 17-year-old girl from the island, Sachi Moritani, had taken third place in the "Miss Manzanar" beauty contest. Finally, camp officials and building council members had worked out a wage agreement: Professional or technical workers were to receive $16 a month, skilled workers $12 a month and unskilled laborers $8 a month.

Will read the report, pumped his fist and ran Paul's story on page one.

Will and Molly were still writing to an island population that was divided, if not in half, in significant splinter groups of Americans who were mad at, and afraid of, the Japanese. It seemed not to matter how the Japanese acted or where they were. Will had pledged to himself and to Molly that he would continue to run "The Open Forum," a place in the paper where any and all residents could voice their opinions. He stuck by his word, and often winced when he saw what ran in his own newspaper.

> "Bainbridge Islanders took naturally to the Japs who came here. We knew them as neighbors and as the smiling and inscrutable drivers of trucks, the owners of grocery stores and schoolmates. Our constitution reminds us that some of them are actually citizens, even though they may be monkey-jawed and yellow skinned. We learned to like them and so we try to close our eyes to the reports of Jap treatment of American boys in prison camps.
>
> "Whether Nesei or not, whether loyal or not, Japs who return to Bainbridge will be met with insults and abuse, if not worse. Not as long as the youngest of them lives could he ever surmount the curse that has been laid upon his race. But if there were no curse, the Jap is not assimilable. You would not have your daughter marry one, ever, not even one that is one-tenth Japanese. Because they really don't belong here and know it, they will be vengeful, hateful and resentful when they return. Could we ever trust the Japs again? Could we put faith in people who know they are despised?"
>
> Robert Rutherford
> Winslow RFD

And, in the same issue:

Editor:

> "There is something going on in this country and in myself that is deeply troubling and I must confess to it, if indeed it is a confession of guilt."

"When I look around me, the faces of the Japanese, maybe all Asians, don't seem to fit anymore. They stand out and it troubles me a great deal. Since the Dec. 7 attack, when more than 2,000 of my fellow Americans were killed, I can't look at my Japanese neighbors in the same way. The inhuman and ruthless killing of so many young men and women has scarred me and I believe it has scarred our country."

"I don't want to be consumed by the hatred and anger that the enemy apparently has toward our country. I want to remain compassionate, but it is proving to be difficult. I have some sympathy for all the Japanese Americans who have been carted off to camps, but deep in my heart I think it may be right somehow, or at least necessary."

"How am I to distinguish, when I walk down the streets of Seattle, between a Japanese man who loves this city and this country and one who may be wishing he were in on the first wave of zeroes that swooped down on Pearl Harbor? How can I really know if or when the young people attending our colleges may turn on the rest of us without warning? I wish I knew."

"December 7 changed everything. I've decided it is not up to me to determine who is loyal and who is not, but it is up to the Japanese in this country to prove their allegiance and loyalty to the rest of us. Do you love America? Show us. Do you pray for our victory in Europe and in the Pacific? Show us. Are you grateful for the freedom and choice this country affords you? Show us."

"I am not interested in sympathy or expressions of remorse. I am interested in action and evidence that you really are American. I want to see more of you enlisting. I want to see you turning in those people among you who are not loyal. I want to see you cease the celebrations of religions and philosophies of the "old" country."

"You 120,000 Japanese are part of the greatest country in the world and the freedom and rights we have here are of an untold value to me and to everyone I know. I think we have the right to know where you stand and what you will do. Under the circumstances, I think we deserve an oath of undying loyalty to this flag and this nation, under <u>our</u> God."

"Show me. Then, and only then, will I welcome you as my neighbor and my friend. There can be no middle ground."

"Sincerely,"

"Michael Thompson, a veteran"

Frank walked over to Will and Molly's house early on a Saturday morning and knocked on the door.

"Hey, you got a minute?"

"Sure. Come on in and have a cup of joe"

Frank had been using Will as a sounding board and resource, trying to sort out his feelings on the internment. After they took a seat at the kitchen table, Frank revealed the reason for his visit.

"There's something troubling me Will. On the West Coast, we've rounded up and sent away more than 100,000 Japanese, or Japanese Americans, if you prefer." He smiled at Will. "And in Hawaii, where there are many more Japanese, they're not doing the same thing. And they're so much closer to Japan. What's the deal?"

"That's a really interesting question Frank. I've been wondering that myself, so I did a little research, a little reading of the Hawaiian papers and talked to some friends of mine at the Times. It's been quite informative. It turns out that one-third of Hawaii is made of people of Japanese ancestry – one-third."

"Wow." Frank rubbed his black hair at the nape of his neck and pulled up closer to the kitchen table.

"And they did take some people into custody. Right after the attack they arrested about 1,200 community leaders, priests, Japanese language teachers, newspaper publishers and heads of various organizations – people they thought of as having a lot of influence over others I guess. These folks they are still holding, as far as I know."

"So the rest are free?"

"Well, yes. And the reason is both cultural and economic _and_, from what I hear, a matter of one man's different personality, believe it or not."

"How can that be?" Frank was full of genuine curiosity.

"Well, consider this: What would they do with a third of the population of the islands? Put them behind bars? They couldn't send them all to the mainland. So I think part of it was practical. Then there's the climate, if you will, in Hawaii. The islands are such a mix of races and I don't think racism is the issue that it is on the mainland. I've never lived there, but from everything I hear, there's much more acceptance there."

"Yeah, I can imagine that, more of a melting pot then we are."

"Right. Then there's the economic factor. How do you think it would affect the Hawaiian economy if you picked up 140,000 people and took them out of the work force? It would cripple the whole economy."

Frank nodded, deep in thought. "So what about the guy you mentioned?"

"Right. His name is Emmons, I think. And he is the military commander of Hawaii. He's the counterpart to our General DeWitt. Apparently this guy believes he can manage the people there and get what the military wants without coming down so hard on them. He's been working with local leaders and holding meetings with all the races and keeping things together. Basically, he thinks he can get more flies with honey than he can with vinegar. That's what I understand."

"Don't you think that's a little strange?"

"What?"

"Not his approach," Frank said. "But the idea that one man could do things so much differently and affect the lives of so many people. It kind of stirs up my brain. You know what I mean?"

"Definitely. It boggles the mind. And it also makes me mad, as if I needed more things to make me mad." Will started shaking his fist at Frank. "But, Frank, it points out what could have happened here, with a little more enlightened leadership."

"Hey, you're right. It's sad."

"That it is."

CHAPTER TWENTY-SEVEN

"Will," Molly shouted at her husband from the front door as she came in. "Are you home?"

"Yeah, I'm out back." He rushed in through the screen door on the small back porch and met Molly in the living room. She was wide eyed and out of breath.

"Are you OK sweetie," Will said, unconsciously glancing at her stomach.

"They want us off the island."

"Who? What are you talking about?" Will took her gently by each arm and steered her to one of the comfortable green chairs.

"It's Rutherford and some of his cronies. They've called a meeting for next week –you should see the notice—and they're trying to start some effort to get us to leave the island and give up the paper. It's at the Grange Hall next Wednesday."

"Oh, sweetie, calm down. We can handle this."

"What do you mean 'handle it?' What if a whole lot of people want us to leave Will?"

"Take it easy. This is still a free country, despite what you may have heard. There's 7,000 people on this island. A 'whole lot of people' would have to be about 3,000 to sway me. I think our odds are pretty good for not getting voted off the island."

"Oh Will." Molly was wringing her hands. "I don't like this. This could get ugly."

"Molly, we don't how many people are behind this. Let's not get our drawers in a knot just yet. This Rutherford is some kind of nut case."

"Is this going to be the place we want to live out our lives, to raise our children?"

Will paused for a moment and looked in her eyes. "This is a fine place, this is a paradise and we love it here. That hasn't changed. What's changed is that some nut cases have come out of the woodwork and are exercising their free speech to be hateful and racist. That will not win out. Believe me Mol, that will not win out." He raised his voice and stressed the last five words.

The following Wednesday Will approached the Grange Building feeling a little nervous. A large wood-frame building near the center of the island, the Grange meeting hall, as most people called it, sat alone in the midst of a magnificent stand of Douglas firs. It was open to rental by any organization. Not sure what to expect, Will clutched his 5x8 spiral notebook in his left hand, playing the reporter to whatever he might encounter. Robert Rutherford, tall, bony and distinguished looking in and English sort of way, met him at the front door.

"Well, Mr. Whitman. I certainly didn't expect to see you here. Kinda like going to your own funeral, isn't it?" He watched Will closely for a reaction. Will suppressed a smile and looked him in the eye. The two men were identical in height. Rutherford had small pale blue eyes, ghostly almost, and white jowls that betrayed little emotion.

"Mr. Rutherford, I wouldn't miss this for the world. I'm assuming I won't need a press pass." Rutherford chuckled and stepped aside to allow Will to enter the room. He saw two men standing behind Rutherford, partially hidden by the tall man's body in the door. Rutherford, acknowledging that Will was looking in the room, commented:

"These are two of my friends, Julian and Fred Orr. We're not sure what kind of crowd to expect, but we still have fifteen minutes before seven."

"Right." Will stood there nodding and Rutherford shuffled his feet. Will nodded to the other two men and took a folding chair at the far end of the hall. The two men remained at the door and Will guessed they were there for some kind of security.

Will looked around at the inside of the hall. It was unfinished and the wooden beams and siding had turned a dark umber. At the front of the hall there was a small platform about a foot above the floor level. He counted ten lights hanging down from the ceiling in two rows of five. There were rows of simple wooden chairs, maybe 30 of them. It was quiet and every movement the other three men made echoed in the hollow space. No one entered for nearly half an hour. Near 7:15 one other man, a short, tough-looking young man with a farmer's tan, poked his head in the door, looked at Will and the other two men, turned and left. Will shifted in his seat, smiling now at the other men. Another fifteen minutes passed.

"Well, I guess we can call this a night," Rutherford said to the cavernous room. "We'll just continue our efforts in another forum."

"Yep, I guess you will," Will said and walked out of the building with a large grin on his face.

CHAPTER TWENTY-EIGHT

The purple edges of the two-cent stamps showed just above the pocket of Bert's light blue denim shirt. He was sitting in a wooden folding chair in the shadow of the recreation building, where the new band was practicing. Close as he could figure the youngsters were playing a Sousa march, but it was a little too disjointed to really know.

Linda had written every day. The last letter was filled with worry and questions. Did he arrive OK? Was he safe? Why hadn't he written? What was the camp like? Bert was feeling guilty about not writing so he was taking the time now. He wet the point of the No. 2 pencil on his tongue and started writing on the yellow lined paper.

Dear Linda:

Sorry I have not written. The last week has been like a whirlwind and it has been hard to find the right time and the right place to write. Right now I am taking some time off from the gardening group I am part of to fill you in.

This place is god forsaken, but we are trying to make something of it. We are trying to make the soil somewhat ready to plant vegetables for ourselves. It is very dry but we have a small reservoir where we can get water, so maybe it will be OK. The dust is awful and any breeze scatters the stuff on everything I own and gets in my eyes and nose. Manzanar is not completely without beauty though. The mountains in the distance are still covered with snow and quite pretty. There are walnut trees and stands of poplars here and there. There are also a lot of cactus and I guess the main thing we see so far are dry shrubs—salt brush, bitterbrush and something they call rabbit brush. In the mornings I hear the mourning doves call and it makes me think of you. It is such a sad sound.

I really appreciate your letters and hope you keep writing, even if I don't keep up with you. I know our love is strong and every day I think of you, the house, the fields and Toto.

There are lots of people here, almost 4,000 now and we hear that there will eventually be 10,000 in the camp. It's interesting—they are a mix of age and hometowns and a mix of Issei and Nesei. Most, it seems, are from California, and there are a lot of people from one city or another. They seem different from us farmers from Washington, a little more tough or hard around the edges. They are not very happy...not that anyone here is happy to be here, but the city folks just have a bad attitude, it seems.

So far we have pigs and chickens and even some cattle coming in. It's a regular farming community and that gives some of us a sense of peace somehow.

When I see the conditions here, most of which I have not told you about yet —I know we made the right decision for you to stay home. I couldn't stand to see you here going through what these women have to go through, just to take a shower or use the toilet, not to mention sleeping or just doing their laundry. (The traditional bath has been banned so everyone showers.) On the other hand, this is not easy for me. I miss you so many times during the day and you are on my mind every minute. This is already the hardest thing we have ever been through and who knows how long it will last. I won't even think about that.

Give Toto a little hug from 'dad.' I send you all of my love, all the way from the high desert to that small island.

Yours forever, Bert

Will and Molly were in the Pontiac, making the short drive to the south end of the island, down to Lynwood Center and the movies. It was a mild spring evening and a light breeze came off the water. They decided that Errol Flynn and Olivia De Havilland would be a worthy distraction from the week they had had.

"I wish you could have seen the look on the faces of those guys at the Grange Hall, Mol. Chagrin – is that the word? They wouldn't look me in the eye at the end. Rutherford was a little icier though. He showed nothing. I think he's a little scary, you know, like, could be dangerous."

"I've never seen the guy," Molly said, her eyes on the brick building ahead that held the theater and a small cafe. "But I have heard about him. Kind of a loner I hear."

They pulled in to the front of the Lynwood Theater, just one of half a dozen cars there and Will reached over to put his hand on Molly's leg.

"Wait a sec, will you? There's something on my mind."

"Yes, sure, we've got a little time."

"I've been thinking about these last few months, trying to get my arms around all that's happened and what we've done and how the paper is going. I think Rutherford's meeting, such as it was, was some kind of big 'Hello' for me, a way of saying: 'What is it that you're really doing here?'"

"Yeah. And do you have an answer?"

"Well Mol, on one hand we're standing up for what we believe in. We're talking and writing about human rights and racism, and that's all well and good. I'm not backing away from what we're saying, at all. But -- and there is a but in me – I wonder what kind of influence we're having.

Some nights, after we've put the paper to bed, I wonder if we're just imposing our own will—pardon the pun – on our readers. I wonder if we're one little voice shouting in this great big forest where there's so much other noise going on. And the other voices don't agree with us."

"I sure understand that," Molly said and touched Will's shoulder. "We are just one little voice. That's the truth. But I've never known either one of us to back away from saying what we believed to be true just because it was unpopular."

"Right. But I'm not saying just because it's unpopular. I'm wondering if it's having any effect, any at all. I mean, you have to wonder, Mol, all the things we've editorialized for have gone the other way: the specific choice of Japanese and not other races, the evacuation itself, the timing of it, the places they've gone to – all have gone against us, and them."

"Right, but you can't…"

"And just a minute, sorry, but you know me. It's hard for me when I think I'm just spinning my wheels, when I'm saying something I think is important and it has no impact." Will paused and looked off in the distance. "I had this dream when I was about 20, I think, a really strong image. I was standing up somewhere, kind of elevated, maybe a hill in the country. And I was at one end of a very long, dark tube. It was small at my end, so I could hold it in my hand, and it got larger and ran downhill. So there I was and I was saying things, then shouting things, down into the tube and they were very important things to me, things that meant a lot in the world. They weren't just personal, selfish things, but things like we're writing about now –issues, ideas, values. And I could hear my words tumbling down this tube, echoing a little, and nothing was coming back. Nothing. No one was answering. Just my words fading away down this long black tube."

"Honey, that's awful. That must be terrible, for anyone, but especially for a writer."

"It was. And it is. Whenever I get to that place in myself, it's pretty damn discouraging."

Molly put both her hands on Will's right thigh. And she sighed.

"You know Will I was having similar thoughts a while ago, about myself and about other women in the world, what it's like to have little or no impact on the world around you. I don't want to change the subject, not at all, but I do want you to know I understand."

"Yeah. Thanks. I honestly don't know if it's different for men and women. I don't know if men need to have some kind of power in the world at large, more so than women, I mean. You have so much impact on the people you know, in your friendships. And think, Molly, of the impact you're going to have on this little one we're bringing into this world."

"I do, Will, all the time, every day. But that's something different. I'd like to make the world a better place too and one thing doesn't rule out the other."

"Sure, you're right." He leaned over and kissed her. "Maybe I'm just expecting too much."

"Well, I'm not sure about that. It is a *bit* unrealistic to think that the Bainbridge Review, circ. 1,000, could change the mind of the US Army and the federal government in a time of war."

"I guess you're right."

"But it is very realistic to believe that we might change the minds and hearts of some of those 1,000 people and to remind them of the Constitution and the Bill of Rights and common decency. We can't give up on that."

"You're exactly right."

"Thank you."

"And we won't."

"Good. It's nice to have an impact on you, sweetie." They both laughed out loud.

"Well old girl," Will said, "Let's go see what Errol Flynn can do to the world around him. What are we seeing again?"

"They Died With Their Boots On." They laughed again, harder this time, and went into the theater.

CHAPTER TWENTY-NINE

Molly walked briskly into the small food store. Previously owned by a Japanese couple with three children, the store had been handed off to an older English couple that had migrated to Seattle and then to Bainbridge Island just a year ago. Molly had no knowledge of the relationship they had, but she wanted to believe that the situation was temporary and the store would be given back to the Japanese family when they returned.

She fingered her purse in both hands as she stood just inside the front door. She looked around the store, full of dust motes and the afternoon light slanting in through windows on the southern side. There were stacks of bread loaves and canned vegetables in the center of the store. A wooden half-barrel held fresh eggs. Fruit –apples and pears—was conspicuous by its scarcity and two small bushel baskets sat on the floor near her. She had come mostly for meat and coffee, both rationed, so she made her way down a center aisle to the rear of the store.

A woman, perhaps fifty years old, in a flowered blue dress walked by her, headed to the front of the store. Molly, recognizing her face and not knowing her name, smiled. The woman walked on without any sort of recognition. Molly raised her eyebrows and pursed her lips, saying to herself: "OK, that was interesting."

At the very back of the store, the Englishman who now ran the store stood beside a cooler, his hand resting on the edge, talking to a well-dressed woman in her sixties. She was in a plain dark blue dress and wore a hat with a pheasant's feather stuck in the band. As Molly drew near, she recognized Marjorie Hamilton, a woman she knew from the volunteer pool at the high school. Molly scanned the cooler, stocked with ground beef, pork chops, a couple of chuck roasts, several whole chickens and one meat loaf.

At a lull during the conversation between Marjorie and the short, balding Englishman, Molly said, "Hello Marjorie, how are you?" The woman wheeled around as if startled by a threatening noise.

"Molly Whitman. You surprised me."

"I'm sorry. I didn't mean to startle you."

The woman turned to face Molly and the Englishman slowly walked off.

"Actually, it's not the only way you have surprised me lately. You and that husband of yours."

Molly could feel her face begin to grow pink and warm. She started to pull back inside, readying herself for the blow.

"Yes? How is that?"

"Well. It's the stance you have taken in that newspaper you own, as if you didn't know. It's disgraceful. I'm sorry to say this, but I believe I should be honest with you. I think you have disgraced the island by coming out against the government. After all, we have young men giving their lives to save our country from those terrible people and you are taking their side." The feather on her hat shook as she spoke. She was breathing hard and flushed with the excitement of her own honesty and righteousness.

Molly took a step backward. She took a deep breath.

"Marjorie, I honestly don't feel we are taking the side of the Japanese Army, just the Japanese Americans who live here, most of whom are citizens. Just like you and me."

The older woman pulled herself up to her full height and clamped down on her brown leather purse tucked under her arm.

"Those people are loyal to their native country. They are not, as you said, like you and me. They are not our kind, they never will be. They are sneaky and they never show you how they really feel. The attack on Hawaii was a perfect example. All the while they were talking to our President, they were plotting to attack us. And then – then -- Molly Whitman, they bombed us without warning and killed thousands of our young men. How can you," she said slowly stressing each word, "take their side?"

Molly squared her feet and dropped her arms down in front of her, holding tight to her purse. "I see that this is hard for you to believe, but Will and I are holding to a belief in law and our constitution. We think it is wrong to send these people away indiscriminately, without a trial or any kind of due process." She paused but kept eye contact. "This is a terrible, terrible war and I am just as scared as you are, believe me, but we have to say what we think is right."

Marjorie shook her head slowly. Her eyes bored into Molly's. She straightened her dress on her chest with an open hand. "The Japanese are not right. I don't care if they live here, in Japan or in Hawaii, they are not right. I don't see how you can hide behind some idea of 'due process' when Japs are killing our men every day. All I can say is I wish someone else owned a newspaper on this island. Good day."

She was away quickly and Molly stood staring at the pork chops, breathing heavily, her pulse racing. "Breathe, girl, breathe," she said to herself.

Linda pulled off her gray work gloves and wiped her brow. She left the gloves on the kitchen table and walked down the dusty dirt road to get the mail.

One envelope lay in the box and she recognized Bert's handwriting immediately. She felt the weight of creamy white envelope in her hand and turned and walked back to the little house. Once inside she sat the letter down on the wooden table next to her gloves and went into the bathroom to wash her face and hands. She enjoyed the feel of cool water on her face and the smell of the soap. She put the water on to boil and made a cup of jasmine tea. Once she was settled at the table, she opened the letter and unfolded the yellow paper. Her eyes filled with tears as she read and she nodded her head and smiled as she went through the hand-printed letter. She immediately read it a second time. Then she drank her tea and looked out the kitchen window at the beet fields. The ground was dry and an afternoon breeze softly moved the young maroon and green leaves. When she finished her tea, she read the letter a third time, then fetched her fountain pen and some crisp white paper and began a letter back.

Dearest Bert:

    I can't tell you how much I enjoyed your letter. It was like hearing you talk for a few minutes. Thank you for the descriptions of the place. That helps me to picture where you are, even though it is not nearly as pretty as home I'm sure.

    I was happy to hear about the vegetable garden you are starting. That will be good for you I hope. I know you will show the others a thing or two about growing things as you have such a green thumb and care so much about plants. It does sound very dry and I hope the reservoir idea works.

    Ten thousand people! My gosh, I can't imaging living with that many people in such a small space. It must be like a small city, crowded and noisy with people you don't know running about everywhere. I hope you can adjust to all that.

    Mom and dad have been helping around here. Since we are a ways away from harvest, there are no real problems yet. We've had a little rain so the beets and the lettuce are doing fine. Our friends and neighbors, as you can imagine, are being great. They've all offered to help whenever they are needed.

    Toto misses you. He goes and stands at the bathroom door in the morning, as if you might be in there taking a shower. And in the evenings he lays out on the porch watching the road up to the house. Poor baby. But he is probably doing better than I am. I miss hearing your voice and I miss feeling your body next to mine. I miss being outside and working with you in the yard. So many things...

    Many things here are rationed now – coffee, tin foil, sugar—and there are more things coming I hear. People are pulling together and helping each other on the island and that's great to see. I read that nightly blackouts have started on the east coast and everyone must pull their shades and cut off all of their lights. And, you might like to know, Jackie Robinson, a colored baseball player, has been working out with the Chicago White Sox. He's supposed to be pretty good. Do you think you're going to be playing baseball in the camp? I know you love it.

Bert, I know our love is strong too. And, as you said, I know this is going to be long and hard. I do know that we're not alone in this, that many wives and husbands are separated by the war and many families have been torn apart. Many people are a lot worse off than we are, if that's much consolation. Just know that I love you and will never, ever stop.

OK honey. This is kind of like hanging up the phone when I'm not ready to, but I'd like to get this back to you as soon as I can. Don't worry about us or the place. We're doing fine. Please treat yourself well.

All my love, your Linda.

CHAPTER THIRTY

Molly rolled over in the bed and drew herself into a fetal position. She held onto her knees and took a couple of deep breaths. She felt a little disoriented. She was in the house alone. Will was up and out early to take some pictures of the new American Legion hall. The house was quiet. She could hear the robins and jays outside chattering away. She began to feel a little light-headed and felt a dull pain across her torso. Her hips hurt like a dull toothache.

She rolled over to her other side. She sat up on the edge of the bed and put her bare feet gingerly on the cold wooden floor. Then a sharper pain shot through her abdomen. She shook her head in confusion. She felt wet between her legs and lifted her flannel nightgown and put her right hand under it, sliding it slowly along her thigh. She pulled it out and her fingertips were red with blood.

"No." she said out loud. "No, no, no, please God." She looked around for Will, knowing that he was not home, but she looked anyway and felt the emptiness of the house.

Molly made her way to the small bathroom and sat on the toilet. She was shivering and began to cry. She felt cold in her body and warm on her face. She felt something let go, low in her abdomen and she heard the blood hitting the water. No, no, no, she said to herself. She leaned forward and put her elbows on her knees, crying silently and she began to pray to herself. "Please God, don't let me lose this baby. Don't let this happen to me and to Will. Please don't take this baby; it will break his heart. Please God, have mercy on us. Have mercy on us."

She leaned back and pulled her nightgown up around her belly. She was cold and afraid. Her hair hung down over her eyes. She slowly looked down into the toilet bowl. The water was dark red and there was something thicker in the water too, something that she didn't want to see. Her belly ached. She felt several stabbing pains in her abdomen. She sobbed, just once, a deep throaty sob. Then she pulled herself up off the toilet, grabbed a towel, shuffled back into the bedroom and slid under the covers. She remained there until Will came home for lunch.

Nothing mattered now; not the war, not the country, not her house, not the newspaper—nothing mattered. Her chance to give life to another being had ended, she knew it. Nothing else had the slightest bit of importance.

CHAPTER THIRTY-ONE

In the summer of 1942 the farmers in Idaho and in eastern Washington, Oregon and California realized that they would not be able to bring in their crops without a lot of outside help. Potatoes, beets, lettuce and berries would dry up in the fields without some labor to harvest them. Many of the young men who had been on these farms had been drafted and were now in Europe or the Pacific fighting a war. The farmers, desperate not to lose their crops, turned to the War Relocation Authority and the US Army. With their cooperation, the farmers began recruiting able Japanese American men to pluck their berries off the vines and pull their potatoes and beets out of the ground.

In Manzanar the word spread quickly and the camp was buzzing with talk about getting out and doing something productive. The young men were especially enthusiastic about leaving the camp, if only temporarily, and about making some contribution to their country. The farmers, *and* the large corporations that owned the farms, did what they could to fuel this fire. In the Manzanar Free Press, a full-page ad from the Utah-Idaho Sugar Company shouted to the confined Japanese Americans: "YOU DON'T NEED TO WAIT ANY LONGER TO GET OUT."

The advertisement, speaking in the voice of the evacuee who is longing to return home, read: "'Someday,' he has said, 'I'll leave here, to return to my family home, or to start over in a new and friendly community. Some day I'll be a part of America again, to produce or fight for it.' Well, that day has come…"

The sugar company, which represented thousands of farmers in five western states, outlined the rewards for any evacuee who would come to work for them in the summer.

1. Freedom to work for yourself and your family for prevailing high wages.
2. Adequate housing.
3. A new chance to make friends for yourself and for all persons of Japanese birth or ancestry.
4. A stepping-stone to permanent year-round employment.
5. Healthful employment, for you and your family, even down to 14-year-old boys and girls.
6. An opportunity to produce more food for freedom, thereby helping America win the war and the peace to follow.
7. A means of earning money for education or for profitable investments.

Paul Hamada and his friend Rick Kobori stood side-by-side reading the ad, which had been posted on the bulletin board inside the recreation building. It was hot and dusty and the two 18-year-olds had just come inside from working on a pipeline that was to run from the reservoir pond to the new vegetable garden.

"This looks pretty good to me," Paul said. "We'd get to leave this place and get out in the fields in some decent countryside."

"What about your stories for Mr. Whitman?"

"Good question. Maybe I could write about things there. And maybe I can get someone to help me from the camp."

"Yeah, I guess. But you know this thing smells to me." Paul knew his classmate to be smart and skeptical. He was known at the high school for his direct, honest comments, comments that sometimes stung. He was a head taller than Paul and had short black hair, cut close to his skull.

"What do you mean?"

"Look around you Paul. Everybody here was forced out of their home with absolutely no choice. My parents and yours had to give up their homes and their businesses, all for the protection of our precious country." Rick paused to take off his dusty red baseball cap and beat it on the side of his leg, causing a minor dust storm in the space between them. 'Now—again for our country and, what'd they say? 'An opportunity to produce more food for freedom, thereby helping America win the war.'" That's horse pucky Paul. Food for freedom?! Bullshit. What we're doing, pure and simple, is bailing out some farmers and large companies who can't harvest their crops. We're saving their asses and, remember, they didn't want us here in the first place. It's hard for me to swallow."

"Yeah, I see that."

"First they tell us we're the enemies of America and cart us off to a concentration camp." He looked at Paul as if to say "don't you get it?" "Then they get us to work here for practically nothing, now they're yelling at us that it's our big chance for freedom and money. Jesus."

'Yeah, Rick, but....'

"I was talking to this guy in the building next to mine. I guess the guards have singled him out for some reason. Do you know they come in at all hours of the day and in the middle of the night? They wake him up and ask him—you'll never guess—'Who's going to win the war?' The guy always answers: 'I don't know.' They leave and then they come back the next night and ask him again. It's ridiculous Paul. It's just harassment. They don't care about us."

Rick swung his dusty hat around and slapped it on the bulletin board.

"You know Rick, maybe you're right, but I look at the big picture a little differently." Paul wiped his brow with his forearm, swabbing off dust and sweat. "I don't like to think about all those beets drying up and dying. That's a huge waste. Sugar is rationed. And the beets do go for sugar and the sugar goes into food and that food does go to all Americans. I know it's a stretch, but I do see it as making a contribution in some small way."

"I don't know. I guess."

"And look, individually, you and I would be out of here. Besides that we'd make a little pocket money."

"Yeah, where would we spend it?"

"I dunno Rick. We could save it." They both turned to walk back outside. "Man, you sound pretty down and pretty angry too."

"I guess I am," Rick said. "I guess I'm not over what you call 'the big picture' yet, just the whole idea that we're citizens and they whisked us away and jailed us, just like that. It sticks in my craw."

"Well it can stick there for a long time, if you let it. Pretty soon you'll choke on it."

The following week, The Review reported: "Barred by circumstances from harvesting their own strawberry crops, five Japanese American Islanders left Manzanar last week to aid in gathering Idaho's sugar beet crop." Paul and Rick were two of the five.

Two weeks after Rick and Paul arrived in a small town in southern Idaho, Will received the following letter:

"Dear Mr. Whitman -- Paul and I are in Idaho, as I guess you know by now, sent here to save the beet crop and keep American in sugar. That's what they're telling us anyway. We're sweetening the pot, I guess you could say.

"I know Paul is filing a report to you, but as usual, I wanted to add my two cents. When we arrived, the field supervisor for the farmer we're working for led us and two other guys to a large old horse barn, where there were a couple of horses and some chickens, but most of it was filled with hay. He said—and this was all he said— 'This is where you all will sleep. I'll see you in the morning.' The next day, six more guys like us got here from Minidoka. They were 'escorted' to a shack beside the beet fields. It had a small coal stove inside and they had to bathe in an irrigation ditch. There were no bathrooms. Sounds swell doesn't it?

"Yours, deep in the heart of the land of the free and the home of the brave, Rick"

CHAPTER THIRTY-TWO

A heavy gray shroud hung around the Whitman cottage during the last days of May. A thick cloud cover blanketed the Puget Sound as well and an occasional light rain sprinkled the woods each day for a week before moving east to the Cascades. Molly walked slowly, deliberately around the house and, at Will's insistence, did not work on the paper. She had visited Doc Martin the day after the miscarriage and listened quietly to his words of support and encouragement. She would be fine, he said. They could try again in a while. It was a stressful time, he had told her, and there was no way she could blame this on herself.

Molly heard the words her doctor said and clung to her feelings, harboring them, embracing them, as if the emotions themselves were her children. She was saddled with the loss of their first child, with her own grief, sadness for Will and with guilt. All the "what ifs" began to surface: what if I had eaten better, what if I'd been more careful, what if I'd exercised more, what if I'd seen the doctor more often, what if I'd gotten more sleep, what if I weren't engaged in this battle royal, what if we weren't at war —anything that would have changed the reality she was now faced with. In the end she couldn't blame anyone or anything outside of herself. Her body had failed her, she reasoned, and the fault was hers.

Colleen was a frequent and welcome visitor. They made tea together, took slow walks in the woods and would occasionally just sit together in the living room and read. Occasionally Molly would look over at her friend and take in her long, glowing blonde hair and appreciate the beauty of it. But she could not dwell on beauty for long, lest she be swept away with grief and the loss of her one, infant beauty that would not be. After the first couple of days, there was not much to say but just the presence of another woman was comforting somehow. They talked about sewing, the books they were reading, the chickens, the Andrew Sisters, the coming of warmer weather, Frank, Will, rationing, the island couples they knew and the war. Everyone talked about the war.

Will handled the loss of his child in a different way, inside himself, hidden away from everyone else, including Molly. To share with Molly would add to her sadness and guilt. To talk about his own loss would increase the weight of hers, a burden he witnessed every day, took measure of, and kept his feelings to himself. This late afternoon he stood in the woods, barely a hundred yards from the house and looked directly up, following the magnificent columns of the Douglas firs, raising straight and true up to the gray sky. He thought about the life of these trees, about the years it took to grow, about the conditions they must have to be so tall, about the life that surged up in them, from the earth, up those singular columns to the top. He knew in his heart that life was in these trees, was in the woods, was in him and was in Molly. He knew the life force that almost hummed through all of nature around him. He watched a rambunctious small red squirrel scramble up the trunk of a big leaf maple and his lips moved just a bit; not a smile, not yet, but a recognition that life was still here. It was here, in this forest, in this house, and he and Molly would have life once again.

And then, his mind came back to the war. And death. So much death. He thought of the American men in the Pacific, lodged in small holes on tiny islands, holding onto their rifles, curled up and waiting, waiting for hundreds of Japanese soldiers to come running, shouting, crazy with lust for death, out of the jungle. He didn't know how he would act in their shoes. He didn't know if he had the courage; the guts seemed a more appropriate word. How would he behave? What would he do if he were lying in that hole and the wave of men came at him in the night, shooting, stabbing, exploding around him? How was it that he was so privileged that he could stay in the comfort of his own home and drive to his office by the water and write about fairness, racism, justice and what the government could do? Just because he was a little older? Just because his eyes were weak? He did not take these questions lightly and on this early evening, as the sun went down on the other side of his small house in the woods, he was profoundly grateful to these unknown men who were thousands of miles away fighting for him.

The Philippines had fallen to the Japanese army and thousands of American troops were now prisoners of war there. The US aircraft carrier Lexington had gone down during an intense battle in the Coral Sea, even though the engagement was called a strategic loss for the Japanese Navy. This was proving to be a costly summer for both sides of the conflict. At home the news was grim nearly every day. How many ships sunk? How many men died? How many planes were lost? How many prisoners were taken and placed behind barbed wire? The war's demands placed a tighter grip on people's lives. Rationing was nationwide. Gas, up to twelve cents a gallon, was now a luxury. Tires were scarce. New appliances in any one's home were rare.

Even though Molly and Colleen talked about these worldly events, Molly's thoughts eventually came back to the loss of her baby. Most of the day she was alone. She walked around inside the house. She napped during the afternoon. She sat and stared out the kitchen window. She watched the rain slide down the dark gray bark of the apple trees and rest in droplets on the new light green leaves. And she kept asking why.

She took some solace in the garden. The earth and growing things had always been a part of Molly's life. She still remembered the large garden her parents maintained in the home near Yakima. Lettuce, beets, corn, peas, string beans...they had a bounty at the table for summer suppers. And she and her sisters were expected to work in the earth. What was at first a chore, dirty and wet, had become a time for stillness and peace outside. Eventually she realized it was good for her, a kind of therapy, to be in touch with the earth, pulling weeds, propping up lilies, watering zinnias, nurturing the things her family loved and took pleasure in. Molly especially loved the bulbs and marveled at how they lived year after year and what they produced. Tulips were her favorite. She pictured these pale, innocent-looking life forms, resting in the ground, no more than golf balls in size, waiting for the first signs of spring. What was it that told them to start coming out? Resting in the cold ground most of the year and through the cold winters, these little beings pumped out a sprout, then a stalk and then a magnificent blossom -- yellow, red, purple, pink, fringed, tipped with a second color. They were a miracle to her, how life itself was contained in these bulbs, waiting to be reborn year after year. And she could hold it in her hand.

    Will devoted himself to Molly and the newspaper. He put out four issues of the Review by himself. The work distracted him. At home he was busy with the household chores and trying to keep Molly as cheerful as he could. That too was a distraction. After two weeks he broke.

    He came home as it was getting dark. He could see lights on in the kitchen. Molly greeted him at the door, hugged him, kissed him and said she had dinner ready. She stepped back from him, looked him in the eye and said: "And how are you Will Whitman, my love?"

    He looked her in the eyes and he could feel that stinging feeling coming up in his eyes and nose. He began to shake his head and dropped his beat-up leather briefcase. He started crying, slowly, silently at first. Then a loud sob. He went on for a few minutes and Molly just held him, gently rubbing his broad back.

    "Oh, Mol, I've missed you so much."

    "Well, I'm back. And we're going to be OK."

CHAPTER THIRTY-THREE

Breaking ground in the Owens Valley earth was hard work. There were many days when Mutt and the others felt like part of a chain gang, working together in the heat and dust, watched over by several soldiers with rifles. The intensity of the work and the stress wore some men down -- the pick, the shovel, the hoe; rows of men leaning forward, breaking into the hard earth again and again and again. The digging was hard enough and the dust was maddening, enough to send a man toppling over the edge of his composure and self-respect. When the wind blew, which was nearly every day, the dust found it's way into every crevice of a man's body. The mouth was the worst. The dust crept in steadily and coated Mutt's teeth, staying there until he was able to get back to his building and brush his teeth. The dust mixed with his saliva and formed a crust on his teeth and tongue and lodged in the corners of his mouth. It was a menace, a constant curse. As the sweaty, tired men dug, the salty dry earth cracked and fell aside in large chunks. Mutt thought there might be something more promising below the surface, that the crusty veneer might crack and reveal some soil, or something else, that would show some kind of life, but it was always the same, dry, hard and salty, suffering from years of no grass, little rain and no care. Some of the farmers were used to this kind of work. They knew the strength of their backs, legs and arms. They knew how to stand and lean and throw a shovel full of dirt. But even they were accustomed to working at their own pace, taking a rest when needed, sitting a while in the shade, seeing their family nearby and working for something that was theirs. Here, they were captive and worked as dictated to and the days were long.

The men from the city were used to something else entirely: standing behind a counter, sitting behind a desk, driving a bus, lifting a small box or standing behind a barber chair. As they worked, an emotional distance grew between the farmers and the men from the city. It was easy to resent a man who was comfortable when you were not, or a man who did not carry his weight. It was easy to judge a man who could not keep up the pace of the others.

Any one of the men on his own would have given up after a quick look at the soil. But there was something larger about this effort that kept the men going, beyond what they were forced to do. There was some force present in those empty acres, something that Mutt felt but did not talk about. There was something growing in the men, not in the soil yet, but in the hearts of the men who worked together. Some of this feeling was an inner strength that was welling up in each man who was forced to work this hard, as if there were something to prove. Something in them was saying, "I will not be broken. I will not allow you to run my life completely. You will, in the end, not define who I am." And an equal part of this force in the fields was the growing sense that they could do this together, the sense that if they stuck together and worked together that they could build something together, something that would be their own. Mutt knew this sense in the men was there as he looked at the other men, as he stood and wiped the sweat from his brow. This was a powerful thing, something that could sustain a man and keep his spirit alive. In Mutt it became a hope, hope that not only he, but all of the men would somehow catch this, that it would grow into something they felt together.

The determination, the work ethic and the perseverance of the men and women in Manzanar began to shine through. That first summer, of 1942, was busy for everyone in the camp. The camp was changing from an empty piece of land in the high desert into a small city, into a community of men, women and children. In March the Army had announced that Manzanar would be a "temporary transfer point," where evacuees would be reassigned to more developed camps elsewhere in the interior. On June 1, the WRA announced that was officially a "relocation camp" and the men and women there would be there for the duration of the war. That announcement brought about a subtle but powerful change; this was it, this piece of land was where they would stay.

The central, more developed part of the camp covered about 540 acres. Eight three-story watchtowers dotted the perimeter by the end of the summer and a five-strand barbed wire fence surrounded the central area. Dirt roads or oiled roads, designated by a number or a letter, divided the area into 67 blocks. There were larger blocks outside of this central area devoted to the Military Police, warehouses, a hospital, a light industrial park, an administration building and various factories.

By the early fall the evacuees had developed several parks and picnic areas complete with walkways, ponds, bridges and open-air fireplaces. They built a nine-hole golf course around a small creek. The largest park, named Rose Park, was built very near the center of the acreage. The men and women in the camp who loved gardening started planting by grafting domestic roses to native rootstock. When word of the project spread, a nearby nursery wholesaler donated a thousand cherry trees and wisteria plants. The gift lifted the spirit of the whole camp and hundreds of people came out to join in the planting. The park eventually included a large hand-built atrium, two large ponds, a waterfall, a wooden bridge, a Japanese teahouse and more than one hundred species of flowers.

Camp residents would devote 240 acres to vegetable farming. Five hundred hogs, 4,000 chickens and more than 80 head of cattle would help feed the evacuees. Everyone had a job and most had more than one.

A small army of carpenters hired by the WRA still roamed the camp, throwing up frames of buildings almost like they were building driftwood houses on a beach. Raw fir and hemlock frames sat on small concrete footings and were wrapped with black tarpaper. Every building looked the same, that is until whoever occupied it moved in and applied their own stamp of ownership, landscaping and decoration.

Mutt had volunteered for the group that worked on Rose Park and he threw himself into the project, working a few hours after his regular workday, which was developing large scale farming just outside the central area of the camp. His wife Suki had joined the sewing group, which led to her being employed in the garment factory on the south edge of the camp.

Amy, wanting to contribute and not wanting to be alone in the building, volunteered to help in the camp orphanage.

In the week immediately following the evacuation from the West Coast, the WRA decided to send any and all Japanese American orphans to the same place, Manzanar. A separate building was hastily constructed near the camp's center and about 100 children, from one to twelve, were housed there. Amy begged her mother to let her go. She read to the toddlers, changed diapers, washed dishes and made friends with a few other pre-teen boys and girls. It gave her a sense of importance and belonging that was invaluable. The orphanage itself took on a larger meaning for most of the evacuees and they formed a strong attachment to the boys and girls who lived here in the first years of their lives.

Things were changing fast. Every morning that Mutt walked out to the fields, it seemed as if a new building had been dropped down on the desert floor and there were people busy inside. There was the garment factory, where Suki worked, a post office, a town hall, a mattress factory, a food processing plant, a typewriter repair shop, a sign shop, a sewing machine repair shop, an auto repair center, an elementary and high school, two outdoor theaters, nine warehouses and a refrigerated warehouse for meat, fruits and vegetables.

Mutt was amazed when he saw a Judo school open. Already there were two baseball fields, a football field, volleyball courts and several basketball courts. And just about every day of the summer a new hen house was built, adding up to fifty houses by early fall.

The Manzanar Free Press, housed in a small building at the camp's center, was thriving. It was now distributed outside the camp, to subscribers in the states and in Japan, and carried advertising from local merchants and from sympathetic companies back home. It carried news of the war—Brazil had joined the allies in their fight against Germany, Italy and Japan, blackouts had begun in San Francisco, the baseball player Ted Williams had volunteered for the Navy and a small Japanese submarine had been spotted near the mouth of the Columbia River, at the Washington-Oregon border. The war seemed to have its own momentum and it was very much in the consciousness of the men and women at Manzanar.

CHAPTER THIRTY-FOUR

It was a sunny Monday afternoon. Will sat in the small back room of the Review offices in a well-used red wooden chair. He leaned over the keyboard of the linotype machine; the stiff keys clacking away and the lead type dropping down into a rack as he wrote about the impact the various rationing programs were having on islanders. He was dressed for the heat the old linotype gave off -- khakis and a sleeveless ribbed undershirt.

There was a knock at the door. Annoyed and then curious, he finished a sentence and made his way to the front room. There were few visitors here in recent months. When he opened the door he saw a short, thin man in a black suit, a black tie and hat and, slightly behind him, a woman companion in a dark blue suit. The man had extremely short hair and immediately impressed Will as being wound pretty tight. A few years ago he could have been a high school wrestler, 155 pounds maybe.

"Mr. Whitman?"

"Yes."

"You are Will Whitman, who owns the Bainbridge Review with your wife Molly?"

"That's right. And you are?"

"I am Harris James, a special agent for the Federal Bureau of Investigation, and this is my colleague, Janice Clarendon, also an agent from the bureau. Here is my identification."

Will wiped the sweat off his hands on his khakis and reached for the badge James held in a black leather wallet. What kind of man has a name with his last name first, he thought to himself.

"I'm sorry sir. I have to hold onto this," James said and kept holding the badge in front of Will's face. Miss Clarendon showed Will her badge. Will nodded and shrugged his shoulders as if to say "OK, now what?"

"We would like to come in and ask you a few questions sir. May we?" James looked past Will into the small office. Will stepped back into the room and pulled two chairs up in front of his desk.

"What can I do for the FBI?"

"I don't need to tell you what's been going on in the past few months, not only in your area of circulation, but in Seattle, San Francisco, Los Angeles—all up and down the West Coast," James said as he sat down and folded one leg over the other. Miss Clarendon sat in the chair next to him, both hands on her thighs. She didn't look comfortable. "I'm sure you're aware of the issues of the evacuation and the controversy surrounding it and how it relates to the war effort."

"Well, I read the papers just like you do, I suppose, and I do have some first hand information from what's happened on the island. But I'm not sure what you're driving at." At that moment Will thought of Molly and wondered what she was doing.

"Mr. Whitman, the FBI continues to investigate the ties that many Japanese have to their homeland. We have, as I'm sure you know, since late last year investigated many individuals and organizations all over America that could potentially be harmful to our country's interests and to the war effort."

Will's mind began to spin. What was behind this visit? Is this guy after me or does he want names? What's the penalty for lying to the FBI? He concentrated on the top of Harris James head, so as not to look him in the eyes. James' hair was blond and scattered amongst the short bristles were beads of sweat. His brow seemed permanently wrinkled.

"Sure, and I'm wondering what that has to do with me or the Review, or Bainbridge Island for that matter." Will leaned back in his chair pulled out a bottom drawer of his desk and put one foot up on it. He was aware of the fact that his armpits were visible under his sleeveless undershirt and it amused him.

The woman leaned forward. She had short straight blond hair and icy blue eyes; pretty and remote, Will thought. I wonder what her parents are like? She probably doesn't have any children.

"Mr. Whitman, because of the ties of race, the intense feeling of filial piety and the strong bonds of common tradition, culture and customs, the Japanese population presents a tightly-knit racial group. The Japanese community, if you will, includes in excess of 115,000 persons deployed along the Pacific Coast. Whether by design or accident, virtually all their communities are adjacent to vital shore installations or war-related plants." She tilted her head as if to gain Will's agreement. He saw what she was looking for but said nothing.

"While it is believed that some are loyal to America, we know that many are not. It was—and is—nearly impossible to establish the identity of the loyal and the disloyal with any degree of safety. There was insufficient time in which to make such a determination. We – the federal government and the armed forces -- had to face the reality that a positive determination could not be made, that an exact separation of the 'sheep from the goats' was unfeasible. Would you agree?"

"Well, I'm sorta stuck back on filial piety," Will said with a smile.

"Miss Clarendon was a college professor before she joined the bureau," James said, "and she has studied international relations for some time. She simply means that there is a very strong family and generational loyalty among the Japanese."

Will noticed the sun shining through the south window and landing on Miss Clarendon's shiny black shoes, which were tucked between the legs of her chair and very close together.

"Yes, thanks, I know what she meant. Then I got stuck on 'the sheep from the goats.' That seems to be a little, uh, unfortunate way of referring to human beings."

"Yes, of course," Miss Clarendon said. "I'm trying to impress on you the difficulty we –all of us – have had trying to sort out who is loyal to the United States and who is not, especially when these people stay so close in their families -- and organizations -- and generally keep to themselves."

"You really don't' have to impress on me that difficulty Miss….uh…"

"Clarendon."

"Sorry, Miss Clarendon, I have seen the difficulty the government has had with my own eyes and so far the solution has been just round 'em up and herd 'em out. Seems to me that someone is loyal until they are proven to be disloyal. And even if they are 'close-knit,' as you say, people have been using that observation almost as if it were an accusation, a crime, to stay close to one's family." He paused and sat up. "I think I'd stay close to my family too if I were as subject to as much prejudice and bias as some of these people have been."

"Mr. Whitman," James said, shifting in his chair and moving closer to Will. "We did not mean for this to be a debate, by any means. "But there are some facts we need to establish. Are you willing to listen?"

"Sure," Will said with some resignation and leaned back in his chair.

"Our research has established that, just before war broke out, there were more than 120 Japanese organizations along the Pacific Coast engaged in what we call pro-Japanese activities. This number does not include local branches, of which there were more than 310. We have further identified more than 100 fascistic or militaristic organizations in Japan that have some either direct or indirect tie with Japanese organizations or individuals in the United States. We have definite information that the great majority of activities followed a line of control from the Japanese government. This happened through key individuals, or organizations, who were Japanese residents in the United States. Are you with me so far?"

"Sure. There are people here in the states who used to live in Japan and who still have ties with people and groups in Japan."

"Mr. Whitman, I don't know why you feel the need to oversimplify what is in reality a very serious subject. These are facts that ought to be of extreme interest to anyone who is loyal to the United States government. That the ties to Japan and these Japanese organizations aided the military campaigns of the Empire of Japan is beyond doubt."

Will felt his ears getting hot and noticed that his jaw was tight. He wasn't entirely sure where this was going but he knew he didn't like it. He folded his hands in his lap, as much to control himself as anything. "Please go on Mr. James."

"Allow me to read you something. It's brief but I think you will appreciate the impact." James cleared his throat and read from a single sheet of paper Miss Clarendon had handed him.

"As a matter of historical fact, whenever the Japanese government begins a military campaign, we Japanese must be united and everyone of us must do his part.

"As far as our patriotism is concerned, the world knows that we are superior to any other nation. However, as long as we are staying on foreign soil, what can we do for our mother country?" James raised his voice on the last half of the sentence. "All our courageous fighters are fighting at the front today, forgetting their parents, wives and children in their homes! It is beyond our imagination, the manner in which our imperial soldiers are sacrificing their lives at the front line, bomb after bomb, death after death! Whenever we read or hear this sad news, who can keep from crying in sympathy? Therefore, we the Japanese in the United States have been contributing a huge amount of money for war relief funds and numerous comfort bags for our imperial soldiers. Today, we, Japanese in the United States, who are not able to sacrifice our lives for our national cause are now firmly resolved to stand by our nation and settle the present war as early as possible." He raised his eyes to look at Will, as if to say "do you get it now?"

"We are proud to say that our daily happy life in America is dependent upon the protective power of Great Japan! We are facing a critical emergency, and we will take strong action as planned. We do hope and beg you all to cooperate with us for our national cause."

"That's impressive, no doubt," Will said. "Where's it from?"

"It's an organization called the Heimusha Kai, one of the groups we have referred to."

"Well I never heard of it here, and by here I mean the Northwest. No knowledge of it at all." Will noticed that the woman had taken out a small notebook and was writing in it as he spoke.

"How about Japanese language schools?" James said. "Or Judo clubs or clubs that teach tea ceremonies or Japanese dancing?"

"Yeah, sure. What's the point?"

"It's our job to investigate any organization that encourages support of or contact with the Empire of Japan, now that we're at war. Any kind of sympathy or support for the Japanese cause, since December seventh, is of keen interest to the FBI."

The guy talks like a robot, Will thought to himself. No expression, he just reels out the words, the recorded FBI message.

"OK, I get it. And I'm still looking for what brought you here, to my humble offices."

James looked at Miss Clarendon, who was still writing in her notebook. "We'd like your help Mr. Whitman in identifying any organization or individual that might have ties to the enemy's home country. And…"

Will spoke before James got another word in. "Sorry, don't know any. Can't help you." The woman seemed to be recording Will's answers. "Anything else?"

"There is one more thing we need to settle," James said and lowered his voice slightly. "Would you call yourself sympathetic to the Japanese?"

It was like a combination lock inside Will clicked on its final number and the conversation fell into place. First the FBI wanted him to inform on people he knew from the island. Failing that they were going after him and The Review for the things he had written. His ears grew hot again and he narrowed his eyes.

"Sympathetic to the Japanese?"

"Yes sir."

"Which ones?"

"Any Japanese that are tied to their homeland or support the war effort of their home country in any way. Or do you think of yourself in that category? It's just a question Mr. Whitman."

"Well, I'll give you just an answer Harris. I'll tell you what I'm sympathetic to and in support of." Will leaned forward in his ribbed undershirt and put his elbows on the desk. "I'm in support of free speech, the right to bear arms, the idea of innocence until guilt is proven, the writ of habeas corpus, the right of an American citizen to own land and keep it and the right of a man —and a woman—to pursue life, liberty and happiness, regardless of where their parents came from or the color of their skin. That's what I support and will continue to support."

James did not back down. "That's all well and good Whitman, but some of your editorials have bordered on outright support for the Japanese and have consistently been against the policies of the US government. The bureau could not help noticing that you have opposed the evacuation and everything about it all along."

"Dissent is at the heart of democracy Mr. James. Anyone in his right mind can see that what's happened to Japanese American citizens is not right."

"So that must include President Roosevelt."

"What? President Roosevelt? The truth is he's probably not got much to do with this. Are you trying to claim I'm not loyal to the President?" Will was genuinely surprised.

Will then turned to Miss Clarendon and said: "I want you to take note that your companion brought the President into this, Miss, I didn't. Now, I have a paper to put out and my patience is growing very thin. Unless you have some action to take here, I think we're concluded." He looked at each one of them and pursed his lips.

"Mr. Whitman, we'll leave, but I want you to know that your activities are being monitored and your preferences for the Japanese have been noted."

"Oh, I'm sure of that Mr. James. I consider it a compliment that you will continue to read The Review. Goodbye and good luck in your patriotic efforts."

CHAPTER THIRTY-FIVE

Sadness. The deep experience of loss. Mutt sees it in Amy's face when she wakes in the morning, when she walks out to the women's toilets, when she settles down to sleep for the night. Only when she walks back from her time at the orphanage can he detect a glimmer of some kind of pleasure or happiness. It's then, he figures, in her time with the children, that she can be herself and connect with the life energy of the young boys and girls who will play with her, talk to her openly and hug her without reservation. In those few hours Amy can, as the children do, forget about the world outside and what they used to know. In this room, there is a sense of life and play, sometimes even abandon. Mutt is, at least, grateful that she has that.

Sorrow is in Suki's eyes too. She and her daughter have lost their home, their friends, their daily routine and maybe, Mutt suspects -- because it's true of him too -- their sense of who they are. Seeing their sadness day in and day out cripples him. He can nearly physically feel his spirit folding in on itself, layer upon layer, getting smaller and tighter; becoming harder.

Suki maintains a sunny exterior, as she usually does wherever she is, but Mutt knows her. Even though they don't talk too much about it, they both realize they want to maintain an attitude that will not poison their daughter. He asks himself: what can I do to stay steady and even? How can

I maintain some kind of positive outlook, some kind of hope, and give that as a gift to my wife and daughter? That struggle is a daily exercise for him. It is perhaps the biggest challenge of his life.

As he lays on his Army cot mulling this over this morning, Suki silently gets off her cot and comes to him. Without saying a word, as if she knows what he is thinking, she slowly drops to her knees and puts her arms around his chest. She lays her head down on him and Mutt smells her hair, thick and tousled from sleep.

"I love you," he says.

She nods her head and holds on to him.

Paul and Rick were put on a bus back to Manzanar in October. They had saved about $20 in three months, picking beets and potatoes in southern Idaho, a hot dry climate in the summer and early fall. The ride back was long and tiring, and through some beautiful country. In the Sierras the leaves were turning and the air was crisp. Paul, who was about to turn 19, was in good spirits.

"I'm anxious to see Mom and Dad," he said to Rick as they both looked out the window of the bus. "I want to catch up on what's happened in the camp and get back into my writing for Mr. Whitman."

"Sounds good," Rick said, "but I think what we both have to look forward to is more hard work. I'm sure we'll be digging ditches the day after we get back."

Elaine and John Hamada were very glad to see their son, reassured to see him healthy and in a good mood. There was not much communication to or from the camp and the fields of Idaho, so they could only hope the two young men had taken care of themselves. And they were back to work the day after they returned. The Army had stepped up work on the large scale farming just outside the camp's fences and Rick and Paul were soon throwing shovels full of compost and manure off the back of a large Army truck.

"Here we are, shoveling pig shit as part of the war effort," Rick said.

Paul laughed but didn't take the conversation any further. He had learned not to contribute to Rick's cynicism and anger.

In his first story since his return, Paul reported on the marriage of a woman from Los Angeles and a man from Seattle who had met the first day they came to camp, a baby boy born to a couple who had ties to Bainbridge Island and a short feature story on Amy Sugimoto's work in the camp orphanage. The next day he wrote about his return to camp and some of his impressions. His report was more of a letter to Will and Paul wasn't sure it would make the paper.

"Two of us, Rick Kobori, and this correspondent returned to Manzanar after three months in the fields of Idaho picking sugar beets and potatoes. It was backbreaking work, even for our young backs, and it was often near 100 degrees in the fields. We were glad to do it, thinking that our labor contributed somehow to our country and it sure helped the Idaho farmers.

"Back in Manzanar we were given a very warm welcome from the families who knew us and, of course, our parents. They got word we were returning and fixed us a feast—well, as much of a feast as anyone can have here. They have had a good harvest here and we did have plenty of fresh vegetables and even a little stewed chicken.

"A lot has happened here since we were gone. The amount of building is fantastic and now there is an outdoor movie theater, so we can have some night time entertainment, at least until it grows too cold. Rick and I are working just outside the camp's fences on a large-scale farm that will eventually feed much of the camp's residents. It's exciting to see the population here begin to take control of some of the things that matter.

"There is some troubling news to report. With all the cooperation and hard work here, there are some divisions among people that are upsetting. People from rural areas, such as Bainbridge Island and the outlying farms near Seattle and in Skagit County, don't have a lot of respect for the "tough guys" from the cities—especially California -- and vice versa. There is a real different work ethic, for one thing, and different ways of dealing with the War Relocation Authority and the Army. There have been some harsh words exchanged in public meetings and some fights, mostly after dark between small gangs.

"Even more troubling to your correspondent are the rumors about informants in our camp. Apparently the Army has asked certain people to keep an eye on others and report any signs of resistance or rebellion to the officers in charge. As you can imagine, this has led to a lot of arguments, finger pointing and shouting in public meetings. It is proving to be very uncomfortable for the older folks here, who do not want to see the camp divided or see any trouble with the MP's, and is not a good thing for the camp in general.

"Signing off from Camp Manzanar, Paul Hamada."

CHAPTER THIRTY-SIX

Frank and Colleen were walking the last fifty yards to Will and Molly's house on a cool, clear night. Frank cradled a six-pack of Miller High Life under his arm and Colleen carried a basket of warm biscuits she had made, knowing how much Will liked them. They were looking forward to a nice evening together with their good friends.

"Do you suppose Molly's OK now?" Frank asked his wife.

"I think the worst is over. It was a real blow at first but Will's been real supportive and I think she's bouncing back." Colleen was thin and athletic and full of optimism. She brushed a few strands of her blonde hair off her face. ""It's hard to know what this is like for her, even though I'm a woman too. I think I know, but I've never been pregnant."

"Yeah. I just hope she's all right." He put his arm around Colleen.

Molly was better and she was glad to see her visitors. She and Will greeted them with handshakes and hugs and settled into getting some beef stew, coleslaw and biscuits on the table. After dinner, Molly was serving cups of coffee.

"That stuff's going to be on the short list pretty soon I hear," Frank said.

"You're right," Molly said, "so we better enjoy it while we can." She wore a loose fitting rose-colored dress and had piled her hair up behind her head.

"You look very pretty tonight Molly," Colleen told her.

"Why thank you. Aren't you sweet." The sugar and cream was passed around the table. The little cottage was warm and comfortable. Here and there a table lamp glowed and Molly lit two candles on the dining table.

"Will, did you see that the federal court upheld the whole internment thing?" Frank said, somewhat nervously, as he was well acquainted with Will's attitude.

"I did," Will answered. "No big surprise. They pegged it all on, quote, military necessity. In a way the court said that we were under marshal law and, after Executive Order 9066, the Armed Services could do just about anything they wanted."

"Honey, I don't think it was quite that sweeping," Molly said. Will looked at her and smiled.

"I suppose you're right, but it's pretty damn close."

Colleen was looking back and forth at the two of them and then looked at her husband. Frank seemed ready to carry the conversation further. He spoke to Will.

"I've been thinking about the conversation you and I had some time ago, Will, and I'm feeling somewhat guilty." His eyes dropped and he turned in his chair to face Will.

"Oh? How so?"

"Well, I just think I came off as some kind of bigot, some super prejudiced guy and I don't really think I am. I think I'm probably just your average Joe." Colleen reached over and patted Frank on the arm.

"That's brave of you to say Frank," Molly chimed in.

"Thanks Molly. You know, I've been reading some things that have really upset me and I was hoping we could talk about some of this so I could learn something. Geeze, all of us might learn something." Will was nodding his head.

"Great idea Frank. What have you been reading?"

"Well, first of all I saw an article in the Times about —and these are not my words—Jap hunting licenses. They actually ran a small picture of the license some guy was making, that you could actually pin on your coat, and it said 'open season on Japs, unlimited season,' or something like that. It really bothered me."

"God, that's sick," Colleen said.

"And then in TIME or maybe it was LIFE, I saw a picture of a poster the government is using to sell war bonds. It had this drawing of a Jap -- Japanese-- soldier and he had really big teeth, narrow eyes, glasses, and a skinny mustache and he was holding a white woman from behind her and he had a big knife on her throat. And the message was something like: Protect Your Country, Buy War Bonds. I mean, is that what we have to do?"

"It's harsh Frank, it's really harsh," Will said. "I've seen Japanese characterized as rats, snakes, sea monsters, beasts from the forest, octopus, subhuman, vermin —you name it. Apparently our propaganda machine is pulling out all the stops. Apparently we think we have to dehumanize a whole race of people in order to defeat their army. It makes me sick."

Molly, who had been quietly sipping her coffee, spoke to Frank.

"Sometimes I think it's simply, but profoundly, about differences, the differences between us as humans. Sadly I think some of this is built into us."

"What do you mean built into us?" Frank asked.

"I had the professor at the U. who said that human beings, when they see another human, have this built in need to identify the sex and race of the other and if they don't do that in the first five seconds or so, they get agitated. It's almost as if we need to know who, or what, we're dealing with so we can decide whether they are a friend or foe and decide if we need to protect ourselves or not. So when you see a stranger you have this unconscious instinct—or so the theory goes—to determine whether it's a man or a woman and if they are Negro or Asian or white, or whatever."

"So once we know that, what happens?" Colleen asked.

"I'm not an expert on this, believe me, but what we discussed at length in the course was prejudice, stereotyping and discrimination and how those things all spring from determining differences."

"So, Molly," Frank said, "I'm different than you. I'm a man and I'm Italian. So what?"

"Well, that's probably a good example Frank. That's all well and good, IF I see that you're an Italian man and I _accept_ the fact that you're different. I think the key idea is to accept and, hopefully, appreciate differences.

Stereotyping happens when I perhaps dislike something you do, assign that to the fact that you're A, a man, or B, an Italian, and then categorize other Italian men by saying they're all like you."

"Well, they just wish they were like me."

The four of them laughed loudly. Will, who had been watching Molly with interest and pride, wanted to go on.

"So what about prejudice Mol?" He wanted to encourage her to speak.

"Prejudice is pre-judging, or deciding ahead of time because someone is an Italian, for instance, that they have a certain characteristic, just because they are Italian. I have an opinion ahead of time about Frank because you tell me he's Italian. I don't know anything about him except that I'm sure he is a certain way because he's from Italy. Discrimination is more about behavior, if I remember correctly. I discriminate when I act on my prejudices. I _do_ something to you or against you because you are Italian. I make you drink from a separate water fountain or go to a different school or I don't hire you, for instance."

"This is, after all, the same country that has separate neighborhoods and different restrooms and different schools for coloreds and it is the same country that would not let women vote until twenty years ago," Will said.

"You're absolutely right," Colleen said. "But why are we doing this to our Japanese neighbors?"

"The truth is, Colleen," Molly said, "that we've prejudged, stereotyped and discriminated against people who were different from us for a long time. And we're not the only ones. The Chinese do not like -- to put it mildly -- the Japanese. We have awful names for Mexicans and other Latin people, the Irish, Italians—you've heard them, I'm sure—people from Poland and Germany and Arabs and Jews...it's a long list."

"And they all have hateful things to say about each other," Will said. "It's not a very hopeful thing for the human race."

"But this is America," Colleen pleaded. "We are supposed to be the great melting pot, where all these different people can come together."

"That's the ideal sweetie," Frank said. "I guess we've got a ways to go until we get there." He paused for a moment. "But I have to admit you guys, when a country does something like Japan has done, it's hard not to blame the people who live in that country. It's hard for me—I mean before they all left—it was hard not to look at some of these older guys who came over here from Japan and say to their face: 'What the hell are you guys doing?'"

"I know what you mean Frank, I do," Will said. "But I have to remember that in our own country, in the revolutionary war, when we began as a nation, that not everyone was behind that war. There were lots of people still loyal to England and there were great divides in our own people about whether or not we should be fighting the Redcoats. I have to think the same is true in Japan. There must be divisions there. "

"Yeah, I get it."

"And, even so," Will went on, "today we're dealing with people who are American citizens, who have never known Japan or set foot on that soil. This country is all they know and all they care about. And we have deprived them of their rights."

"All in the name of military necessity," Colleen said. All four of them drained their coffee cups at the same time. Seeing that they chuckled and sat them back down.

"I think it's just about fear," Molly said. "Maybe the greater the differences between me and someone else, the more susceptible I am to being afraid of them when I feel threatened. And we all know that when we're afraid we act in ways that aren't entirely logical or don't make much sense."

"You're right Mol, absolutely," Will said, "AND those are the times when the rational and reasonable among us have to step up as leaders, that's when our laws have to be applied. Otherwise we are destined for chaos." They sat silently for a moment before Will spoke again. "What keeps coming back and biting me is the speech Roosevelt gave, the 'all we have to fear is fear itself' speech. I think he was exactly to the point. We just couldn't live up to it."

After Frank and Colleen went home, their bellies and their heads full, Molly took Will by the hand and led him to the bedroom. She took off her full length rose colored dress and threw it over the chair, slipped out of her underwear and tucked herself quickly under the covers.

"Hurry up you. This is going to be good."

She took Will in her arms, pulled him over on top of her and kissed his chin, his nose and his lips. He was smiling. She pulled him into her and they lay still for a moment, savoring each other. It was their sweetest sex in months.

The following afternoon Will sat outside in the front yard, the September sun warming him. He turned his attention to the smoke bush growing just a few feet away. It was still small, two feet at the most, and it's lime green leaves were shimmering in the light afternoon breeze. The leaves were nearly round and he could see the veins as the sun illuminated the leaves from the back. They shook as if nervous or chilled and he fixed his attention on them for some time. His thoughts wandered and landed on Molly and he felt his heart drop. Life is so fragile, he thought, so fleeting and so susceptible to things we cannot control. They had lost a baby and he was fully aware that the loss was so different for Molly, a fully alive woman, a natural mother, a loving human being. The child was part of her in a way that it was not part of him, could not be, at that stage, and maybe never. He wondered then if that was how men could go to war and how old men could send young men to battle, because men did not, could not, feel deeply what a woman felt about a son or daughter. Was that the truth? Who would ever know?

CHAPTER THIRTY-SEVEN

A high-pressure area over the California coast boosted the temperature in Los Angeles to 79 degrees and post-Thanksgiving shoppers were out in their short sleeves and sandals. To the northeast, above the Owens Valley the wind moaned around the 14,000-foot peaks, raced down the mountains and blew straight down the length of the valley. The sand and dust kicked up around the wooden Manzanar buildings, lashing the windowpanes and rattling the black tar paper. Inside, Mutt, Suki and Amy huddled together on their straw mattress. Mutt held Amy in his arms, heating both their torsos, but his legs and feet were numb from the cold. Suki lay on the other side of her daughter and extended her arm across her so she could put her hand under Mutt's arm.

It was a couple of hours before midnight and the camp was dark, save for the spotlights on poles above the barbed wire. All the evacuees had been ordered to stay in their own buildings and the lights went out at 9 p.m. The tension in the camp was as thick as the oatmeal they served for breakfast in the mess hall. There had been death threats against members of the Japanese American Citizens League and rumors of a black list of JACL officers who would be beaten or killed.

Mutt had warned Suki and Amy of the dangers in the camp and forbade them to go anywhere alone. At the recent community council meetings and other public gatherings he had heard the rumblings of violence, the arguments, the heated accusations of betrayal and informing. JACL members, who were young, second generation men for the most part, were more Americanized than their parents and, from the beginning of the evacuation process, had been cooperative with the War Relocation Authority and the Army itself. Issei, first generation Japanese, had learned to protect themselves over the years from racism and persecution by white Americans. They had pulled into their own organizations and families as a way of buffering themselves from the culture at large. The Issei —stubbornly in the eyes of some of their sons and daughters-- emphasized their roots in the Japanese culture and their solidarity as a group.

Their children stepped more fully into the American dream and the larger culture, embracing, to the extent they were able, white America's values and customs. These differences between the two generations, apparent for years, burst into full blossom following the attack on Pearl Harbor and during the evacuation process itself. Life in the camps only served to underline the loyalty issue. The harsh conditions, the surrender to authority and the daily tests of will power, patience and acceptance chafed many of the more seasoned Japanese as much as the dry, cold wind that was nearly constant now.

The Army, not blind to these currents in the camp population, seized on the differences and actively recruited younger Japanese and specific members of the JACL to help them keep in touch with what was happening under the surface of daily events. The Army and War Relocation Authority went so far as to rule that only Nisei could hold offices in the community councils, politically castrating many of the older Japanese men; this in a culture that valued the wisdom of its elders and the unity of the family.

In early December, as the first anniversary of the Japanese bombing of Pearl Harbor neared, the camp was filled with suspicion, resentment and anger. Families were arguing. Community council meetings were filled with shouting and angry accusations, one generation against another, one faction of the camp dead set against the other. Some of the more angry men, men who had attempted to organize their followers and who spoke in the harshest terms about the JACL members, publicly called the young men *inu,* or dogs. Posted on the bulletin board in the recreation hall was a hand scrawled note: "We are going to kill all the dogs."

One of the most political JACL members, Fred Oshima, was named as a target. Oshima, from the Bay Area, had worked hard to organize the Citizens League before the evacuation and carried that zeal into the camps. He believed, as many others did, that cooperation with the Army, the FBI and the WRA would be the easiest path for all the Japanese to follow. He met WRA officials regularly and consciously tried to build a harmonious relationship with them and with the camp director, William Madison, a 51-year-old career government executive from Los Angeles. Madison, in turn, seemed to favor members of the JACL in day-to-day decisions.

On the morning of Dec.3, two soldiers on patrol found Fred Oshima, in a sitting position, leaning up against the side of building 22. He was barely conscious and visibly bruised on his head, neck and face. His speech was slurred and he told the two soldiers that he had been beaten by a group of men during the night, but he couldn't identify any of them. The soldiers put Oshima in a pickup truck and took him to the camp hospital, where he was cared for and placed under guard.

Mutt and Suki had heard the pre-dawn beating outside their building and remained inside. They didn't even look out the window. Mutt, like many of the Japanese from Bainbridge Island and other rural areas, were not that political and tried to avoid the rancor and divisive talk in the camp. He again warned his wife and daughter against getting involved or walking around the camp alone.

The next morning Mutt was walking to breakfast by himself. He would bring something back to his building, to Suki and Amy. He heard loud voices before he saw anything and as he rounded the corner of the building across the street from his, he saw four MP's forcing a man he knew into a jeep. Harvey Nuino, who Mutt had met in their work on the garden and whom he had heard speak up in many community meetings, was forced into the back seat between two MP's and placed in handcuffs. Their eyes met. Harvey's face was dark and angry. Mutt remembered now that he was openly critical of the JACL and the men who ran it. He knew also that Harvey was active in organizing the workers in the kitchen into a union, which would have been the first in the camp. Mutt watched the jeep drive off and turned his attention to several other Japanese men in front of the building.

"The *inu* sold us out."

"They turned on us. This is their way of getting us back."

"Harvey didn't do anything. He was in his bed yesterday morning, I saw him."

Mutt hurried off to the mess hall, where he scooped up some oatmeal and three apples and hurried back to Suki and Amy.

That afternoon several hundred men gathered in front of the camp administration building. Most of them wore heavy topcoats and hats pulled down over their heads. At first they were talking amongst themselves but when William Madison came out on the front porch, they began to shout at the camp administrator.

"Let Harvey go."

"The citizens league dogs are spies for you."

"Give us our vote."

"Give us Harvey back."

"Free Nuino."

The crowd inched forward until it had surrounded the little wooden porch. Madison, who had been listening, began waving his arms to quiet the crowd, and then stepped back inside the building to speak to an Army officer. Moments later soldiers with rifles and MP's with clubs moved into the crowd from the rear. One MP spoke with a bullhorn:

"Return to your own building immediately. This assembly is over. Go back to your building NOW." The soldiers were separating groups of men with their rifle barrels and forcibly moving two or three men at a time away from the porch. The Japanese men, still talking loudly and shaking their fists, dispersed. The MP's remained around the administration building while the soldiers fanned out down the rows of buildings to make sure there was no more trouble.

Paul Hamada and Rick Kobori had watched for the last hour from a safe distance, their eyes wide with curiosity and fear. The two Bainbridge High School graduates had never seen their elders in such a public display. They immediately knew the gravity of the situation and the risk involved. Before the soldiers could get near them, they returned to their building and told their parents what had happened.

That evening the camp was eerily quiet. Harvey Nuino was in a cell at the north edge of camp. Fred Oshima was still under guard in the camp hospital. The lights were again turned out early and Paul could hear the soldiers walking up and down the rows of buildings and see the erratic arcs of flashlights dancing on the walls of his little room.

The following morning, as the sun cleared the mountain peaks to the east, groups of men in threes and fours moved from the mess hall to the administration building. In less than fifteen minutes there were 500 men crowded up against the building. Shouts began and got louder.

"Let Harvey go."

"We want our lives back."

"Give us a voice."

"Get rid of the spies."

Men were yelling and pumping their arms in the chilly December air.

Paul and Rick, on the edge of the crowd, watched in silence. The energy of the men was compelling and Paul could feel himself being caught up in the emotion. He looked over at Rick, who was standing with his fists clenched and his body tense. The shouts grew louder.

Near the back of the crowd half a dozen evacuees were straining to push a large Army truck forward. Others joined them and the truck gained momentum. A roar went up from the crowd as the truck started rolling toward the building that housed the administration offices. Just as the truck rolled through the crowd and crunched into the timber of the small porch, tear gas canisters were lobbed into the crowd. The roar grew louder.

Mutt, Amy and Suki stood together at the window of their building, arms around each other, unable to turn away.

A voice over a bullhorn ordered the men to disperse and return to their buildings. Two more tear gas canisters plopped into the middle of the crowd and white smoke formed a horizontal trail out into the rows of buildings. At the edges of the crowd three trucks full of soldiers rolled up and helmeted men jumped out with machine guns, shotguns and rifles. They quickly formed lines, shoulder to shoulder, and aimed their weapons.

Shotguns, aimed above the crowd of men, boomed out into the desert air. The mob grew even louder and continued to move toward the administration building. And rifles, now leveled at the Japanese, began to pop, one after another.

Paul watched as man near the Army truck that had rammed the porch dropped to his knees. A cry went up from the men around him and faces turned to the soldiers with guns. Men called for help for the man who had been shot. Others, caught in the flow of the tear gas, were coughing and choking and crying for help.

Rifle shots were still popping to the left and right and across the crowd from Paul and Rick. A soldier was randomly firing a shotgun into the air. Paul could smell the gunpowder and the fear. Suddenly he sensed, out of the corner of his eye, that Rick was not beside him. Paul turned his head, scanning the crowd. Where had he gone to? Then, out of the corner of his eye, he saw a dark form on the ground to his left. A chill ran through his body as he turned and saw his friend crumpled on the dry ground.

"Rick!"

Paul squatted and grabbed Rick's dark blue winter coat. He lifted and turned his friend, at the same time opening the lapel. A dark red stain covered Rick's white shirt. Rick only stared at the clear, cold sky. Paul called his name. And again. Tears formed in his eyes and he looked out into the crowd, looking for something or someone who would change this brutal reality. He picked up Rick's arm, limp and lifeless and lowered it to the earth. His high school friend was dead.

Paul dropped his head and sobbed, struggling to breathe, and put both his arms around his friend, as if to protect him from the chaos that was around them. The crowd thinned out as men ran alongside the wooden buildings and sought refuge in any corner of the camp that felt safe. Two soldiers, rifles held out in front of them, walked slowly to Paul's side and he slumped to the ground, weak and lost, beside his friend's body.

Rick Kobori and one other man, from Santa Barbara, were killed that day by Army gunfire. Five more were wounded. Harvey Nuimo was freed to resume his life in the camp. Fred Oshima and every other officer in the Japanese American Citizens League were immediately removed from Manzanar and taken to other facilities.

Mutt, Suki and Amy, as most of the other families in the camp, huddled together in the darkness and tried to protect themselves from the cold and the thoughts of what would happen next. After Suki and Amy fell asleep, Mutt lit a single candle and turned to his journal. His short wooden pencil scraped along the page slowly, deliberately:

I cannot write everything for it is too ugly
I cannot write about the ground itself

Rising up and gouging each barrack's windowpanes or even of
Sand crystals falling from the sky like snow

I cannot write how our silence and shame
Make all of us insane
How the searchlights at midnight
Seek us out and fill our nights

I cannot write of syrup on rice
And a cook's fight for life
For this is the night of Manzanar's riot
The night of the ground rising up and gouging us

I cannot write how they shout "Quiet!"
Or how the searchlight replaces the moon
And young men die
And old men weep

I cannot write about the fumes that fill
Our lungs and how our children must hide
Their eyes and their mouths to live
And how the earth is no longer ours

I cannot write about myself
So much is missing
And all that is left
Are sand crystals falling like snow

Whatever name you have god, please take care of the spirits of these two young men and be generous with mercy on their families. And please give the rest of us the strength to endure this horror."

Mutt read over what he had written with tears in his eyes, closed his diary and blew the candle out.

Paul Hamada, two buildings away, had cried until he was empty. He lay on his mattress and stared into the darkness. He kept picturing the black coat, the white shirt and the red stain.

CHAPTER THIRTY-EIGHT

This was another one of those mornings for Will when it was quiet and he was contemplative. He had put the current issue to bed late last night and he was tired of writing about traffic accidents, meetings and rationing. He sat in front of the Royal typewriter he had written on since college and looked at the keys. He felt the keys, smooth, shiny and slightly concave. He looked at the levers that arced back and forth and the small steel letters at the end that were covered with ink and remnants of the buff colored paper they repeatedly struck. He wiggled his fingers on the keys, moving the levers forward without striking the paper. He just wanted to write about what came to his own mind, not what someone else was doing or saying, just to let go for a few moments.

I am an ordinary man, he wrote. He looked at the words and nodded.

I am an ordinary man in extraordinary circumstances. (Plenty of men and women must feel that way.) These circumstances, this war and this evacuation, are calling something out of me.

I am sure of some things. I am sure of the principles involved and the legal issues, but I am not sure that what I am doing is endearing me to this community. Is this

the right thing—whatever that means - to do? Maybe, just maybe, I am being divisive and not contributing to the good of the whole.

No. I am not being divisive. The community itself is divided and I am reflecting that. I am sure there are plenty of people who think the way I do and there are plenty of others who are against the Japanese -- all of them -- because of what their country has done. I can't blame them for their opinions. But it is how we act on these thoughts that makes the difference.

I am an ordinary man. They are ordinary people. We have our biases and our opinions and so many of them are part our culture, part of the way we grew up. Culture is a very strong thing. Those first years in the bosom of our family and in the place we are, and the time we are - all those do so much to shape who we are. So much of that we can't help.

How do some people escape hatred and racism, while others are immersed in it? How do some people learn to love those around them, while others are filled with suspicion and fear? It can't be just our parents. It's got to have something to do with the way we all interact and the things we say to each other as young men and women.

We—yes, there's a definite 'we' here—Molly and I have got to keep saying and writing the things that we grew up with, that we learned from our families and the people we know well, that we learned from each other. She has taught me so much about love, about accepting another person for who they are and not trying to make them into someone you need or want them to be. She is so good at that. And it just seems to come naturally to her. But is it really 'natural?' Doesn't it have to do with her parents and her upbringing on the farm and what they valued together? It's got to.

We are so lucky to have grown up with people who loved us and saw in each one of us kids someone unique, who had their own way of doing things and their own path. She will do that, and, God help me, so will I, with the children that we have. And we will have children. I'm sure of it.

Well, I feel a little better. I'm sure of one more thing now -- we have to keep on this path together. We have to keep saying what we believe in.

The news of the Manzanar riot took some time to filter back to Bainbridge Island. After hours of trying to reach a source at the camp, Will connected by phone with William Madison. Madison did not mention Rick Kobori's death, only saying that there had been "a disturbance." The details would have to come later, after responsibilities were sorted out and families notified.

The next issue of the Review carried this front page headline: NO ISLANDER IMPLICATED IN CAMP RIOT and an editorial: YOU SHOULDN'T PACK APPLES WITH LEMONS. Will took the point of view, supported by Madison, that the disturbance was the product of "a few pro-Axis agitators" and that the majority of evacuees in the camp, especially the Japanese Americans from Bainbridge Island, had nothing to do with the demonstration or the ensuing violence. Will used the occasion to campaign for the removal of the evacuees who had come from the island, under 300 people, to another camp.

Bainbridge Island's contingent of Japanese Americans and Japanese aliens should be moved forthwith from the relocation center at Manzanar, Calif. to one at Camp Eden, Ida.

The Review hereby publicly pledges itself to work for that removal. It hereby petitions for the aid in that effort of all others who may feel as we do, that such a move is the only humane thing to do.

Far off Manzanar never was the place to send our Island Japanese colony. At the time of the hasty evacuation from the island -- ahead of evacuation in other Northwest communities—the Army said it had no choice. There were no other location centers set up. So it was that our Islanders were transported more than 1,000 miles and plunked down amid thousands of California Japanese with whom they had nothing in common. They were placed in a hot, dry desert country amid geographical and weather conditions entirely foreign to them. There are 10,000 California Japanese at Manzanar. There are about 275 Bainbridge Island Japanese there. That is like putting a Washington State apple in a crate of California lemons.

The Review has a pitiful file of letters -as do many Islanders—from our evacuated residents, telling how utterly foreign they have found some of their California 'neighbors' to be. Our Islanders, like a transplanted Washington rhododendron in a California desert, are existing - not living. We do not ask pampering for them, but we do say they have a right to live. The recent riot at Manzanar of pro-Axis Japanese brings matters to a head. We maintain that the riot only serves to emphasize the point that our Northwest evacuees belong in a Northwest relocation center, not in California.

Every single other Northwest evacuee, so far as we know, is in Camp Eden, Idaho. Our Islanders belong there too. The Review intends to see that they are moved there.

The next day Molly, who was in the Review office paying some bills, received a phone call from the father in a Filipino family who were friends with the Kobori's. Their son was dead. The Army command at Manzanar had allowed only a small service for the family, inside one of the camp's recreation halls, for fear that a larger gathering would get out of hand. Rick's body, at the family's request, was being shipped back to his island home for burial.

The news of Rick's death hit Molly and Will hard. Molly, remembering her recent loss, was especially impacted and cried openly, only when she found Will and was safely in his arms. They decided to run a story in the next week's edition, something that honored Rick but would not incite any more divisiveness or violence, on the island or in Manzanar. They knew the Review was well read in the camp. Molly wrote the story. She wanted to.

The loss of the young Japanese American stuck in Will's craw and strengthened his resolve. An innocent boy, he thought, who, with his family in a strange and hostile place, was only trying to survive until he could get back home. He wished he had written an even stronger editorial. That evening before dinner, Will and Molly raised a glass of whiskey to Rick and wondered aloud when they would hear from Paul.

A letter was in the next day's mail. Paul wrote to say that he could not write any story about Rick or the riot. It was just too emotional for him, he said, and he could not find his rookie reporter's voice to write in any objective way. Enclosed was a request for letters of recommendation that would support Paul in leaving Manzanar, moving to Hunt, Idaho and finding work. He asked Will to write a letter as well as the Bainbridge High School principal and any other "prominent islanders" Will could find. Paul asked the Whitmans to save his $5.50 monthly salary until he was sure where he would end up.

That spring and early summer, most of the evacuees from Bainbridge Island were reassigned to Idaho and more of the young men took jobs in the beet, corn and potato fields of the interior west. Some were petitioning to leave camp life altogether and attend college in the Midwest and east. Paul recruited a new reporter for Will, to file reports from Manzanar, a young woman named Kiyoka Fujita who worked in the camouflage factory.

The Review continued to run stories that connected evacuees with their home community and informed the island residents of accomplishments and events in the lives of the Japanese. In every issue there was a story, long or short, about the camp and/or the displaced citizens…ISLANDERS AT MANZANAR TO MOVE SOON,
THE NISEI GET A BREAK,
T. SAKUMA LEAVES MINIDOKA FOR MIDWEST FARM,
SGT. MOTO VISITS FAMILY AT RELOCATION CENTER,
KOBA BROTHERS JOIN FAMILY AT MOSES LAKE,
NINE ISLAND NESEI IN ARMY -- SURVEY SHOWS,
ISLAND NISEI VISIT HERE,
BI GIRLS SOFTBALL VICTORS AT HUNT CAMP and
LEGION HITS U.S. JAPANESE.

The last was a tough headline for Will to write. It galled him. The American Legion, in its annual state convention that included several delegates from Bainbridge Island, voted unanimously to urge the President and Congress to oust all Japanese from the United States after the war ended. It was beyond imagination, Will thought, to even think of removing a whole ethnic group from a country. What were they thinking? Who were these people? He ranted at Molly most of the evening.

That story and a public statement by Army Gen. John DeWitt, that the Japanese were still "a dangerous element," whether they were citizens or not, or loyal or not, fueled the fire in Will's belly. He lashed out at DeWitt again:

Highly indignant, we were about to give a hot answer to Lt. Gen. John L. DeWitt when we came across an editorial in the Minidoka Irrigator, the newspaper published at the relocation center in Idaho where many of our Bainbridge Island Japanese are now stationed.

The general, in a statement about Nisei loyalty that sounded like something out of a dictator nation and not from free America, will draw protests from Japanese Americans who have volunteered to serve as front line shooting fighters in the same army to which the General belongs. Then, in better words than we could have chosen, the camp newspaper's editorial concludes:

"There is no point in disputing here the General's plainly off-center allegation that we are a 'dangerous element, whether loyal or not.' It would be a waste of time and space to comment at any length upon the utterly ludicrous absence of sense, discretion and logic in the statement. Even the loyal may be a 'dangerous element' to the General, but the War Department knows different.

"General DeWitt is a thoroughly efficient and capable military commander, as the evacuees well know – but as a commentator on Japanese American loyalty, he is something less than admirable. It shouldn't be necessary, but somebody ought to tell the General that most Americans accept the word of the President that this war is being fought for the Four Freedoms and is not a race war."

It gave Will some satisfaction to publish that in the Review, but his stomach still churned when he thought of DeWitt, the power he had and the way he used it.

CHAPTER THIRTY-NINE

Bert left the men's bathroom, situated in between rows of barracks on each side. He had a small white towel draped around his neck. Still he felt the evening breeze cool on his shoulders. He looked around him. The camp, for the moment, seemed empty, save for the sounds of voices coming from inside the buildings.

After standing still for a moment, he walked slowly to the west, toward the outline of the mountains, still framed by the setting sun. He could hear quail calling outside the camp and he thought of the same sound at home, around his own farm, the shrill, plaintive call alone in the evening air. He left the protection of the buildings and the wind picked up, stirring the dust around his feet. The fences, topped with barbed wire, came into focus, black against the fading light. He walked closer, wary of the guard towers. He took a long look to his left, then right; seeing nothing, hearing nothing, he walked on, closer to the fence.

His thoughts were about Linda and his house. He pictured her there, sitting at the kitchen table by herself. Toto was probably at her feet. The kitchen was warm with light and Linda was eating dinner, slowly bringing some salad greens from the plate to her mouth. As she chewed she stared off into space. Bert longed to be with her.

He walked slowly toward the fence, surprised that he had seen no one. He was ten feet from the fence and stopped, afraid to walk up and touch it. He thought of the soldiers in the towers, looking down at him, perhaps even moving their rifles up to their shoulders. He could feel chills go up the back of his neck. He looked out over the land beyond, flat, dark and desolate. He could see the silhouettes of tumbleweeds and a few spindly trees.

Nights had turned into weeks. Weeks had turned into months and months into a full year. Where was his home? Tears formed in his eyes and swelled up over the lids.

Bert stood there until all the light disappeared and found his way back to his building and fell onto his cot.

In the spring and summer of 1943, called by some the "middle year" of WWII, US forces, slowly, painfully and at a great cost in lives, began to exert their dominance in the Pacific theater. It seemed as if the Marines were taking back small, desolate islands yard by yard, treading painfully and slowly along stepping-stones to Japan. Seven thousand Japanese were lost when four destroyers and 25 airplanes were brought down in the battle of the Bismarck Sea. In April, an American P38 shot down Admiral Yamamoto's plane over the Pacific, killing the master strategist of the Pearl Harbor attack and a national hero. Victories at sea and in the air, at New Guinea, Guadalcanal, the Solomon Islands and Tarawa gave Americans a growing sense of confidence and made even more remote the possibility that Japan would attack the US, much less win the war.

At home, this growing feeling of security brought into even sharper focus the issues of evacuation, imprisonment and eventual release of "aliens." The government still had in camps surrounded by barbed wire more than 100,000 people, two-thirds of them American citizens. The evacuation itself had been called "an emergency measure," but fear, racism and politics had, in effect, sentenced these people to indefinite confinement and a way of life that was, physically and mentally, very taxing. Now that the emergency seemed to be over, would the nation relax and let the Japanese Americans come home?

No charges of espionage or aiding the enemy had been filed against any of the evacuees, nor was there any basis for charges. The legal basis for detaining them was highly suspect. The question of loyalty, one of the burning issues in the confinement, was just that – a question that was virtually impossible to answer, though the government and the Army had tried and would continue to try. The "military necessity," the foundation of the claim for exclusion and evacuation, was plainly wearing thin as each week passed.

Still, more than a year into the war and the imprisonment, the government had no idea who to release or when any kind of release would happen, if indeed it was to happen. The norm now, as it had been since March of 1942, was total control of a population of more than 100,000 citizens. It was as if the federal government had imprisoned a whole city on false premises and now did not know how to set the city's people free, or even if it wanted to.

Related to the larger issues of evacuation, imprisonment and release was the issue of serving in the military. There were already thousands of Japanese men and women in the armed services. Many more, in and out of the camps, wanted to enlist. In June of 1942 the War Department had announced that it would not accept for service any more Japanese "regardless of citizenship status or other factors."

There was growing pressure, in and out of the government, to "allow" the Japanese to serve. Within the War Department itself civilian officials were pressuring President Roosevelt with a three-point argument for second generation Japanese in the armed services: (1) there was general agreement that Nisei were loyal, (2) citizens have a fundamental right to serve their country and (3) service would have an important psychological effect internationally.

Eventually these arguments won out. In early 1943 Secretary of War Henry Stimson issued this statement:

"It is the inherent right of every citizen, regardless of ancestry, to bear arms in the Nation's battle. When obstacles to the free expression of that right are imposed by emergency considerations, those barriers should be removed as soon as humanly possible. Loyalty to country is a voice that must be heard and I am now able to give active proof that this basic American belief is not a casualty of war."

Any program of release or service was strongly opposed by Gen. DeWitt and the Western Defense Command. DeWitt held fast to his view that the disloyal Japanese could not be distinguished from the loyal Japanese.

Less than a month later the first significant signal that detention might end for thousands of Japanese Americans came from President Roosevelt:

"No loyal citizen of the United States should be denied the democratic right to exercise the responsibilities of his citizenship, regardless of his ancestry. The principle on which this country was founded and by which it has always been governed is that Americanism is a matter of the mind and the heart; Americanism is not, and never was, a matter of race or ancestry. A good American is one who is loyal to this country and to our creed of liberty and democracy. Every loyal American citizen should be given the opportunity to serve this country wherever his skills will make the greatest contribution – whether it be in the ranks of our armed forces, war production, agriculture, government service or other work essential to the war effort."

If there was one word that focused this issue and this time, one word that would bring so much opportunity and so much pain, it was the word the President used three times in this short statement: loyal.

And, if this was indeed the first idealistic statement that signaled an eventual end to the imprisonment of 120,000 people, there were months of tough, painful realism ahead. During 1943, 21,000 Japanese would leave the camps on leave, for work or education in the Midwest or eastern United States. The following year, 18,500 more would follow. But the exodus to new towns and new jobs was not without its conflict and anguish, and nearly 80,000 people still remained in camps.

Proving that any person is loyal is improbable. It might take a lifetime to show that he or she wouldn't swerve from devotion. Proving that a whole ethnic group is loyal seems impossible. Proving that one person is disloyal would involve some kind of demonstration or proof, at a trial for instance, that some act of treachery was committed. Proving that a whole population is disloyal boggles the mind. And yet, there they remained, a population that was overwhelmingly innocent of any crime, suffering in shacks through heat and cold, away from families and friends in many cases, existing behind barbed wire and under guard towers.

CHAPTER FORTY

Bert Kobiyashi and Mutt Sugimoto had become good friends. Though they knew each other back home, it was only at wedding receptions, large picnics and public meetings that they said hello and exchanged pleasantries. Here at Manzanar, working together, thrown together through hardship and necessity, they formed a strong bond. Mutt shared his experiences in the "old" Japan, before any of this had happened, and the way he and Suki had worked together on Bainbridge. He introduced Bert to Suki and Amy and they took him into their family circle. Bert loved to talk about Linda and what they had built together on their small farm.

During the winter in the camp they spent many hours in the fields together and more time around meals in the mess hall, talking about their lives and when they might return to normal. Both had the firm intention to return to their homes on Bainbridge Island and pick up their former lives, but when, and how? In early spring the first indication of any kind of possibility of freedom presented itself in the camp. It was called an "Application for Leave Clearance."

"Registration teams" had fanned out to the camps, initiating a new program —still hotly contested in the federal government – that would allow individuals to leave the camps, after addressing the "tendencies of loyalty or disloyalties to the United States." The Army clearance questionnaires explored personal backgrounds, group memberships, work histories, skills and two questions that would become known simply by their numbers: Question 27 and Question 28. The government, in short, instead of deciding who was loyal or not, had decided to administer a loyalty oath.

Bert and Mutt had seen the questionnaires -- copies were circulated secretly around the camp shortly after the government agents arrived -- but had not yet been interviewed. One Sunday afternoon they sat drinking tea in the mess hall and talking.

"Are you going to go for this?" Bert asked. The men had isolated themselves in one corner of the building, making sure they weren't overheard.

"I'm not sure. Suki and I have been talking and it's a tough choice."

"I know; it's a real dilemma. First they ask you if you're willing to serve in the Army and go into combat, wherever they tell you to go. Then they ask you if you will swear—what do they say? — 'unqualified allegiance' to the US and forswear any allegiance to Japan. I mean on the surface it seems like a 'yes-yes', but when you think about it, it puts some of us in a real bind."

"Right." Mutt sipped his tea and adjusted the dark red cap on his head. The cap was stained with his sweat and the bill was powdered with gray dust where he had repeatedly put his fingers. Outside there was a light wind and it was growing dark. "Take us, as a for instance. If I, as an Issei, renounce any ties to Japan and I still can't become a US citizen, I'm left out in the cold. I have no country. And, if I say yes to both 27 and 28, and I am taken away to the Army, or probably a factory somewhere, what happens to our family. What will Suki and Amy do, stay here by themselves?"

Bert was shaking his head. "And if you say no?"

"Yeah. If I say no, then I'm branded some kind of security risk, someone who can't be trusted and who knows what they will do with me then?"

"Yeah. I can imagine them taking all the 'no-no's" --they both smiled-- "and sending them to some high security camp and saying something like…'OK, you guys admitted that you're not loyal to the US. Here you go, more prison time.' I hate this. We can't trust them anyway." Bert paused and finished his cup of tea.

"And you, you've got a family to think of, like you said."

"Right," Mutt answered. "I'm a head of household and I earn a little money and we're together. I'm probably too old for the Army, but if I sent off to Pittsburgh, say, to work in a steel mill, I'm breaking up my family and, at least for a while, taking away their income. How can I say yes to this?"

"I know. It's a horrible bind. I thought this morning about saying yes to both questions. I'd probably end up in the Army, fighting for my country, which has declared me an illegal alien, fighting for liberty, justice and equal opportunity for all and I still don't know what would happen to my citizenship. I mean, what would happen when the war is over. Then what?"

"You know Bert, if you answer yes, it's the same as volunteering for combat?"

"Yeah, I thought about that. Linda would have a fit. I'd end up in Germany killing Germans. They wouldn't dare send us to the Pacific."

"No. I can't imagine that." The two men leaned back in their chairs and looked around them to see who else was in the mess hall. A few men were gathered around a table in the back talking. They guessed the conversations were similar.

"You know, there's another issue here," Mutt said. "Some of our people here have parents, who aren't getting any younger. Some people your age or younger, like Paul Hamada, he's got parents here. What if they don't want to leave the camp? What if they need him? You could look at this as making the Nisei leave, forcing them out of the camps. How can someone like Paul—or anyone with older parents—honor his parents, keep his family together and still not be seen as a traitor?" Mutt paused and rubbed his forehead. "These are like trick questions, when you get down to it."

"I honestly feel insulted." Bert took his cap off and knocked some of the dust out. "I was born in America. I've never left the country. I own land and a home. I'm married to an American woman, a citizen, _another_ citizen. They've taken me away from my home and locked me up in here. And now—and this pisses me off Mutt –they want me to swear that I'm loyal to my country. What about their loyalty to me? What happened to that? Is loyalty just a one way deal?"

"I know, my friend, I know. But pretty soon they're going to be knocking on your door and asking you to answer these questions. What are you going to do?"

"I don't know yet. I just don't know." He paused and looked out the window into the evening. "One thing I do know Mutt. I miss Linda terribly."

News of the questionnaires and the responses to them spread quickly from camp to camp. Camp newspapers carried stories and opinions on the issues. Block councils held forums on the questions, giving evacuees a chance to blow off steam and clarify their choices. The questionnaires quickly became divisive, in and of themselves, and the individuals answering them were thrown into conflict with each other. .

Mutt and Bert went to a block meeting to hear what choices others were making. The large wooden building was nearly full by the time they got there. The group was made up almost entirely of men, most still dressed in their dusty work clothes. Only a few bare bulbs hung over the group, casting shadows over the men's faces and giving the hall an eerie glow. A young man, wearing a clean white shirt and khakis and standing on a raised platform at one end of the building, called for silence.

"We are here tonight to voice our point of view and answer questions about the Application for Leave Clearance and related issues. Your block leaders will take questions and comments to the War Relocation Authority staff. Please keep your comments as brief as possible."

"Are you saying that what we're saying here tonight will be recorded and passed on to the government?" The speaker was an older man with short white hair in the front row of folding chairs.

"Well, not specifically," the younger man answered. "Your names will not be used -- and we will try to convey the flavor of what is said tonight. Please do not worry about being recorded." He turned to an older man next to him who whispered something.

"Perhaps I should read the two questions aloud so we will all know for sure what they say exactly." The young man reached back and took some papers from the older man. A wave of words spread through the crowd. The young man on the platform, because he was young, because he was well groomed, clean and articulate, was immediately suspected of being aligned with the WRA or the Army. He found the sheet of paper he wanted and spoke to the group:

"Question 27 – 'Are you willing to serve in the armed forces of the United States on combat duty, wherever ordered?' Pretty straightforward... you are willing to fight for this country. Not that you will have to, but you are willing, if called."

Bert made a mental note that the man said "this country," not "your country." He looked at Mutt but remained silent.

"Now, question 28 – 'Will you swear unqualified allegiance to the United States of America and faithfully defend the United States from any or all attack by foreign or domestic forces and forswear any form of allegiance or obedience to the Japanese emperor or any other foreign government, power or organization?' This asks you to swear allegiance to the U.S., without any qualification, and to deny any allegiance to any other country. Those are the two questions everyone is talking about."

A man on the end of the front row, in a blue denim shirt stained with sweat, stood up. "I answered the questionnaire and I answered yes-yes to 27 and 28 and I'll tell you why: I feel this is the only country I've got now. Where else can I go? What other choice do we have? It's not that I don't have feelings about this—I just don't see many choices." He sat back down, nodding at the men around his chair.

"My whole family answered yes," said a voice from the back of the room. "We thought about the old Japanese saying and applied it to our country: 'Your adoptive parents are your real parents—umi no oya yori mo sodate no oya.'"

"These are not our parents," said an angry man in the center of the room. He stood and faced the man in the rear. "This government has betrayed us from the beginning. I answered 'no-no." He turned and faced the front of the room, his face contorted with the pain of what he was saying and the resentment he had been carrying for months. "I don't want you to think I am proud of it or just rebellious. I think our rights have been violated and I wanted somehow to fight back, to say something about these policies. I didn't want to take this sitting down and this was my chance, maybe my only chance. I am so damn mad and, honestly, I cannot get over it. This experience is ruining my life. Whatever we do, we get no help," he said and tears filled his voice. "There is no help from the outside. We are forgotten. We are a people without a home. We are a race that does not count. We are forgotten people. I cannot say yes to a government that does this."

The room was quiet. Insects could be heard banging up against the glass windows, along with the constant wind and dust spraying the panes. A moment later a tall man with wild black hair stood.

"We have been forced here. Now we are forced to make a choice that we cannot win. They tell us nothing in the beginning and they tell us nothing about the end. What are the consequences of a yes or no answer? No one can say." He cleared his throat. "Furthermore, we don't even trust each other. We voted yesterday as a block not to answer or sign the form. That very afternoon two men from my block confronted me and said they heard I went to the administration building and signed anyway. I had to take them to my family and have each one say that I had not signed. This is the effect of this form. It is splitting us apart one man at a time and it is splitting us apart as a group of Japanese men. This must be the work of the devil."

Bert and Mutt looked at each other, both faces reflecting the pain of the words they were hearing. Mutt reached for Bert's arm and held it for a moment. Soon another man stood, a middle-aged man with long black hair wearing a worn Lee jacket, and spoke. Mutt noticed that many in the crowd began to nod their heads, as if they knew him and were glad he was speaking.

"Brothers, this is the most difficult time in our lives. On the outside, it seems as if we have lost our way, but we can never lose our way inside. We can never lose our integrity or our honor. We have to hold on to these things. When I was younger I volunteered for the United States Army and some of my own people refused to speak to me. Some elders went to my father and asked him why he let me sign up. He told them I was old enough and had my own mind." The man turned and spoke to the crowd, trying to include everyone.

"Since then I have been tested mightily in my belief in my country and the men who run it. But there is one thing I remember. I have seen men die beside me for our flag. I have seen men make sacrifices you would not believe, all because they believe in freedom. I can't forget that. When they ask me if I am loyal, I must answer yes. And it is not because I am so devoted to a flag or a President, but because of my love for the men I served with and the sacrifices they made. I cannot betray them, their families or their memory." A murmur rippled through the crowd and a few men applauded.

After some minutes a thin young man with high cheek bones, smooth skin and a gentle demeanor stood up to speak. He was one chair away from Mutt, who watched the man's hands moving nervously and the man grabbed onto the sides of his jeans to keep his hands still.

"I am nineteen and I had to make a choice that affects the welfare of my entire family. If I signed no-no I would throw away my citizenship and the government would eventually come after my two brothers and my sister. Being the oldest son I have an obligation to take care of my parents, my brothers and sister. Saying no-no would stain my family forever. We know that. I was torn in half." He stopped to calm himself. Mutt reached over and touched his arm and the man looked down and met his eyes to acknowledge him.

"Yesterday I walked from my building to the administration building and though it was only a quarter mile, it seemed to take hours. All the way

I was saying 'no-no, no-yes, yes-yes,' over and over again. It was torture, not knowing what any of those answers would bring to me and to my family. If I was alone it would make so much difference, but there are others who will be affected by what I do. When I got to the building and stood in the line my head was spinning. Finally an Army officer interviewed me. At question 27 I said to him 'Damn you. No.' He wasn't flustered, just sat there in his uniform making notes. And then asked me question 28. I answered yes, that I was loyal to his country. I said that –'your country." I think he represented the whole government to me. The thing is, I still don't know if what I answered is right and what it will mean to us."

He sat back down with a deep sigh and turned to Mutt. "Thank you," he whispered.

Then a small, wiry man on the right of the crowd stood. He was silent for a moment, drawing the attention of the others. His black hair spiked straight up around his head. It was obvious he had not had a haircut for a while. Bert saw something in his face and turned to whisper to Mutt.

"I think that's Henry Kitano's son, Henry Junior. Remember, the FBI took his father away." Mutt nodded and Henry Junior began to speak.

"I just want to talk to you about one word. It won't take long. That one word is home. I want to go back home. I want my father to come home and be with us again. These other places we could go—Europe, to kill Germans, St. Louis to make tires, Cleveland to make ball bearings to go into tanks—all these mean nothing because we don't have a home to go back to. I want to sleep in my own bed and put my head on my own pillow. I want to see my wife and children in my own home again, look into their dark eyes and hold them in my arms. I want to see the Madrona tree as I drive in the driveway and see the cherry tree outside my bedroom window when I wake up. Do you know what I see now when I wake up? On one side is an Army blanket that separates me from the family next to me. On the other side is a small window and I wake in the morning to see a tall wooden tower. In that tower are two soldiers, one with a rifle and the other with a machine gun. They have taken me from my home without any choice and plopped me down here in this godforsaken desert. I have no idea when, or if, I will see home again. Let me go back to my home. Then, I will talk to you about loyalty and serving my country."

The crowd rumbled with agreement. Henry Jr. sat down with tears brimming in his eyes. Soon the meeting was called to an end.

After the meeting dispersed, men lingered to talk and argue and slowly filtered out of the building. Mutt and Bert found Henry Kitano.

"Thank you for saying what you did."

"Yes. Thank you for hearing me."

"Where is your father?"

"I found out just last month that he is in the high security camp at Tule Lake, in California."

"Is he all right?"

"I think so. I still have not talked to him, but they said he was alive and healthy. That's all I know."

"Well," Mutt said. "I am glad to hear that much. He is a good man."

"Thank you." The three men shook hands and walked back to their buildings, tired and their spirits low.

In the weeks that followed, the Japanese American Citizens League announced in writing that it was purging its ranks of any members who answered no to both questions on the leave application. Any "no-no's" would not be admitted to JACL membership and, further, JACL would expend no further effort on their behalf.

On the other hand, the administrative director at Manzanar, William Madison, expressed a more humane view: In a letter dated February 27, 1943 letter, he wrote:

"It is important to determine whether the "no" answer on the loyalty question actually means a renouncing of citizenship or whether it is a protest indirectly arising from the pressures of the father who is a non-citizen or directly representing the outcry of a man who has, in his opinion, been ruthlessly and wrongfully deprived during the last year of his rights and position as a citizen. When all the motives have been reviewed, it must be concluded that there is no such thing as a line of strict demarcation. . . . It is my considered conclusion that the answer 'No' has many shades of meaning and is prompted by many motives, some of which are attributable to our failure, both past and present, and some of which may yet be modified and reversed without damage to the principles of American citizenship."

Here was at least one voice, from a white WRA official, that recognized the dilemma the loyalty issue posed for Japanese Americans. But the battles within the government, the battles between the government and the Army and the battles between the government, the Army and the Japanese Americans were far from over.

CHAPTER FORTY-ONE

Will was on the front porch painting an old Adirondack chair bright yellow. The sound of Glenn Miller's "In the Mood" drifted from the floor model radio in the living room through the open front door. Will hummed along. It was a bright clear Sunday in the 60's.

Molly steered the black Pontiac into the driveway and strode quickly up to the front porch with grocery bags in each hand.

"Well," said Will, looking up, "if it isn't my Greer Garson, coming home for dinner." Molly shook her head and her auburn hair and smiled.

"Yes, and my Gary Cooper is doing a great job on that chair." Will put the paintbrush down on the paint can, rose to his feet and stuck his thumbs behind his belt.

"Yes, mam, happy to do anything for my sweetheart," he said in a Western drawl. "What is Miss Garson going to fix for dinner?"

"Well, Coop, how about chuck roast, red potatoes and peas, along with a cold beer?"

"Oh, Greer, you know the way to my heart." He leaned over and kissed Molly on the lips. "And how about a little pre-dinner cuddling in the bedroom, mam?" He looked at her, widened his eyes and raised his bushy dark eyebrows.

"Why Coop, you're so bold."

"Faint heart never won fair lady."

"Let me put these groceries way and I'll meet you in the boudoir."

Will turned immediately and walked into the house, whistling "In the Mood."

After they made love on the steel frame bed, they lay on their backs and talked.

"You know we're doing OK financially," Molly said. "I went over the books this morning and so far this year we're in pretty good shape. We've had our share of pulled ads and subscriptions cancelled, but all in all, I think we'll be OK for the rest of the year. We'll survive."

"Good news."

"Yes. And I was wondering if we could get a new rug for the living room."

"New rug? Oh, first she seduces me with food and sex and then goes after what she really wants." Molly poked Will in the side with her elbow.

"Will, you're awful."

"Thank you."

"Have you looked at that rug? It's practically worn through in places."

There was a knock on the front door, which was still open.

"God, who is that?" Will said. He scrambled out of bed, grabbed his robe and peered out of the bedroom door. "Frank! Hi. Hey, give us a few minutes."

Will and Molly reluctantly dressed and went out to join Frank.

"Have you heard?"

"Well, I don't know. Heard what?"

"Mussolini is out. Italy has surrendered and declared war on Germany."

"Wow," Will said, "leave it to those Italians to turn on a dime."

"Will, my clever friend, you don't know what this means. I am free to be myself again. I can walk down the street without shame. Colleen and I can hold our heads up. This is molto bene. This is fantasico." Frank was teary and his face was flushed.

"That's marvelous Frank," Molly said. "I'm really happy for you, for all of us."

Frank took Molly's hand and kissed it. "Thank you Molly. I knew there was someone in this house who had a brain *and* a heart."

"Hey Frank, you and Colleen want to do potluck tonight?" Will asked. "Just bring over what you were going to have?" He looked at Molly, who shrugged and nodded.

"Sure, let's do it. Swell."

The conversation at dinner that night, after Frank had stopped hooting about Italy finally being on the right track and it was OK for him to be Italian again, turned to the departures from the camps. Leave permits were being granted to those Japanese who were considered unquestionably loyal. Agricultural leaves were granted, as were leaves for higher education. In some cases, "indefinite leaves" were granted for four-month trial periods. But relocation was not going easily.

"It must be really hard," Colleen volunteered, "to leave the camps and move to a new city and start all over—new house, new job, new school for the kids, new neighbors."

"Yeah, and I heard they gave them twenty five bucks when they leave -- whoop de do," Frank said.

"I read about one family in Chicago that went to twelve rentals before anyone would even talk to them about renting, Molly said. "And all the time they were lugging their kids and luggage with them."

The four of them sat around the dining room table. Molly and Will had cleared the dishes and now they sipped on a cup of rare and expensive coffee, Maxwell House.

"Did you hear what LaGuardia said in New York?" Will asked.

"Well, it must have been good, his family is from my home town." Frank chimed in.

Will nodded at Frank and smiled then went on: "He's been arguing with the Feds about the number of Japanese that will end up in New York City. The federal government maintains that mayors or governors shouldn't be allowed to restrict resettlement. So La Guardia, in the Times, says something like: 'If we had to evacuate them from their homes, put them in concentration camps' –he used those words—'how can we justify turning them loose all along the eastern seaboard? If California, Oregon and Washington don't want them, what right does the federal government have to dump them in New York?' It's the same argument the western governors used at the beginning of the war –how can you dump them in our states. Jesus—excuse me—but it sounds like they're talking about dumping loads of garbage."

CHAPTER FORTY-TWO

She walked in the front door, weary beyond words, her blond hair stringy and oily and her hands stained with the juice of strawberries and the black dirt they grew in. Her eyelids were at half-mast and her entrance into her house slow and measured.

Linda Kobiyashi had worked her way through two successful strawberry harvests and had sold her crops to wholesalers. She had given up on lettuce and any other secondary crop to simplify her efforts. With the help of her parents and friends she had held her life and her home together. But Bert's departure had left a big hole in her life and it was wearing her down emotionally. She wondered to herself, although never out loud, what it would be like when he returned.

Since an initial flurry of mail more than a year ago, she had settled into a routine of writing Bert a letter every Friday. She washed her hands, poured herself a glass of wine and sat down at the kitchen table, their old meeting place, a cozy spot that always reminded her of their conversations.

Dearest Bert:

    I hope you are still healthy and not working too hard. I was very happy to hear about your friendship with Mutt and his family. I think I remember who they are. They seem like good people and their friendship will mean a lot to you, I hope.

    Everything is fine here. I've put most of the money from our berries into a saving account. I've opened an account in my name because the bank told me I couldn't be sure what will happen to the accounts of Japanese Americans. It's terrible to think that, but maybe it is the safest.

    There are all kinds of rumors here about leaves you all might get and loyalty oaths and when some people might leave. We can't make much sense of it, but we do know that some people are being released to go into the army or into defense related jobs. Please, please let me know how, or if, this affects you. I don't want to get any false hopes.

    Well, your birthday is in three days. I hope the timing of this is right and you get my letter, and card, on your special day. Twenty-seven years old! I can hardly believe it. 'Course that means I'm 27 too. Pretty soon I'll be over the hill.

    So, on your birthday honey, I'd like to tell you how much you mean to me. Since the day we met in the cafeteria at BHS, you have been such a light in my life. You have never said anything cruel or mean to me — always kind and loving, always accepting me as I was. I don't think I am the best wife in the world, but you have never tried to change me. That means a lot to me.

    I think you are a wonderful man and a great husband. We have built a life together, one that not even the US government can take apart. I admire your strength and courage in the face of all that has happened to you (and the others). I know you will get through this and that *we will reclaim our life together. I hope we will even be stronger.*

Never, ever worry -- I am here for you, waiting to see your shiny, smiling face again. I send you the biggest hug, sweetheart, and kisses all over that round face of yours. Be safe and know that you are loved.

Your Lin.

It was difficult for Linda to be happy as she folded the letter and put it, with a birthday card, in the envelope. She loved Bert with all her heart, but the sadness and loss of two years apart was taking its toll.

Kiyoka Fujita, a young, bright woman who had stepped in for Paul Hamada, had been filing short stories for The Review on births, marriages, vegetable harvests and baseball games since her initiation as a reporter. In September she wrote Will and said she'd like to try something "bigger and more important." She called it "segregation." Two weeks later, Will read the story aloud to Molly in The Review's small office.

"The War Relocation Authority, under increasing pressure from the US Senate and the Army, has decided to separate Japanese American evacuees into categories and ship them to different camps, depending on their loyalty to America."

"Pretty good lead, huh?" Will said.

"Yes," Molly answered, "but it's horrible news. I think it means they will separate families, something DeWitt has pledged not to do."

"Yeah, right, since when have you trusted DeWitt?" Will read on.

"Pressure came from many fronts to segregate loyal evacuees from quote disloyal evacuees and quote troublemakers. The Japanese American Citizens League supports the segregation program."

"Wow," Will said. "I wonder what the JACL reasoning is." He went on.

"Certain evacuees, after research and interviews, will be sent to Tule Lake, California, a high-security center. WRA officials cited the type of individuals who will be segregated:

"Those who applied for expatriation or repatriation to Japan and have not withdrawn their application.

"Those who answered 'no' to the loyalty question or refused to answer it.

"Those who were denied leave clearance due to some adverse evidence in their records.

"Aliens from Department of Justice internment camps that have been recommended for detention.

"Family members who chose to remain with their families."

Will was shaking his head as he read the final paragraphs.

"The WRA anticipates that thousands of evacuees will be moved *from* Tule Lake and thousands more will be moved *to* the high-security center. Already, according to camp administrators in Hunt, Idaho, security is being increased. A double eight-foot fence is being built, the Army guard is being increased to a full battalion and numerous tanks will be patrolling the perimeter.

"Evacuees at Camp Minidoka have expressed anger and disappointment to camp officials, especially those who answered one of the loyalty questions unsatisfactorily and family members who say they are being given an impossible choice."

Kiyoka Fujita.

"Wow. Good job girl." Will turned to Molly. "The US Army strikes again. I wish she had named a source over there. But I think we'll run it anyway. What do you think?"

"Yes, of course. But I'm still stuck on the families. What a horrible choice. And it's just one more slap in the face. How much of this can these people endure?" Molly turned away and stared at her desk. She was picturing the double eight-foot fences with barbed wire, the tanks clanking around the perimeter and the machine guns. Then she thought of Paul Hamada, Rick and the Kitanos. "And I think I'm discouraged, " she muttered to herself.

Bert was able to find an empty table in the mess hall with a light over it. Men in the back were still cleaning up after the evening meal. He sat down with several sheets of yellow lined paper and the wooden pencil he carried with him in his breast pocket.

"*Dearest Lin:*

I have your last letter and was cheered up by it. I always like hearing what's going on at the place and in you. I missed some news about Toto. I hope he is doing OK patrolling the farm and keeping you company.

I am doing OK. I am glad to have Mutt, Suki and Amy as friends. We talk a lot. In the last week all of us have been worried about this new policy of separating the troublemakers from the rest of us and moving them to another camp in California. Mutt and I are pretty sure we will not be moved, but it's not very clear how they are going to decide.

People here are very emotional about it. Some people have said they are disloyal just to get out of here and back to California. Others are so frustrated with the Army that they say they're fed up with the whole process and tell the officers to their face that they're not loyal. I don't get that. Still others who are pretty old, or pretty young, or handicapped in some way, almost have to go, if the head of their family goes. It is a mess, again.

Mutt and I agree—this is just one more insult to all of us. At this point in the war and in our imprisonment, what difference will it make? Is this country so insecure about the threat of these people in camps that they have to do this?

Well, not to worry you honey. I think I'll be just fine here, but it is hard to see hundreds of people around me in such distress about this. There are still rumors about freedom for all of us, but they are still just rumors. No one is officially talking about it.

We had a great harvest this year. It's remarkable what we can do together with land that was so barren and in conditions that are not the best by a long shot. We are practically feeding ourselves here and I have learned some things that I think will help us at home.

Home. There's a word. Lin, I love you and miss you terribly.

Keep writing as I live for your letters.
                    Yours always, Bert

PS - Thanks for the birthday card. I celebrated with Mutt and his family and we had a can of pretty good tuna and some muffins after.

CHAPTER FORTY-THREE

In the fall of 1943, 6,000 Japanese Americans were moved out of the Tule Lake camp to other camps, and more than 12,000 were bussed into the California camp, a mass migration by any definition. That fall and winter and into the next summer, 16,400 evacuees were crammed into Tule Lake. More than 11,000 were legal citizens of the United States.

The food, the facilities, the living quarters and the environment were inferior to the camps the evacuees came from. It was a period of turmoil, impoverishment, uncertainty and violence. Suspicion and conflict were plagues on the camp's prisoners. Evacuees were fired from their jobs in groups and, after protests, reinstated. There were strikes, a string of accidents in the camp's light industry, work stoppages and withholding of food. Medical care was spotty at best. The Army became more and more repressive, without explanation.

As 1943 drew to an end, hundreds of evacuees at Tule Lake rioted, after witnessing white men from the WRA taking food from an evacuee mess hall and loading it into their own truck. Hundreds of men gathered around the administration building. The Army moved in with pistols, rifles, baseball bats, tear gas, machine guns and tanks to restore order. For three months following, martial law was in effect. MP's patrolled in tanks and jeeps. There were unannounced inspections of men in barracks at all hours of the day and night. Anything that could be used as a weapon was confiscated, including scissors, garden tools, pocket knives and carpenter tools. Tear gas was regularly fired at men in groups, even if they happened to be waiting to shower or gathering coal for heating.

The loyalty oath and the ensuing segregation policy had divided an entire population of Japanese Americans into camps, literally and figuratively. For thousands, this was the blackest period of their lives.

After her story ran in The Review, Kiyoka wrote to Will and said she wanted to stop writing. It was a great deal of pressure, she wrote, to get everything right and not offend the different splinter groups in the Japanese community, to say nothing of the white community. She was feeling discouraged about the impact her stories might have. Will wrote her back right away.

"No, let's not stop writing, neither one of us, girl. You have done extremely well so far. Your nose for news is a good one and I would hate to see it end, not just for me, but for you and your people.

"The Review has stuck its neck out good and proper for you people, not because you are 'you people' but because you are Americans and, temporarily, have lost the title 'citizen' that this nation guarantees to each of us born here. The news you are reporting, and this may sound like a speech, is a torch held high in the name of good American citizenship. Its flame reminds the people of Bainbridge Island and all who care to read The Review that some of our neighbors—our fellow citizens—are living elsewhere temporarily. It is a torch that has burned steadily since a tragic day in December, 1941. Don't let it go out, not for a moment. Keep this thing alive Kiyoka.

"Sincerely, Will"

By return mail, Kiyoka thanked Will and said she would continue writing.

The Selective Service announced, in December of 1943, that it would begin drafting second generation Japanese Americans into the Army. This announcement was a double-edged sword that sliced through thousands of young men in the camps. On one hand it was opportunity to serve their country, prove their loyalty and bring some degree of pride to their family. For some it was also a way to escape the terrible conditions and the boredom of the camps. On the other hand it was one more humiliation, one more slap in the face for young citizens who had been imprisoned against their will and were now being forced overseas to fight.

Service in the US Armed Services was not new to the Japanese. Nearly 33,000 served in some capacity during World War II. Many were put to good use in the Military Intelligence Service Language School, translating documents, interviewing prisoners, writing propaganda, teaching others the language and helping to break Japanese codes.

Many more enlisted in what began as the Hawaii National Guard unit and became the 100th battalion. Those men were launched into combat in North Africa in September of 1943, then almost immediately sent to Italy, where they slowly fought their way up the Italian boot from Salerno.

In late 1943 the Army put together volunteers from Hawaii and volunteers and draftees from the relocation camps to form the 442 Regimental Combat Team, made up entirely of Japanese Americans. In June of 1944 the 442nd landed in Naples and immediately joined the battle on the beach at Anzio. The men fought almost without rest that summer, and joined by the 100th battalion, fought their way into France, losing 2,000 men to wounds or death in just three months. They suffered 800 casualties in one week.

The regiment pushed on, rescuing the Seventh Army's "Lost Battalion" in France's Vosges Mountains in some of the bitterest fighting in Europe. They moved back to Italy and ended up fighting in seven major campaigns. The Japanese Americans in the 442nd earned seven Presidential Distinguished Unit Citations, one Congressional Medal of Honor, 47 Distinguished Service Crosses, 350 Silver Stars, 810 Bronze Stars and more than 3,600 Purple Hearts.

One Army general said of the combat team: "They bought an awful hunk of America with their blood. You're damn right those Nisei boys have a place in the American heart, now and forever. We cannot allow a single injustice to be done to the Nisei without defeating the purposes for which we fought."

Back on the island, Will ran two stories filed by the AP from Rome and Paris:

"Anzio Beachhead—"For gallantry in action' reads the citation which the tall West Pointer with a proud smile handed to Sgt. Melvin Tesuda and PFC Kaz Yamamoto, winners of the Silver Star.

"One of them continued to lay a telephone wire while a German machine gun killed three men beside him. The other stayed with his mortar, although wounded, and fought off the charging enemy infantry.

"Heroism is a common commodity in this doughboy outfit, in which all the enlisted men and more than half the officers are of Japanese descent. Oddly, they have the slogan: 'Remember Pearl Harbor.' Their record is figuratively written in blood: Three Distinguished Service Crosses, 21 Bronze Stars, 36 Silver Stars and 900 Purple Hearts. A large number of the awards were made posthumously.

"The Japanese-Americans didn't put it into words, but you can feel that they no longer feel it necessary to prove their patriotism. Generals have commended them honestly. They have gone through the infantryman's hell and come out unshaken."

The second story read:

"Sixth Army Group in France—A 'lost battalion' of the Seventh Army, cut off by the Germans for a week in the St. Die area, was relieved by Japanese American troops who fought brilliantly in Italy, it was disclosed today. Japanese Americans who fought their way to the trapped men late on the afternoon of October 30 were of the 442nd Regiment.

"'It was really ironic that we were so glad to see the Japanese,' said Pvt. Walter Yattaw of Providence, R.I., 'but boy, they are real Americans.'"

In the same issue was a letter The Review had received from a Lt. Col. Ernst Witte, a Seattle resident serving in Italy:

"Unless the people at home can really accord the minorities in their midst (where they have shown their trustworthiness) the freedom and tolerance we profess to be fighting for, they had better call us all home."

Will, nodding his head, turned to Molly.

"Geez, Molly, I don't think we can say it any better than that."

CHAPTER FORTY-FOUR

As the leave policies were relaxed, more and more Japanese Americans slowly scattered, like seeds in the wind, to towns in the western interior, the Midwest and the eastern seaboard. Many were reluctant to return to the West Coast, some because their families had been separated and they didn't want to come back alone and some out of fear of the reception they would get in their once hometowns.

On Bainbridge Island, as in many communities, the heat of the debate about their return rose in proportion to the number of evacuees released. The closer the Japanese Americans came to returning home, the more the rancor swelled.

In the "Open Forum" section Will had committed to run in The Review, Robert Rutherford rang the bell for the next round on November 10, 1944:

"I submit that a large majority of residents will either oppose the return of the Japs or would see them return with some dismay. I will tell you why:

"It's apparent that no other community wants them. If they are encouraged to return here, large numbers that didn't live here may settle on the island. Any intelligent person can see the complications and conflicts this would cause.

"I can tell you sincerely, from having lived in Japan, that the way of thinking, the traditions and the customs of the Japanese are so vastly different from ours that it would take at least half a century to assimilate them successfully. I personally think it would be impossible.

"The loyalty and love of America of many of the Japanese along the West Coast, including the Nisei, is *not* above suspicion. Since the removal to concentration camps, their resentment can only have grown. Again, realizing this is simply a matter of intelligence.

"Finally, as for the battalion of Japs now "dying for America" in Italy and France, death in modern war in not necessarily a matter of loyalty or self-sacrifice. It may be simply a case of being forcefully placed in the wrong place at the wrong time, where one fights and dies. Some of the best soldiers in history were quite indifferent to the cause for which they were supposed to be fighting.

"No amount of star-spangled valor on the part of conscripted Japs should change our minds one bit. We don't want any Japs back here, ever."

Robert Rutherford

Will sat down that night, with steam coming out of his ears, and wrote the longest editorial he had written during the entire war. Molly, in the office with him, brought him a cup of tea and read over his shoulder:

We run a letter from Robert Rutherford in this issue of The Review for two reasons - he signs his name, unlike some others, and two, it's a marvelous opportunity to see the difference between personal bias and "intelligence."

We don't think it takes a particularly active intellect to refuse to differentiate between a dogma-trained, culture-ridden native of Tojo's Japan and a freeborn, liberty-loving American citizen who happens to have ancestry from that island. And an intelligent man doesn't argue with invectives like 'Jap", nor does he question the loyalty of men who fight and die for their country.

We think he comes closest to being intelligent when he describes the unhappy lot that Japanese Americans face after this war is over. Because there are people like him up and down the West Coast, apparently they will be despised and hated by some, no matter the sacrifices they have made for America, including giving their lives.

Where would Mr. Rutherford have them go to lead happy lives -- that is if he cares at all? Japan? Has he exercised that intelligence enough to imagine the treatment American citizens might receive in post-war Japan? Couldn't the hatred be even more intense?

Of course some of our white American boys, who are savagely and bravely fighting the despicable "Jap" in the Pacific, will come home with a residue of anger and hatred in their hearts for anything that resembles the enemy they have been face to face with. God will forgive them that reaction, as we should too. But while those shell-shocked, upset heroes of ours are adjusting to the realization that there are some perfectly loyal Japanese American citizens here, it should be our job and the job of every citizen—including Mr. Rutherford—to help ease that transition, NOT to make it infinitely worse by stirring up racial hatred.

And with nothing else to use for argument, Mr. Rutherford's brilliant mind dredges up a grave insult to the Nisei now in the uniform of his own country! But the facts do not bear him out, not in the slightest. Many of our Japanese Americans now fighting and dying in Italy are volunteers, not draftees. For the sake of argument, even if they were drafted, how can Mr. Rutherford, writing from the comfort of his plush island home and far from the fields of battle, dare to question any individual in the trenches? What good can that possibly do?

Where, then, does that leave all the white American boys who were drafted? It leaves them facing death, not because of patriotism and loyalty, according to Mr. R., but merely because of a desire to survive. We hope he doesn't' mean that. A lot of American mothers will be very upset with him if he does. He is, again, drawing the color line.

That, in a nutshell, is Mr. Rutherford's argument: a color line, a yellow face instead of a white one. If we are to deprive people of their citizenship and despise them because of color, aren't we laying ourselves wide open on the fundamental matter of the rights of an American citizen?

Suppose, in your wildest imagination, Mr. R., that tomorrow the President should decree that everyone named Rutherford, or from England, would be removed from their homes and trundled off to the desert, there to be ongoing objects of our scorn. Does it matter that a name is Rutherford, or Whitman, and not Yamamoto?

We don't think it's especially intelligent to shout to the rooftops that 'We don't want any Japs back here, ever.' We are trying to write about a kind of intelligence that this country will need to resolve its post-war problems, including those of race and color.

The Review has, for many months now, stood up for these Japanese Americans, it is true. Basically, to us, it makes no difference whether or not the people we are defending are Japanese Americans, Italian Americans, German Americans, red headed Americans or Rutherford Americans. Each one is an American and, as such, is guaranteed—<u>guaranteed</u>, Mr. R.—certain rights that The Review will always defend.

Molly stood <u>behind</u> Will with her hands on his shoulders. She kissed him on the crown of his head.

"That just smokes, sweetie. I'm proud of you."

Colleen came running up the front steps and banged on the door.

"Molly, are you home?"

Molly strode out of the kitchen and opened the door. "What is it?"

"Have you seen this?" Colleen said, waving a white postcard in front of her face.

"No. Just slow down a minute and let me read it."

"WHAT WILL WE DO WITH THE JAPS? Come to a community meeting Wednesday night, 6 p.m. at the Grange Hall and help us decide. Don't be fooled by The Review -- red, white and blue blood is not improved by yellow blood. Come one, come all."

"God, they're at it again."

CHAPTER FORTY-FIVE

The Grange Hall on Bainbridge Island is a wooden rectangular building built up off the ground level, sitting just off the highway about two miles from the ferry dock. Inside it is cavernous and dark, with no insulation or dry wall. There is a raised platform at one end, just a simple wooden box large enough for a dozen chairs. It is dimly lit and, on this fall evening, chilly.

There are about 200 people assembled on benches, wooden chairs and steel folding chairs as the meeting begins. Will, sitting in the back right hand side, turns and says to Molly: "There must be more frustration built up than we realized. I must admit, I'm a little nervous."

As people filed inside four men handed out pamphlets. Will and Molly read one together. It summarized anti-Japanese opinions and outlined a plan to have all Japanese shipped to islands in the Pacific that the US had conquered during the war. The flier contained some of the ugliest language Will had seen.

The meeting was mostly made up of comments from the audience, with Rutherford at the front calling on people. There were few questions. One-by one, men and women from all walks of life stood up and spoke.

Sometimes there was scattered applause or a wave of muttering in the crowd. Sometimes there was low mutterings of disapproval. But there were no shouts, no accusations, no threats. On the whole, the meeting, despite some of the views expressed, could be called civilized.

An Army veteran of World War I, who identifies himself as a member of Mr. Rutherford's group, "The Live and Let Live Legion," got things rolling:

"Long before Pearl Harbor the Army and Navy intelligence and the FBI knew that a certain number of traitors existed in the Japanese colonies along the West Coast. They also knew that there were still a larger number of their countrymen who were aware of these disloyal Japanese and tolerated them in their midst.

"For this reason, when our fleet was partly demolished and 2,300 of our men killed in Hawaii, every single Japanese American, born here or not, was removed and placed in a concentration camp. The military necessity of this evacuation, which I have never doubted, makes me, and many people I know, reluctant to have these people as neighbors again.

"The fighting spirit some of these Japanese have demonstrated in recent months does furnish an attenuating circumstance. However, I doubt that it will outweigh the serious grievances against the Japanese along our West Coast or make us welcome them back with open arms.

"The newspaper on this island has undertaken a long campaign to persuade us to see the Japanese in a different light. I think this is done, frankly, out of ignorance of what the real Japanese is like and what they are capable of. This is indeed a grave matter for all of us at this juncture and is vital to the future of our small island. Thank you."

A woman saying she was a shipyard worker on the island stood up quickly and said: "I'd like to know who this Mr. Whitman is. Why does he always stand up for the Japs? How did he get to be such a Jap lover? Maybe he *is* a Jap."

"I think we're all one big family on this island," said a frail older woman who said she had a son fighting in Italy. "Now we've got a family problem and I think we ought to keep our heads and work it out fairly. Name calling and racist talk is not going to solve anything."

A middle-aged man in dirty work clothes spoke: "Look, Japanese lives as well as American lives are going to be saved if we don't permit them back on the island. I respect the Japanese, especially those who are fighting for us, but I predict there are going to be race riots here if we don't make them live somewhere else."

A man and woman, both with gray hair, stood in the middle of the room and the man spoke: "My boy just left to fight the Japs a long way from home. I hope to God he comes back safe. If he comes back maimed in some way I don't think he'll take it out on any Japs on the Island, but I don't know how he will react. I don't think he'll want to see them every day. Maybe Mr. Whitman can help. Maybe he can run more things in his paper that will prevent trouble. I think the boys who have served overseas have seen enough trouble."

A young blond man in a rumpled work coat stood up in the back of the room and waved for attention:

"This is a little hard to say at this meeting, but from my point of view we can't just suspend the Constitution and Bill of Rights. I think we've done enough of that so far. Every Japanese I know, or have seen, are law-abiding, hard-working, family-oriented men and women who contribute to our community. They pay their bills, they raise their children to be kind and decent, they don't want something for nothing – in short they are model citizens. How can we separate them from the Russians, Poles, Italians and Filipinos who also live and work on the island? I just don't get it." He paused for a moment and spoke to a man beside him. "This 'Live and Let Live' group doesn't seem to live up to its name. I think that's all the Japanese want, to be left alone so they can live their lives. This island, only twelve by four miles, is ours. We can create something here that could be a model for the rest of the country, but not if it's in the direction this meeting is going."

Some of the older white men in the front booed. One stood and said: "Sit down boy. You're too young to really know what this is about." A wave of low talking swept through the crowd.

An older man with a cane slowly got to his feet.

"I am a veteran. I was born in this country, in Teaneck New Jersey. Do you want to send me home? I have worked for a Japanese man, for three years. He has been fair and decent to me and his children have been very kind. I personally don't see how we can say to any man who has fought for his country, a country he loves, that he can't come home and live where he wants to. I was lucky enough to be born a citizen and I'll tell you one thing tonight: if someone here tried to take my rights away, he'd have an awful fight on his hands."

Will and Molly took notes furiously, helping each other and taking turns as each person spoke. The crowd grew quiet as a tall, sandy haired man stood up from the front row of seats and took the platform. Will stirred in his seat and elbowed Molly.

"Good evening, I'm Robert Rutherford. Thank you for coming tonight." He stood with his hands folded behind him and had the bearing of a military man. He spoke in an even voice that was laced with confidence.

"I'd like to start by suggesting that Mr. Whitman read the Declaration of Independence. When our founding fathers wrote that 'all men are created equal,' they were referring to themselves and other men like them. They meant that all white men are created equal." There was ripple through the crowd and many people sat shaking their heads. "We're crazy in America if we think people of all different races can live together peacefully, that is unless some of them are unsexed.

"The Japanese, as I have said before, are a different animal than us. They're human yes, but cunning and treacherous. Their concept of morality is much different than yours and mine. Believe me, if they come back here there are going to be race riots and they are going to come after us. There is not a doubt in my mind that the Hirohito Japs are in cahoots with our Japs. Mark my words.

"On a personal level, I don't want my kids going to school with them. I don't want my wife rubbing elbows in the grocery store with them. I don't want them causing the kind of trouble that would endanger my family. I just don't like them. Never have, never will, and all of us would be a lot better off if they went somewhere else.

"Now, having said that, I would like to urge you to read the pamphlets that were handed to you and watch for the notice of another meeting of our committee. The meeting is adjourned. Thank you."

Will and Molly sat in their chairs quietly as the men and women slowly made their way out of the large room and into the night. To Will it felt like he was sitting in a bathtub of water that was cooling off and he had pulled the plug, lying there while the water slowly drained out around him and formed a whirlpool around the drain. Slowly the men and women left and the hall grew quiet. He was, at the same time, agitated and empty, angry and grateful, discouraged and determined. He put his arm around Molly and they waited in order to leave last. What can you say to a man like Rutherford? How did we human beings get to be so different from one another? How would he put all this into words? Would his words make any difference at all?

Molly saw that his head was spinning with thoughts like a overloaded Washing machine on a spin cycle. She squeezed his arm and they walked out into the cool, moist air.

Over the next two weeks Molly took control of "The Open Forum." She ran every letter the small weekly received, as long as it was signed. She dedicated page after page to letters, long and short, from all corners of the island, expressing wide ranges of opinion. Included were half a dozen letters from Japanese American soldiers commenting on their return home and what they had heard from their families. One letter, from a first generation Japanese sergeant serving in France, contained one sheet of paper with only these words:

"Give me your tired, your poor,
Your huddled masses yearning to breathe free
The wretched refuse to your teeming shore,
Send these, the homeless, tempest-tossed to me,
I lift my lamp beside the golden door.
        --The Mother of Exiles"

Will was working on an editorial that would pull together varied points of view and express his thoughts and feelings after the meeting at the Grange. At Molly's urging, he wanted to temper the emotion and call up all the logic and compassion he could muster. He sat looking at his masthead "BAINBRIDGE REVIEW —an independent newspaper" and he stared at the cartoon they had used since they bought the newspaper nearly five years ago – a newspaper boy, cap askew, running down the street and offering a newspaper: "Extra," he shouted.

That's what we all need now, he thought, just a little bit extra, and he warmed up his fingers on the old Royal's keys.

THE ANTI-JAPANESE SPEAK

Some 200 of the 7,000 people on this island attended a meeting last week which discussed action to prevent the return here of those of Japanese ancestry whom the Army evacuated more than two years ago.

OK. Factual. Calm, he thought to himself.

The Review fails to see that numbers are important in the basic consideration of this problem. The point is that some free American citizens decided to hold a meeting and speak their minds in free assembly. This, The Review thinks, is good.

Fine. Free speech -- gotta be for that.

The Review realizes only too well that the Island, like many other communities on the West Coast, must face up to a serious problem in the impending return to this part of the country of evacuees. Our readers have always been welcome to use our Open Forum to discuss issues, for only by discussion and thought can America solve its many postwar problems. Feeling this way, The Review certainly welcomes any public meetings to thrash things out.

OK, fine, now get on with it.

The Review, of course, cannot subscribe to some of the extreme ideas presented at last week's meeting. For years now, we have stood by one point and one point only. We still say, despite the gathering here last week, that the majority of Islanders believe with us in that point, namely that citizenship rights guaranteed in our Constitution must not be tossed aside because of war hysteria.

Clear. Simple. Good, go on.

We believe it is a dangerous thing for us to suddenly decide that we will deprive one group of citizens of their inherent rights under the Constitution. We believe we speak for the majority when we say that the destruction of one group's rights could easily lead to the loss of rights for any other group in our country. This is the awful thing that happened in Fascist Italy and Nazi Germany. We are sure America wants none of this.

None of what? Loss of their rights? Maybe you should emphasize that.

Certainly, The Review admires the exercise of free speech demonstrated last week and guaranteed by our Constitution. We hope those who disagree with us similarly respect our use of the right of a free press. In this we regret to note that two people who had the interest and courage to speak out in opposition to the majority of folks at the meeting were heckled and had their patriotism questioned.

OK, don't get petty. Stick to the big idea.

Surely that is not the way to arrive at a sensible solution to this problem. We are very near, indeed, to a totalitarian situation in this country if those who disagree with us must be called unpatriotic.

We hope that those who would bar the return of our evacuee citizens will remember at their next free American assembly that they meet under the protection of the greatest governmental document ever written – the Constitution of the United States.

All right, let's finish strong. Stay reasonable.

Let all of us be guided less by hysteria and blind war-inflamed viewpoints. Let us, instead, turn to logic. Above all, let us take care that none of us destroy the very guarantee that gives us as American citizens – the right to free speech and free assembly.

"Mol. Hey, Mol, will you come read this?"

CHAPTER FORTY-SIX

The following morning Will felt at loose ends, walking around the house, aimless and stirred up. Molly had gone to Seattle for the day, for a doctor's appointment and shopping at Pike Place Market. The paper was done for the week. He poured himself a second cup of coffee and sat down by the phone. He dialed a familiar number.

"Good morning, Seattle Times, how can I help you?"

"Joseph McIntire please."

"May I tell him who's calling?"

"Will Whitman."

Joseph McIntire had hired Will some years ago as a cub reporter and moved him up to the city desk. McIntire was a veteran newspaperman and came from a family of journalists. He was now editor in chief of the Times. Tough, cynical and intelligent, he was well respected in the city and had remained Will's good friend.

"Joe, I just wanted to talk with you for a minute or two. Do you have time?"

"You caught me at a good time Will. What's on your mind?"

"Well, I guess you could say the whole Japanese question; more specifically the internment, their eventual release and return home and what waits for them."

"Yeah. It's tricky, isn't it? I have been reading your stuff."

"And?"

"Well, you're consistent. I admire you and you're out there on a limb nearly by yourself."

"Do you agree with me?"

"Well Will, I wouldn't say I agree with everything you say. I mean there was a military emergency after all."

"Yeah, Joe, but if we hand ourselves over to the military every time there's a perceived emergency and take away rights, we're in deep do-do."

"Maybe you're right. But the Supreme Court has gone along with this. They're ruled it was a matter of military expediency, a national emergency."

"I know, I know. That still doesn't make it right."

"You're stubborn Will; I'll give you that. Also, you and I face a little different situation. You are out there on that island and you're publisher, editor and copy boy. You don't have to answer to anyone but your own conscience. And maybe Molly. I've got to answer to an editorial board and the family that owns this paper, and they're tough. It's more of editorial-by-committee over here."

"I know Joe." Will sighed. "I don't envy you that."

"Well, it is safer, in a way."

"Yes, I suppose you can hide behind that if you want." Will instantly regretted saying it.

"Ouch."

"Don't take that personally. I just mean…what do I mean? That sometimes it gets lonely out here. And you can stand behind the group, the owners if you need to, as long as you all agree."

"Well, I'm holding my own with them and so far we're pretty much in agreement."

"I guess I'm happy for you Joe. I'm just trying to say what I believe in."

"Will, have you ever thought what kind of bind the Army has been in?"

"Sure. First you come out with a plan that says you can't determine loyalty at all. So take everybody away. Then you say, oops, we can determine who is loyal and we're going to let some of these guys back on the West

Coast to work near a high explosives plant or an airport. Then you'd be forced to admit that you made a horrible mistake."

"What about the possibility of landing Jap paratroopers dressed as civilians? That would be confusing as hell. I think things like that are still a real possibility."

"OK, suppose you dropped white folks dressed as civilians. Does that mean you evacuate all white folks? That doesn't make any sense."

"White people are not a threat. The danger is the Japanese."

"Not on the east coast. They're worried about white folks like Italians and Germans...and we can't tell them apart."

"Well, there are just too many of them out there."

"Too many what?"

"Too many Europeans that have assimilated into the general population."

"Well, too many people is not the issue. If we -- your example -- dropped white paratroopers in civilian clothes on the east coast, that would be confusing as hell too. We'd have a tough time saying who was loyal until they started shooting us."

"Well, Germany wouldn't do that on the West Coast."

"That's not the point Joe. It was your example about the threat of paratroopers who look the same and the threat that represents. I think that's remote, no matter what color the paratroopers are. I think this gets back to the loyalty issue and that the entire military is deathly afraid of saying it made a mistake."

"What do you mean?"

"OK, the Army says we've got to send these people away because it's a military emergency and we can't tell a loyal Jap from a disloyal Jap – DeWitt's now famous 'A Jap is a Jap" statement. So we send them all. Then the Army, or the WRA anyway, slaps this loyalty oath on them. Inherent in the loyalty oath idea is that notion that you can determine who is loyal and who is not. Then they say we're going to separate them into categories of loyal, disloyal and troublemakers. And they profess to have way to do that. So they're contradicting themselves. The whole loyalty oath idea destroys the argument that you can't tell one from the other."

"I see what you're saying."

"I mean if I can give a group of people a test of some kind and cull out the bad guys and send them away and let the others live their lives, why the hell didn't I do that in the beginning? Either we can determine who is loyal, or we can't."

"Will, I think you're on to something, but it's an argument that will be lost on the bureaucracy."

"Joe, I'll tell you the truth. The more I do think about this and the longer it goes on, the more it stinks. You might expect that I would get used to it, or something like that. But I just get more and more angry and, frankly, disillusioned."

"You always were an idealistic SOB."

"Yep. I guess it's a blessing and a curse. You know Joe, I think it's the same as with the colored people. We look at them as a group, not as individual human beings. We paint them all with the same brush. Maybe it's us who colors colored people. I just thought of that in that way. Maybe they're not really colored, but we color them."

"What the hell do you mean by that?"

"Well, it's our eyes that do the 'coloring'. Stay with me here. Look what we did to the Indians. We put them all, regardless of what they thought or felt, into 'relocation centers,' if you will. And we brag to the rest of the world about being this great melting pot, but when push comes to shove, we separate them out – these people of color-- and put them into a prison all by themselves. Because—we claim—we can't tell the dangerous ones from the safe ones. So they're all dangerous. And the weird thing is that when we do that do them, they *do* become dangerous."

"Well, Will, like I said, you're an idealist. And there's the ideal and the real. Like it or not, we're still struggling in this country to live up to an ideal. Maybe we'll never get there, but I like to think we're still working on it."

"Yeah, I guess."

"Look, you've given me something to think about. And I hope I've been a good ear. I appreciate you calling Will."

"Thanks Joe. Thanks for letting me vent. And see if you can't push that editorial board my way a little. Let's keep in touch."

Will hung up the phone and wondered if he'd abused an old friendship.

CHAPTER FORTY-SEVEN

Three days later Will and Molly sat in their living room and read an Associated Press account in the Seattle Times of a congressional hearing. Will was ensconced in the old green armchair and Molly was on the arm. He could smell her clean, warm body and enjoyed her hips up against his arm. The story related an appearance before the congressional committee by Gen. John DeWitt. The committee chairman asked if DeWitt had any problems he wanted to discuss, he answered:

"I haven't any except one—that is the development of a false sentiment on the part of several individuals and some organizations to get the Japanese back on the West Coast. I don't want any of them there. They are a dangerous element. There is no way to determine their loyalty. The West Coast contains too many vital installations essential to the defense of the country to allow any Japanese on this coast. There is a feeling developing, I think, in certain sections of the country, that the Japanese should be allowed to return. I am opposing it with every proper means at my disposal.

"This same element that wants to bring them back is the same element that wanted to put them in the Army. As I told the War Department, the Japanese government—finding out that we are bringing them back—will find that the ideal place to infiltrate our men in uniform. A Jap is a Jap.

The War Department says a Jap-American soldier is not Jap, that he's an American. They can say what they want, but I have the Jap situation to take care of and I'm going to do it."

Will turned to Molly.

"Well, I'll give that old Army mule one thing. He's consistent and sticks to his guns, even if he's screwing up the whole country."

Mutt, Suki and Amy sat together in their small space in Building 22. It had been a warm afternoon but the night air was now chilly and Amy sat with a blanket pulled around her. Now 14, Amy had learned a lot in her three years in the camp, including more sophisticated English and she was already more articulate in English than her mother.

"I am not sure, Dad, about going home. I mean, I want to, but it feels kinda scary. I don't know how we'll be welcomed back." Suki scooted over next to her daughter to comfort her.

"Yes, I understand," Mutt said. "What have you been thinking about?"

"Well, you know what we've read in those copies of The Review, about the meetings and all. People there sound pretty angry, so full of hate."

"That is not everyone dear," Suki said.

"Yes, mother, but it's a small island and if a hundred people feel that way it can be big trouble for us. And I don't know what friends will be there. I don't know what happened to some of my friends."

"Yes, it may be a little uncomfortable for a while. But is that worse than where we are now?"

"No, I guess not. But maybe we could go somewhere else, somewhere and start over again. I hear that some families are going to do that."

"No Amy. We will go home, when the time comes," Mutt said. "We have our land and we have our house. Mr. Baker has taken care of our property and we have friends there."

"You have friends Dad. I don't know if I do." Amy's eyes filled with tears.

"We still have each other dear," Suki said. "We are fortunate. We have more than most. Try to be grateful for that."

After Amy and Suki had settled into their beds, Mutt sat down by the low light of a kerosene lamp and wrote in his journal.

"Of all the days and nights in this place that god has forgotten, the times that Amy and Suki are sad or afraid are the hardest for me. It breaks my heart to think of the time that they have taken from my daughter, of the years that she cannot replace. This is only a small piece of my life and Suki and I will be OK, but three years out of Amy's young life is a long time.

"The longer this goes on, the harder it becomes to think about home and going back to the way things were. It seems impossible. So much has changed. The world has changed and it will never be the same. I trust Milt and believe that we will have our property again, but what will it be like? Can we still sell our beets? Is our home still standing? Will there be a community to go home to or will it be groups of angry people?"

Mutt paused and put his pencil to his lips. The wind rattled the windowpanes.

"One thing is very difficult for me. I have lost the feeling that I am a good father and a successful head of this family. I know Amy and Suki still love me, but I have lost so much, so much…what…confidence. I no longer have the feeling that I am in control of my life. My life is not mine. It belongs to the US government, or at least it has for three years. If I have lost that…how much is that worth? How can you measure a man's life as being any good if he does not respect himself anymore? How can I get that back?"

CHAPTER FORTY-EIGHT

The civilian officials in the Roosevelt administration -- in the War Department and the War Relocation Authority – had fought a protracted battle with the generals in the Army –headed by DeWitt – over the return of the Japanese to the West Coast. The Secretary of War and his aides had determined that there was no longer a military necessity to keep thousands of people in prison camps and openly spoke—albeit only amongst themselves—about ending the "exclusion." It was announced that Nisei soldiers on leave would be allowed to return to their home communities. There were rumors that DeWitt was about to be relieved of his post.

But DeWitt was by no means alone, nor was he done fighting. Sentiment in the press, in Congress and in pockets of the public on the West Coast reacted to the leave program initiated by the WRA and the promise inherent in administering the loyalty oath. Civic groups, local governments, state agencies and groups such as the American Legion rose up with a fervor similar to that of December of 1941. Governments at many levels began debating restrictive policies should the Japanese return. The Arizona legislature passed a bill curtailing the liberties of returning evacuees and the

State of Arkansas decided it was illegal for any ethnic Japanese to own land in the state.

Congressman began issuing press releases about how evacuees had been overfed and pampered in camps. One representative claimed there had been a whole division of Japanese soldiers on the West Coast before the Pearl Harbor attack. Investigations were launched and claims were made that spies and saboteurs were being released into the general population.

The press eagerly joined the fray. *The San Francisco Chronicle* sided with DeWitt and, citing the probability of riots, waved aside the "ethical factors, the constitutional factors and the Bill of Rights." *The Los Angeles Times,* apparently waving aside logic, said the end of imprisonment for the Japanese was "stupid and dangerous." The editorial went on to fan the flames of fear:

"How much of the recent smashing defeat for reelection of former Governor Olson of California was due to his suggestion that the Japs be recalled for agricultural work cannot be estimated, but it was undoubtedly considerable. There are worse things than food shortages.

"As a race, the Japanese have made for themselves a record for conscienceless treachery unsurpassed in history. Whatever small theoretical advantages there might be in releasing those under restraint in this country would be enormously outweighed by the risks involved."

Despite this tide of emotional argument, which had prevailed for three years, more compassionate voices prevailed. The WRA itself took on the congressional committee formed to investigate the possible return of Japanese Americans to their homes, openly challenging congressmen.

The Washington Post took on the Army:

"The general (De Witt) should be told that American democracy and the Constitution of the United States are too vital to be ignored and flouted by any military zealot. The panic of Pearl Harbor is now past. There has been ample time for the investigation of these people and the determination of their loyalty to this country on an individual basis. Whatever excuse there once was for evacuating and holding them indiscriminately no longer exists."

Finally, in the spring of 1944, President Roosevelt received a recommendation from the War Department that the Japanese be allowed to return to their homes. The Secretaries of the Interior and Justice agreed. Interior Secretary Harold Ickes told Roosevelt in June: "The continued retention of these innocent people in the relocation centers would be a blot upon the history of the nation."

The blot on the nation's history would remain a while longer. The President would wait to make a public decision – until after the election in November of 1944. Six more months would pass for 100,000 people behind barbed wire.

In the first Cabinet meeting after that election, there was agreement to end the imprisonment of Japanese Americans. On December 15 the Army gave the Roosevelt administration a list of nearly 96,000 names of people who had been cleared for release. Twenty thousand children would be added to that list.

On December 17, 1944, three years and ten days after the attack on Pearl Harbor, Public Proclamation Number 21 was issued.

CHAPTER FORTY-NINE

Will and Molly were in the offices of The Review talking about Christmas cards and what they might give Colleen and Frank. Molly was opening the mail.

"Will, here it is –Public Proclamation 21 they call it."

"Lemme see." He took it from Molly's hand, scanned it and began to read aloud:

"To the people within the states of Arizona, California, Idaho, Montana, Nevada, Oregon, Utah and Washington and the Public generally..."

"Let's see...they cite 'substantial improvement in the military situation.'"

"Whereas, the present military situation makes possible modification and relaxation of restrictions and the termination of the system of mass exclusion of persons of Japanese ancestry as hereinafter provided and permits the substitution for mass exclusion of a system of individual determination and exclusion of those individuals whose presence within the sensitive areas of the Western Defense Command is deemed a source of potential danger to the military security thereof...

"So," Will said, looking at his wife. "That means no more racism, only deciding things on an individual basis." Molly smiled and nodded. Will continued to read aloud.

"The effect of the rescission…and the purpose of this Public Proclamation is to restore to all persons of Japanese ancestry who were excluded ---blah blah blah---their full rights to enter and remain in the military areas of the Western Defense Command. The people of the states situated within the WDC are assured that the records of all persons of Japanese ancestry have been carefully examined and only those persons who have been cleared by military authority have been permitted to return. They should be accorded the same treatment…" Will raised his voice…"and allowed to enjoy the same privileges accorded other law abiding American citizens or residents. Effective midnight Jan. 2, 1945."

"My god! Finally! I've got goose bumps Mol."

"Me too sweetie."

"Let's get our story ready."

The proclamation was posted on the bulletin board in the mess hall in Camp Minidoka and Bert and Mutt stood reading it.

"Is this it Mutt? Is this the end?" He turned to Mutt who had tears slowly making their way down his brown cheeks. He waved his hand, asking for a moment to clear his throat.

"It sure looks that way. It sure does. Let's read the whole thing."

"January 5, that's not even two weeks away."

Henry Kitano walked up behind them and read the proclamation. He stood shaking his head and his breathing deepened and became faster. He looked at Mutt and Bert. "Wow."

"How about your dad?" Mutt asked him.

Henry's face lit up and a slight smile crossed his face.

"I was able to talk to him two days ago, by phone. We talked for half an hour. He's still at Tule Lake and that's where the 4,000 'troublemakers' are. We think they've interviewed him and, knowing my dad, that should go OK. But I really won't know things are for sure until we all set foot on the island."

"How was he?"

"Thanks for asking." The younger man's face dropped. "I think he's depressed. He missed my mom in the worst way. He's worried about what people back home are thinking. He has no idea what his house is going to be like. He sounds sad and lifeless; I can hear it in his voice. He even hinted at staying at Tule Lake, as bad as it is."

"Yeah? Really?"

"Well, at least that's a certainty, in his mind anyway. But you should have heard him talk about the camp. Compared to Tule, we've got it good. There's not enough food for everyone there. The toilets and showers are awful. Every piece of mail is censored and they can't have visitors. But the worst was the bull pen."

"The bull pen?"

"Yeah. Most prisoners live in wooden shacks with no insulation or any facilities, but the so-called hard-core prisoners are kept outside in tents in a stockade in the middle of the camp. Everyone calls it the bullpen. There's nothing there, nothing. There's maybe a thousand people living on the ground, the whole winter, with just a couple of blankets. If they get sick or hurt, too bad. They just lay on the ground and suffer."

"God," Mutt said, "no wonder he's depressed, just seeing that every day."

"Exactly. And I think he has some guilt operating too. Like, if he leaves and all those people stay, he's in some way abandoning them. It's really a terrible situation. And you know he's not alone in the way he feels."

"No, you're right," Bert said. "It sounds like the worst place for him to be. Sorry Henry." He put his hand on Henry's back.

"Well, I wish him the best," Mutt said. I wish there was something we could do. But right now I've got to get back to Suki and Amy. We've got a lot to talk about."

Will was stomping around the office, picking up pencils and odd pieces of paper and setting them down again. He moved the phone over a few inches, picked up the handset and put it back down. He pulled up the belt-line on his khakis. He scratched his head.

The Christmas season was hard for him. He wanted to get into the spirit of the holidays but the commercialism of it all rankled him. He found it difficult to give and receive gifts, believing that whatever he chose to give, it would end up in the back of a closet somewhere and whatever he received he would have to be grateful for it even when he didn't like it. This led him, most Christmases, to a bah-humbug kind of mood, eventually balanced out by Molly's shiny optimism and generosity of spirit.

Today he wanted to write something that was real but not so gloomy. He gave it a shot.

A MOCKERY

Last week's Review was filled with messages from your business and professional friends on the Island, wishing you a "Merry Christmas." This issue has a number of similar messages for "Happy New Year"

The same people at The Review who turned cold type into those warm messages also took other type and, in the news columns, wrote fateful accounts of how the war had claimed this and that Island boy, of how war had turned mass suspicion on a large group of our one-time Island neighbors, of how war in many different ways had done everything to make us forget what the Prince of Peace said.

We got to thinking, what a mockery those good wishes seemed to be. "Merry Christmas" must be an awful mockery for nice Mrs. Majors, whose young husband, Stan, lies dead in France. "Happy New Year" must be a miserable mockery to Jim Tanaka, one of our finest citizens, who sits down there in Manzanar, a pall of suspicion on him and his kind. How can anybody see anything in this world to make him "merry" or to give him hope for future happiness?

That was my dour outlook until last Saturday, when we heard a New Zealander speak on the radio. He told us that a lot of time was being spent on the form that the forthcoming international organization of free nations would take. He said the form was not important. He said there was only one thing that caused success or failure in international peace plans.

He said, and we were mighty thrilled to hear his words, that the separate nations must adopt the same kind of morality that is adopted by individuals who live together in peace in their own nations, that there can't be one code for individuals and one for nations.

Civilized individuals, he said, live together under a code based on right and wrong. Nations can too, he said. There is no hope for an international peace organization that lives by appeasement and power politics. Our only hope lies in nations getting together on the basis of right or wrong.

It wasn't a particularly emotional speech. It sounds less thrilling in the words we have used to condense it. But, to us at The Review, it means everything.

This kind of philosophy can only be lived out from the individuals who make up the peace-loving nations. That means you and me and the fellow next to us. It doesn't mean an ambiguous, mysterious "leader" will save us, for our leaders in this democracy reflect only the temper of their people.

So we feel a little calmer in our troubled mind; we think less of the mockery there could be in our seasonal greetings. We think of what those messages have meant down through the ages as mankind has struggled and continues to struggle for the things we know are right, fair and just. We think there is hope in the death of Stan Majors and the evacuation of Jim Tanaka.

We think there is still hope as 1945 approaches—hope for a world where enough individuals shall insist on the Golden Rule and hope for Merry Christmases and new years to come.

I've got to add something a little more upbeat, he thought to himself. Where is Molly when I need her? Thumbing through his Roget's Thesaurus, he came across a quote he had marked several years ago. He added it to the end of the editorial.

"Nothing that is worth doing can be achieved in our lifetime; therefore, we must be saved by hope. Nothing which is true or beautiful or good makes complete sense in any immediate context of history; therefore, we must be saved by faith. Nothing we do, however virtuous, can be accomplished alone; therefore, we are saved by love."

Reinhold Niebuhr

CHAPTER FIFTY

In the first three months of 1945, there was a trickle of Japanese Americans out from the camps. Many Nisei were either in the service, on farms in the Midwest or had migrated to the east coast, leaving their parents, and sometimes their children, in the camps. The men and women in the camps were not at all sure, in many cases, where or when to go, once they decided to leave. A mass movement was about to get underway, slowly and carefully. Older men and women would move east to join their children. Some children would move west to rejoin their aging parents and some families would head back to their homes, farms and businesses, uncertain what they would find or how they would support themselves.

Finally, the War Relocation Authority scheduled closing dates for all the camps, save Tule Lake. The agency gave the evacuees train fare and an allowance of $25 and put them on a train. Housing for those returning was uncertain. Employment, food, family reunions, and personal safety – all were up in the air.

One thing was certain. Racism was alive and well in the California, Oregon and Washington communities they returned to. "No Japs allowed" "Japs go home" "No Japs here" signs greeted some in their home cities. Violence, to their bodies, their homes and their businesses greeted others.

One hundred thousand people were now facing the task of beginning their lives all over again, many of them in a context they had ever faced before, an atmosphere of mistrust, alienation and hatred.

Mutt, Amy and Suki stood just outside the camp, two battered suitcases and a large duffel bag lay at their feet. They each held a small paper envelope with $25 in cash in it. They squinted against the afternoon sun and the swirling dust. They looked for the bus, keeping their backs to the camp. Hundreds of other evacuees made their way out of the big wooden and barbed wire gates that had been closed for three years. The dust swirled around them, nipping at their eyes and mouths, and out of the north an old gray and red bus pulled up beside them.

Henry Kitano Sr. was reunited with his wife Edna, his son and his wife Carol and their children in a shelter in downtown Seattle. They had taken separate trains into the city and been led to a large room in a basement of an office building, taken over by the WRA to organize and escort evacuees back to their homes. Henry Sr. walked into the dimly lit room and saw his family sitting together in a small circle of chairs in the back of the room. He could barely walk to see them, shuffling his feet and crying until they saw him coming and ran to surround him, hugging each other, crying out loud. The old man would have dropped to his knees, but the family held him up and helped him to a chair. Soon they looked around the big room and saw that other families were having the same tearful reunions.

On the ferry back to Bainbridge there were many reunions, old friends greeting each other and talking in hushed tones. Henry Sr. sat with his family in a booth, his arm around Edna, talking to his son, Carol and the grandchildren. To Henry, his family seemed comfortably familiar and, at the same time, different. What he had seen and experienced, beginning with the forced removal from his home and in his three years behind fences, remained in front of his eyes, coloring the present, staining his reunion. Still, he tried to connect.

"You know, once upon a time a good many of us old folks talked about, and maybe hoped, to go back to Japan to spend the last few years of our lives. But the war, and this evacuation, ended all that. Now I just want to go back to the island and live out my life in some peace. My son will take care of me," he said and patted Henry Jr. on the knee. "In a funny way it'll be like going back to Japan. Bainbridge has been my home for over 30 years, and although I do not know many of the Caucasians I meet on the street, the streets are still there, the ferry dock looks the same, the same beaches, the same trees, and the buildings have the same corners that they occupied when we left. It may be a fine thing for the Nisei to pioneer in other parts of the country, but when you are 64 years old, you want to return home and this is home to most of us older people. The pigeons and the seagulls are probably not the same pigeons and seagulls that we saw in 1941, but they will look the same to me. I'm just glad to be on this ferry."

Once on Bainbridge Island, the family was greeted by a federal employee from the WRA. He would escort the family home, he said. The ten-minute drive seemed to take a very long time. Finally the black Chevrolet sedan pulled into the long dirt driveway to the older man's home, the family craning their necks to get a glimpse of their home. Henry and Edna were out of the car first. They stood and stared at the house. The front door was open. Weeds had taken over Edna's flower beds. Windows were broken. Paint was peeling off the outside walls. They both remembered the damage inside that the FBI had done three years ago. The old man turned to look at his son, standing by the car. Henry Jr. was crying.

"At least it's still here," Edna said to her husband and smiled. "We still have a home." She hugged her husband, still looking at the house and afraid to go inside.

Mutt, Suki and Amy got off the next ferry from Seattle. They walked down the steel off ramp and paused at the bottom, Mutt in front. Suki and Amy stopped just behind him.

"Tell me this is real Suki. Tell me I'm not dreaming." Suki dropped her bags and hugged her husband from the back. Amy did the same.

They caught a ride to their farm, from a man they knew only slightly, a familiar face. They were silent in the car until they made the turn into their driveway.

"I'll bet you're glad to be here," the man said.

"You have no idea," Mutt said. "You have no idea. Thank you so much for the ride." Mutt opened the door before the car came to a stop. He pulled Suki and Amy out with him.

"We're home. We're back," he said, barely holding in his tears. The beet fields had grown over with weeds but the house seemed intact and the cherry trees were in full bloom. A slight wind out of the south rippled through Amy's hair as she ran to the house, burst through the door and ran to her room. Mutt slowly turned in a full circle, holding Suki in his arms, looking at his land.

"God! I can hardly believe it. We're home." He reached down and grabbed a handful of dirt and threw it up into the spring air.

Linda could hardly contain her feelings. Bert had called her from Seattle and now she was dashing around the house, picking up, tidying the kitchen and making the bed. Finally she scooped up Toto, tossed him on the front seat of her car and headed for the Winslow ferry dock.

It stole her breath to see Bert. He was thin and moved slowly, walking unsteadily as he came off the ferry ramp. But when he saw her he dropped his suitcase and ran for her. Toto dashed alongside her, at first not knowing why, then he recognized Bert and picked up speed. The three of them came together at the edge of the parking lot, Linda and Bert, high school sweethearts, crashing into each other and holding on tight. Toto bounced up and down like a pogo stick until Bert, at last, picked him up.

"Let's go sweetie," Bert said. "I can't wait a moment longer." They got in the car and drove back home.

Will was at the office alone. Molly was in Seattle for a doctor's visit. He had been sitting out front in the spring sunlight most of the morning, drinking coffee and thinking about the editorial he wanted to write. Just before eleven, he walked inside and settled into the familiar position in his old chair in front of his Royal. He reached out and rolled a sheet of fresh paper into the carriage and snapped the paper holder against the rubber roller.

No one can undo history. We can only hope to learn from it. To right the wrongs that have been done to a sizeable part of our society, we can only take full stock of our individual and collective consciences and move forward in a way that heals wounds and makes amends where possible.

In hindsight, the Executive Order that excluded 120,000 people from their land and homes three years ago was not justified, by military necessity or by the protection of those evacuated or for any other reason. We have to face it -- people were taken from their homes and deprived of their incomes by the powerful forces of racism and fear. The evacuation happened because of who these people are, not because of anything they had done. This is a sad, profound learning for us Americans.

We white Europeans are largely ignorant about the Japanese people. Out of that ignorance and the fear that often follows ignorance, we committed grave injustices to so many individuals and so many families. We granted them no voice, gave them no individual review and gathered no evidence against them.

They have suffered enormous damages, to their incomes, their families and their psyches. Perhaps the most lasting damages we will be unable to see, including the shame and loss of self-esteem that many will carry with them.

The worst part of this whole affair of evacuation and detention is that it was not carried out by an angry mob or by a few evil men, but it was initiated, approved and conducted by our executive branch, our congress, our armed services and our courts. Everyone, it seemed at the time, had given into fear and to racial hatred.

As Americans and as a new nation, we often look overseas and shake our fingers at others and say, "That would never happen in our country." To our credit, we have carried the banner of freedom, justice and equality high for others to follow. But there are times when we have stumbled and that banner has dragged in the dirt. It must now be our strength and our commitment to acknowledge our mistakes in this last war and to see that our imperfections are there to be learned from.

War and threats to our national security have invaded our rights and civil liberties before, more than once. During the terrible times of our Civil War, that pitted brother against brother, fear held sway in many parts of our population. Martial law was imposed by the victors and the Supreme Court, ruling against that imposition, wrote something we think it appropriate today:

"When peace prevails and the authority of the government is undisputed, there is no difficulty in preserving the safeguards of liberty...but if society is disturbed by civil commotion -- if the passions of men are aroused and the restraint of law weakened, if not disregarded – these safeguards need, and should receive, the watchful care of those entrusted with the guardianship of the Constitution and laws. In no other way can we transmit to posterity unimpaired the blessings of liberty."

We at The Review remain invested in "transmitting to posterity unimpaired the blessings of liberty." We will be looking hard in the coming weeks and months to see how we can safeguard our rights and how we can make our Island community a better place to live for each one of us.

He finished typing and stared out the windows into the woods. There was a good, loose feeling in his chest for the first time in a long while. The phone rang.

Will leaned back in his chair and picked up the black handset.

"Will, it's me babe. I'm pregnant."

"Halleluiah. I'll be right home."

The End

"We are now in possession of substantially incontrovertible evidence that most important statements of fact advanced by General DeWitt to justify the evacuation and detention were incorrect, and furthermore that General DeWitt had cause to know, and in all probability did know, that they were incorrect at the time he embodied them in his final report..."

Justice Dept internal memo dated Apr. 13, 1944 commenting on General John DeWitt's "Final Report," which was written in 1943.

"On the same day that we decided the evacuation case we held that there was no authority to detain a citizen, absent evidence of a crime. Meanwhile, however, grave injustices had been committed. Fine American citizens had been robbed of their properties by racists – crimes that might not have happened if the Court had not followed the Pentagon so literally. The evacuation case...was ever on my conscience."

William O. Douglas, Supreme Court Justice, 1939-1975

By most estimates 120,000 Japanese immigrants and citizens were moved from their homes to camps in the western and southern United States in the 1940's. Two thirds were American citizens. The government tracked what happened to them, during the incarceration and after the war:

Four people were listed as "unauthorized departures."
1,322 were sent to other institutions, including mental hospitals
1,862 died
2,355 joined the US armed forces
3,121 were sent to a higher security camp (Immigration and Naturalization Service.)
4,724 moved or were moved to Japan
52,798 stayed somewhere in the interior United States
54,127 returned to the US West Coast

References:

Personal Justice Denied
Report of the Commission on Wartime Relocation and Internment of Civilians
Univ. of WA press, 1997
And the Civil Liberties Public Education Fund

In Defense of Our Neighbors
The Walt and Milly Woodward Story
By Mary Woodward
Bainbridge Island Japanese American Community and Fenwick Press, 2008

THE BAINBRIDGE REVIEW, 1941-1945

The poem in Mutt's diary is based on a poem by an evacuee, Claire Kageyama-Ramakrishnan.
Thanks to the Kitsap Regional Library, Bainbridge Island

A book from ZEN 'N' INK
Small publishers for big minds
Suquamish, WA
Copyright 2012
Editorials written by Walt Woodward
Cover art by John Wood

www.ingramcontent.com/pod-product-compliance
Lightning Source LLC
Chambersburg PA
CBHW071304110426
42743CB00042B/1170